NAVAJO NATION PEACEMAKING

NAVAJO NATION PEACEMAKING

Living Traditional Justice

Edited by Marianne O. Nielsen and James W. Zion

The University of Arizona Press   Tucson

The University of Arizona Press
© 2005 The Arizona Board of Regents

Manufactured in the United States of America

10 09 08 07 06 05 6 5 4 3 2 1

Library of Congress Cataloging-in-Publication Data
Navajo Nation peacemaking : living traditional justice /
edited by Marianne O. Nielsen and James W. Zion.
p. cm.
Includes bibliographical references and index.
ISBN-13: 978-0-8165-2471-6 (pbk. : acid-free paper)
ISBN-10: 0-8165-2471-8 (pbk. : acid-free paper)
1. Navajo courts. 2. Navajo law. 3. Dispute resolution (Law)
—Southwest, New. 4. Justice, Administration of—Southwest,
New. I. Nielsen, Marianne O. II. Zion, James W., 1944–
KF8228.N3N38 2005
340.5'2'0899726—dc22
                                                    2005005821

Publication of this book is made possible in part by the proceeds
of a permanent endowment created with the assistance of a Challenge Grant from the National Endowment for the Humanities,
a federal agency.

DEDICATION

To the peacemakers:
changing the justice system, case by case.

CONTENTS

PART 4 CONCLUSIONS

FOREWORD

The Honorable Robert Yazzie
Chief Justice Emeritus of the Navajo Nation

Marianne O. Nielsen and James W. Zion have done an outstanding service in compiling this collection of articles on Navajo common law and peacemaking. Looking over the themes of this book, I see parallels to my life; that is, I entered law school thinking that American law had all the answers I needed as a Navajo who wanted to be a lawyer. The Navajo Nation Council thought the same thing when it created the modern Navajo Nation court system in 1959. I became a trial judge in 1985, and over the years, I got a nagging feeling that something was not quite right with the law I had learned. I focused on polishing my Navajo and learning more about my people's philosophy, spirituality, beliefs, and thinking. The Navajo Nation courts did the same thing, as it became apparent by 1981 that Navajo law had gone too far down the *Bilagáana* path. I now know that despite the value of the law I learned, if the Navajo Nation courts are to survive and work well, they must be *Navajo*.

It took me a while to understand Navajo peacemaking, from getting an appreciation of how it fits into our (Navajo) court system, to working with peacemakers to know what they do and how and why they do it. Once I acquired that understanding, I gave my full support to the development of peacemaking, just as my predecessors had done. Former chief justice Tom Tso once had a vision that peacemaking would totally supplant litigation in our system. I do not feel the same way, because I can see that adjudication in litigation will continue to be needed in the Navajo Nation. However, the possibilities for peacemaking are many.

This book should help promote both peacemaking and Navajo common law development. It lets us look at the past to understand where we've been; it tells us the foundations of peacemaking, how it works, and the proven fact that it does indeed work and work well. It gives a vision of the future and tells Navajos that their future is up to them. It explains peacemaking to the world because, as the authors indicate, there are lessons in Navajo peacemaking for those who want to approach old problems in sensible new ways.

This work is a prologue for new ways of thinking. When I made my journey home as a judge and a Navajo, I learned to insist upon Navajo thinking. We use it in Navajo Nation court decisions, and we use it to develop court policy and make daily decisions. Navajo common law and Navajo peacemaking are not legal philosophies or techniques. They are a way of thinking and living. Peacemaking transforms individuals and communities as its dynamics of participatory democracy, talking things out, consensus, and respect-based communication move from formal courthouse settings for peacemaking sessions to internalized habit in the people who come to know it. Navajo common law and peacemaking teach us that we need to take the feelings and attitudes we see described in these pages and learn to live them as habits. We have come a long way, as you will read, and we have a long way to go to revive the spirit of Navajo thinking in law and procedure.

This book is a dream that has come true. One summer, I had a student worker compile a collection of articles on Navajo common law and peace-making in a ring binder. I hoped they would be published one day. Marianne O. Nielsen, a true friend of our courts, took up the challenge to publish a collection of the best pieces on the subjects covered here, and expanded the collection far beyond what we collected. Her organization of the chapters, introductory comments, and editing are magnificent. She drafted my good friend and former solicitor of the judicial branch of the Navajo Nation, James W. Zion, to help her compile and edit the collection and attempt to identify the growing literature on peacemaking.

There is a growing appreciation around the world that indigenous law can inform the law of the future, and it takes partnerships such as the one that produced this book to get that information out. It can rightly be said that this book is the legacy of the pioneer Navajo Nation justices and judges who revived Navajo common law and peacemaking. It is their legacy to the Navajo Nation, and it is their legacy to all our relatives around the world.

ACKNOWLEDGEMENTS

We would like to express our appreciation to the scholars who agreed to let their work be included in the book or who produced original chapters for us. *'Ahéhee*. Thank you. A lot.

We would also like to thank the office staff of the Department of Criminal Justice at Northern Arizona University, Ingrid Davis and Cathy Spitzer, for efforts to make this a presentable manuscript, and student workers Joanna Labastida, Mary Powell, Laniel Biakeddy, and Deborah Madrigal. Their assistance was invaluable in carrying out the day-to-day production details. We owe you chocolate for a long time. We would also like to thank graduate students Holly Vargas and Varvara Harvey for their work on developing the reading list, judicial branch extern Susann Skogvang for her preliminary work, graduate student David Berg for his excellent editing suggestions, and graduate student Anna Nalwood for her assistance with ensuring the correct spelling of the Navajo words. We would also like to thank the University of Arizona Press for their encouragement of this project. Finally, we are very happy to tell you that all royalties from this book will be given to the Native American Criminal Justice Scholarship and other scholarships at Northern Arizona University, through the NAU Foundation.

NAVAJO NATION PEACEMAKING

Introduction to Peacemaking

Marianne O. Nielsen and James W. Zion

This is a book about peacemaking as it exists in the Navajo Nation justice system. Peacemaking is a form of conflict resolution that is rooted in Navajo culture and practices but has been modified to take into account present-day issues and resources. Depending on the individual, it can be practiced as a way of life or simply as an alternative to the court process. It is not mediation, and it is not alternative dispute resolution. It has been called "reparative justice" and "participatory justice" (Zion 1999). It *is* restorative justice, but not exactly the same kind that has been rapidly gaining popularity in the field of criminology. To assume that peacemaking is simply another kind of alternative dispute resolution or mediation is to impose European-based models and standards on the Navajo system of justice (Austin 1993). The term "peacemaking" is becoming more common in criminology and criminal justice; some scholars, such as Pepinsky and Quinney (1991), see it as the wave of the future in both theory and practice. Though there are striking resemblances between this new criminological model and Navajo peacemaking, they are not the same. Navajo peacemaking came first—by many centuries.

Because this book is about Navajo peacemaking—its origins, history, context, and contributions to Navajo criminal justice—it is also, to some extent, about the history of the Navajo people themselves, their resistance against colonialism, the social issues they must face on a day-to-day basis, and their struggle to regain sovereignty. Unfortunately, because of space limitations, this book cannot provide a discussion of the complete context of Navajo peacemaking, such as the impact of colonial processes on the Navajo people, Navajo history within colonial theory, the impact of legal and governmental policy changes on the Navajo justice system, other traditional justice practices of the Navajo people, and comparisons to the justice practices of indigenous peoples worldwide.[1]

The concept of peacemaking is found not only in Navajo culture and current criminological theory, but also in the cultures of other indigenous groups (see, for example, Lednicer 1959; Price and Dunnigan 1995; Houston 1995; UVic Institute for Dispute Resolution 1997; Stuart 1997). Peacemaking, as it exists in the Navajo Nation, is what former chief justice Robert Yazzie (1993) calls a "horizontal system of justice." In a horizontal system of justice, all participants are treated as equals, and the purpose is to preserve ongoing relationships and restore harmony among the involved parties. This is in sharp contrast to the American criminal justice system, which is based on European common law and justice procedures. American criminal justice is what Philmer Bluehouse, former peacemaker coordinator, calls a "way of war" (1996, 55). In peacemaking there is no coercion, and there are no "sides." No one is labeled the offender or the victim, the plaintiff or the defendant. As Yazzie (1993, 41) writes, "The ultimate goal of the peacemaker process is to restore the minds, physical being, spirits, and emotional well-being of all people involved." The process is guided by a *naat'áanii,* or peacemaker, who is an active part of the process, ensuring that all participants speak, underlying issues are uncovered, a plan to resolve the issue is developed, consensus is reached, and the participants understand the issues as they relate to the spiritual world and the community.

The contrast between the two systems is described by former justice Homer Bluehouse, in the words of his brother Philmer Bluehouse (1996, 55):

> "The adversarial system," he said, "is not fair. I have had people come into my courtroom, come before me on the bench, and at the end we find that it is not fair. I see my own relatives walking out the door. One group is dancing around with their tails up in the air. The other group is moping and walking out with their tails dragging on the carpet." . . . What about emotions? What about the physical comfort that all human beings desire? When you go into an adversarial court, you don't address those things.

The Cases

To introduce the scope and processes of peacemaking, this section provides brief synopses of eleven cases that cover a wide variety of disputes, including criminal offenses. These are all real, well-known cases ("cases" in the anthropological or Navajo common law sense, not in the western legal sense as reported in law journals).[2]

The Case of the Parents Who Knew the Truth

A young woman brought a paternity action in court against a young man. When the man appeared, he told the judge he was not the child's father. The judge referred the case to the local peacemaker, because the couple could not afford blood tests or litigation.

The young woman's and young man's parents participated in the peacemaking. The parents said they were there to talk about "their" grandchild, and that they had known what was going on between the couple all along.

They knew about the relationship and told the couple they could not deny that they were the parents of the baby. On admitting he was the father, the young man said he could not afford to support the mother and child because he was unemployed. Family members worked on an arrangement whereby the young man would cut and haul firewood until he was able to get a job.

The Case of the Broken Home

A woman's daughter and son-in-law lived with her, but the son-in-law often got drunk and beat up the daughter. The mother's frustration led her to file a criminal battery complaint against her son-in-law. The couple moved out, leaving their children in the grandmother's care. The grandmother was the victim of "dumping," a common practice of parents in the drinking culture leaving their children with family members, usually grandparents, to support the children without help. The husband continued to beat his wife and to ignore his obligations to his children. The grandmother wanted to do something about the violence directed at her daughter and about the parents' responsibilities to their children, so she sought peacemaking. Peacemaker Division staff told her how peacemaking restores harmony and relationships using *k'é* (a strong emotion that is difficult to define but can mean "respect" and refers to the process of maintaining solidarity).

The peacemaker was able to get the parties talking so that the man recognized his alcohol dependence and neglect of his children. He also acknowledged the link between his drinking and the abuse of his wife. He then asked for help. The peacemaker listened to the emotional experiences related by the parties and offered traditional Navajo counseling. A representative of the Navajo Nation behavioral health organization was invited to participate and offered services. The man received alcohol counseling and a referral to Alcoholics Anonymous, and the couple got marriage counseling. The mother returned to the Peacemaker Division a few months later to offer her thanks and to report the success of the peacemaking. The couple had received their own home through the Navajo Housing Authority, and the husband had gotten a job promotion.

The Case of the Troubled Veteran

Navajo individuals enlist to fight in America's wars in numbers that far surpass their proportion of the American population (see, for example, Nichols 1998). Decades ago, judges who presided over criminal cases involving violence began to recognize the existence of post-traumatic stress disorder (PTSD) as a sometimes-contributing factor. One veteran complained that since his return from Vietnam, he had trouble sleeping and had developed a drinking problem to forget memories of the war. He also had difficulties dealing with his family, given his sometimes violent behavior. He consulted with a peacemaker about what to do.

Navajos are aware of the horrors of war because of their historical conflicts with the Spanish, Mexicans, and Americans to keep their independence (see, for example, White 1983). There are special ceremonies to prepare for war and to remove the stain of war. These cleansing ceremonies have been perceived to prevent PTSD. To Navajos, PTSD is a "monster" or an evil, similar to the monsters that exist as part of the Navajo journey narratives, monsters that must be eradicated or weakened using ceremonial healing.

At first, the man said he did not believe in the ceremonies; then he said he could not afford one. Finally, as his problems continued, he agreed to have the ceremony performed. Following it, he was able to sleep without bad dreams, and he had achieved a sense of peace. The peacemaker supplemented traditional counseling in peacemaking with a specific healing ceremony to address the psychological problem.

The Case of Assault with a Cinder Block

A woman tried to get her son to stop throwing pieces of cinder block at her and her house. He kept doing it, despite her protests, and he finally picked her up and threw her into the house. She got a cut to her skull when her head hit the floor. She called the Navajo police, who took the son into custody.

In peacemaking, it was discovered that the man had a mental disorder caused by sniffing gasoline over a long period of time. He said he had no memory of the incident that had put him in jail. He had not been taking his medication for mental problems for six months. He depended on his mother to take him to the clinic for it; however, she could not take time off from work to transport her son for medical treatment. When the problem was clarified, the son recognized the importance of taking his medication and promised to get treatment. The mother agreed to provide transportation or make arrangements for other family members to take him. Peacemaking was used to supplement and reinforce an existing medical treatment program for a mental disorder.

The Case of the Denied Compensation

The Navajo Nation was treated as a "national sacrifice area" when the Navajo uranium deposits supplied material for weapons during the Cold War. There were massive mining operations, and Navajo workers were exposed to radiation poisoning (see Eichstaedt 1994). When Congress enacted a uranium compensation program for Navajo workers, a man was denied benefits because his documents showed two names. He went to peacemaking to get his records corrected.[3]

The man, his relatives, and representatives of the Navajo Nation Office of Vital Statistics attended a meeting to discuss the man's identity and documentation. They were able to agree on his proper identity, and the peacemaker made a recommendation to the court for a correction of Navajo Nation public records to reflect the man's proper name. The court accepted the recommendation, entered an order, and it was recorded with the Office of Vital Statistics. The court order was accepted by the uranium compensation program, and the man received benefits.

The Case of the Death Certificate

Navajo people retain many traditional practices, including the practice of traditional burials. When a child died at about one year of age and was buried without the assistance of a coroner, her brother and sisters, who had been in school when their sister died, wanted a death certificate. In peacemaking, the parties discussed the facts of the death and burial, testified about the traditional burial and the fact that no one could write to record the death. The peacemaker reported the facts to the court, which issued a decree for a death certificate.

The Case of the Stolen Necklace

An elderly Navajo woman who lived in a nursing home accused her daughter of stealing a turquoise necklace worth $950. The daughter denied this, saying the mother gave it to her as a gift. A sister insisted that she return the necklace, but the daughter refused.

In peacemaking, the sisters discussed their mother's forgetfulness and the fact that she had forgotten that the necklace was made up of several turquoise strands. The mother was thinking of the whole necklace, which she had divided up into strands and given to her daughter and grandchildren. When the accused daughter realized the importance of the necklace to her mother, she agreed to gather up all the strands and return them as one necklace. The peacemaker received them and gave the necklace to the elderly woman. That concluded the family dispute.

The Case of the Sex Offender

An Indian Health Service (IHS) psychologist who specialized in the treatment of sex offenders called the Office of the Chief Justice for assistance. He explained that he operated a special program for sex offenders and that a Navajo abuser had reported himself to it. The man had dropped his denial, and the IHS official felt that peacemaking would be an effective means of dealing with his sexual abuse. Arrangements were made for a referral to peacemaking, with protections of confidentiality, given the likelihood that the Federal Bureau of Investigation did not know about the underlying crime.

On another occasion, a specialist in treating sex offenders called the Office of the Chief Justice for information on how peacemaking works. He, too, agreed from his professional point of view that peacemaking was an effective tool in dealing with sex-related crimes.

This is a controversial subject that is clouded by the anger that sex offenses generate, leading to a lack of focus on solutions. While James W. Zion, one of the co-editors of this book, was teaching a Navajo common law course, a student who was a lawyer asked his opinion about a case in which the child was being sexually abused but the lawyer did not know if the abuser was the child's father or maternal grandmother. He asked how peacemaking would address such a case. Zion explained that he had seen a similar case in which the family, with the assistance of the peacemaker, had put the problem on the table in the hope that the ensuing discussion would prompt a confession. The lawyer then asked what would happen if neither admitted it. In the case that Zion was citing, the family isolated the child from both people and made sure the child was never alone with either. The lawyer expressed his amazement at the simplicity of the approach and said that he has been so focused on the notion of identifying and punishing the wrongdoer that he had not thought about simply protecting the child in the future.

The Case of the Corporation in Peacemaking

Some children were playing in a Chinle (Arizona) laundromat, and a child was scorched to death in a clothes dryer. The child's parents brought a wrongful death suit against the laundromat and the dryer manufacturer, with their lawyer using a products liability theory against the manufacturer. The defense attorney attempted to survey the likely jury verdict in the event the plaintiffs were successful and obtained figures from one dollar to five million dollars. As a result, his non-Navajo clients—who included two insurance companies—were very nervous. The defense attorney persuaded his clients to try peacemaking. The manufacturer's administrators went into a room with the parents, family members, and the peacemaker. The lawyers had to wait in the hallway. The parties negotiated a settlement sum that the defense lawyer later said fell within an acceptable range for rural Arizona settlements and jury verdicts, which pleased both the manufacturer and the insurance company representatives. The child's parents explained that they did not consider their child's death to have a price tag, but that they wanted just compensation in honor of his memory.

▼▼▼

The diversity of cases described above and the wide range of underlying problems resolved indicate that the European-based criminal justice system could learn some valuable lessons from Navajo peacemaking. Whereas European-based restorative justice programs are, relatively speaking, a new paradigm in American justice and as such are still developing procedures, handling issues, and finding acceptance, Navajo peacemaking has been operating for many years, even centuries if we go beyond the current model. Peacemaking has already developed and tested procedures, found solutions for issues, and earned acceptance. It is true that some aspects of Navajo peacemaking are deeply rooted in Navajo culture, such as the Navajo clan structure (Bluehouse 1996), and cannot effectively be adopted by another program (such as using the Navajo journey narratives as part of counseling). But this still leaves the prospect that the philosophy and processes of peacemaking are adoptable (such as the *idea* of using counseling based in the spiritual beliefs of the participants). Some scholars disagree (see Goldberg 1997); however, previous research suggests that indigenous justice ideas and processes are quite transferable to other cultural groups. For example, research with the Youth Justice Committees of Alberta, Canada, gives evidence of this generalizability. The youth justice committees started in First Nations communities in Canada are now widespread and operating successfully in non-Native communities (Nielsen 1998). Other scholars and practitioners agree with this potential transferability. As former United States attorney general Janet Reno (1999) stated,

> About 150 years ago, Abraham Lincoln said: Discourage litigation. Persuade your neighbors to compromise whenever you can. Point out to them how the nominal winner is often a real loser—in fees, expenses and wasted time . . . Even earlier than Lincoln, the Indians of the Navajo Nation created a peacemaking system to dispense justice, using a simple form for dispute resolution that focused . . . on problem-solving rather than winning and losing. I agree wholeheartedly with the commentator

who said the Navajo goal in dispute resolution of preserving the community and seeking peace is one our own system of justice must embrace.

The sharing of knowledge between Navajo and European-based criminal justice systems is the first reason this book was produced. The second reason for the writing of this book is that Navajo peacemaking has gained international renown for its success. Many people do not realize that Navajo peacemaking is one of the most researched and cited restorative justice programs in the world. Window Rock has a steady stream of visitors from the international criminal justice and legal communities: Canada, Zimbabwe, Namibia, South Africa, Australia, New Zealand, Fiji, Papua-New Guinea, Sweden, and the United Nations, not to mention other parts of the United States. Many different international and national audiences are eager to learn more about Navajo peacemaking.

Third, the Navajo Nation is fortunate that it has a group of insightful and articulate scholars who are currently working for, or have worked for, the judicial branch. Some of them are traditional in their perspective, and some are nontraditional. They include Raymond D. Austin, Philmer Bluehouse, Tom Tso, Robert Yazzie, and James W. Zion. The fact that four of these scholars are Navajo is important. The issue of indigenous voice is almost a cliché in academic circles, but it is also an ethical principle that is too often violated. When Navajo scholars have analyzed and written about their own justice system, it behooves scholars to pay special attention to these writings. Their voices capture peacemaking more intimately than those of any non-Navajo Nation scholars. As well, their work needs to be made accessible; too much of it is scattered through a wide range of legal and popular journals. Some of their work is included in this book; the rest is listed in the final section called "Peacemaking Reading List." Other talented scholars also have worked with the cooperation and permission of the Navajo Nation to bring a comparative perspective to peacemaking research. A listing of their work also can be found in the final section. In addition to original contributions, this volume takes some of the "classic" articles and puts them together with less accessible (but equally valuable) conference papers and internal documents.

Finally, the Navajo Nation has overlapping jurisdictions with criminal justice systems in Arizona, New Mexico, and Utah, and with the federal government. There are many criminal justice practitioners who would like to and, in some cases, know they need to learn more about the operation of Navajo Nation peacemaking. This book provides legal and criminal justice practitioners with information about aspects of peacemaking such as structure, procedures, and outcomes that will be useful for them as they work with the Navajo courts and the peacemakers.

Themes

The chapters in this book contain a number of underlying themes that require additional clarification for the reader. The first theme is the *impact of colonialism*. According to Jurgen Osterhammel (1997, 16), colonialism is "a relationship of domination between an indigenous . . . majority and a minority of foreign invaders. The fundamental decisions affecting the lives of the colonized peoples are made and implemented by the colonial rulers in pursuit of interests that are often defined in a distant metropolis. Rejecting cultural compromises with the colonized population, the colonizers are convinced of their own superiority and their ordained mandate to rule." The United States remains a colonial society today. From the point of view of the colonized, the arrival of European settlers was an invasion. Just as other Native Americans were pushed to the margins of colonial society—economically, politically, and socially—so were the Navajo people.

Colonial history is ugly. It began with the importation of diseases to which the indigenous inhabitants of North America had no resistance. These diseases killed anywhere from 10 to 90 percent of their population (Snipp 1989). Colonialism continued with the social disorganization that followed as economies collapsed, social institutions changed, and traditional knowledge was lost. Exacerbating this tragedy was the greed of resource-hungry European powers that saw "the New World" as a treasure trove of gold, spices, slaves, and land. They used military might to acquire them. This sorry episode in North American history has been well described in many excellent books (see, for example, Nies 1996; Jennings 1993; Wright 1992; Deloria and Lytle 1983) and won't be repeated here at length. Nevertheless, there are three aspects of colonialism that are referred to directly or by implication in many of the chapters.

The first aspect is the ideology that was used to justify colonization. It stated that indigenous peoples were inherently inferior, first because of their "heathen" spirituality, and then later, with the advent of social Darwinism, because of their supposed low rung on the evolutionary ladder. When colonists were still dependent on the indigenous peoples for food, shelter, companionship, and trade, they were described in romantic terms such as "noble savages" and "innocent children of nature." When they became invaluable allies in the wars between the European colonies, they were described as "bloodthirsty savages" and "red demons" (the better to terrify their enemies). The missionaries who needed to justify funding for their missions described them as "heathens" and "pagans." When Native Americans defended their lands against the invading settlers, the settlers described them as "animals" and "vermin," to justify massacres. Currently, Native Americans are seen by many non-Native people as incompetent, drunken, and welfare dependent (Trigger 1985; Mihesuah 1996). In the past, these stereotypes informed the treatment of Native Americans by government and by society. Even though many Americans today no longer believe these stereotypes, some policy makers are still influenced by them. They expect Native Americans to assimilate and give up their legal rights to land and other natural resources. Some individuals believe Native Americans should accept second-class citizen status. Some use this ideology to justify hate crimes against Native Americans.

The second aspect of colonialism is assimilationist government policies. Since the early years of colonialism, there has been a movement to remake indigenous peoples into the image of Europeans. Colonial ideology was used to justify the efforts of the "superior" Europeans to change Native Americans through religious conversion by missionaries, education at boarding schools, the economic dependency arising from the reservation system, and laws forbidding cultural practices. In the early 1950s, assimilationist policies reached their depths when the federal government adopted a policy of termination. The goal was for the federal government to end its relationship with Native Americans. They were to be assimilated into mainstream American culture. This would free up their lands for non–Native Americans to take over (O'Brien 1985).

Termination was a failure and was abandoned in the early 1970s. Native Americans refused to give up their culture, land, or sovereignty. Many scholars, however, believe an assimilationist ideology still informs policy making by state and federal governments (Trafzer 2000). Native American nations must struggle continuously for their right to remain diverse groups—culturally, politically, and legally. This pressure to conform to non-Navajo society also exists in the criminal justice system. One theory in the field of complex organizations argues that organizations are under pressure to conform to the structure and operations of other organizations in their area of service or business (Zucker 1977). It is a situation comparable to fashion trends, but in organizations, trends include business concepts (quality control, accountability), management style (management by objectives, new management), technology (management information systems, dot.com ventures), and many other organizational characteristics. Some of these fads become permanent parts of the organizational landscape, while others fade away. Organizations are pressured to adopt them even if they are harmful to the organization's goals or clients. This book argues that peacemaking is not the same as other forms of conflict resolution; it should not be judged by inappropriate non-Navajo organizational or justice standards; and clients would only be harmed by efforts to turn peacemaking into the image of European-based dispute resolution. In other words, peacemaking is also under pressure to assimilate into the non-Navajo model of criminal justice. The political pressure exists in conjunction with organizational pressure (Nielsen 1998).

The third aspect of colonialism is the use of law to control indigenous peoples. Laws were used, for example, to foster assimilation. Laws banned ceremonial practices, removed children from their families, took away Native American land, confined Native Americans to reservations or forced them off the reservations if the lands were later found to be valuable, prevented Native Americans from voting, forbade Native Americans from developing businesses, and interfered in Native Americans' maintaining their culture (see, for example, Deloria and Lytle 1983). Sociolegal control of Native Americans continues. They still have only limited sovereignty; that is, there are still legal limitations on what kinds of decisions tribal governments are allowed to make about their social institutions and their communities. Native American police forces and courts are limited in what kinds of crimes they can process and what severity of punishment they can administer (see, for example, Pommersheim 1995). Reasserting control of law and justice is therefore an important step in regaining sovereignty.

The Navajo Nation is taking this step; it is resuming control of the justice system on its own terms. The Navajo people in earlier times were organized in small clan-based communities. The chapter system that now exists approximates this structure but is not the same. Chapters are local units with elected officials who carry out the wishes of the people as expressed at regular meetings. The Navajo Nation is made up of 110 such chapters. A current issue related to sovereignty is how much decentralization of centralized Navajo governance is possible. This includes the criminal justice system. Since peacemakers are a return to earlier days of locally administered justice, they are a step in the direction of decentralization. The Navajo Nation Local Governance Act of 1998 provides that one of the general powers of the 110 chapters is to establish peacemaking at the chapter level. Most recently, peacemakers have been incorporating as nonprofit, tax-exempt organizations to increase their prestige and ability to network for mutual benefit. This process is comparable to lawyers forming bar associations or judges participating in judicial conferences.

The Navajo Nation is one of the most assertive Native American nations in the struggle for legal sovereignty. This book describes how the Navajo Nation took control of its own criminal justice system. Fear of state interference through the potential adoption of Public Law 280, which moved Native American nations from federal to state jurisdiction, originally kept the Navajo court system modeled on non–Native American courts. This changed as soon as the Navajo Nation judicial branch felt that state usurpation was no longer a danger. One of the most important changes that occurred in the Navajo Nation criminal justice system was the reintroduction of peacemaking. We use the term "reintroduction" deliberately to emphasize that peacemaking did not begin with the start of the peacemaker courts in 1982. Because of its legal status, peacemaking is able to avoid some of the legal restrictions faced by the courts. Many judicial branch personnel believe peacemaking is the future of Navajo justice.

Colonialism is an important part of the historical context for peacemaking, but it is not the only context. *Understanding the context of peacemaking* is the second theme of the chapters. Learning about the history of the Navajo people and their present socioeconomic situation is necessary to understand fully the importance of peacemaking. Although the Navajo Nation is different from other indigenous communities in the United States and Canada, it also has some similarities. These include the social problems it must resolve, the lack of funding and other resources for operating its justice system, the distrust of the American government and its representatives felt by many Native American people, and, as mentioned earlier, the lack of control the Navajo Nation has over some of its social institutions.

The Navajo Nation covers about 25,300 square miles, is home to about 169,000 people (of whom all but 6,500 are Native American), and is situated in three different states (Navajo Nation 1995). The people of the Navajo Nation have some characteristics that make them different in significant ways from their non–Native American neighbors: The average per-capita annual income is $4,106 compared to $14,420 for the United States population; 56 percent of individuals and 57 percent of families live below the poverty line compared to 13 percent and 10 percent of the United States population; 59 percent do not graduate from high school; 77.5 percent live in homes with no telephone; and 82 percent speak a Native American language at home (Navajo Nation 1995). These statistics only hint at the economic, cultural, and social differences that might make a European-based, adversarial justice system ineffective and inappropriate in dispensing justice to this population.

The *battle for legitimacy* is the third theme and is related to the theme of colonial ideology. For many years, Navajo Nation scholars have fought to convince others that traditional Navajo justice processes in their modern-day incarnation of peacemaking are a viable alternative, that they are still relevant and effective. There is a need to educate non-Navajos about peacemaking, but also a struggle to achieve legitimacy for Navajo justice practices in general. Because of persistent stereotyping, Native American nations must continue to justify their traditional social institutions. This battle for legitimacy was once fought on a daily basis by members of the Navajo Nation and is reflected in the content of their scholarly writings. As the non-Native world has become more aware of and better educated about Native Americans, there has been less need to justify peacemaking. The educational process now shares information with parties who realize peacemaking's value.

Effectiveness of Navajo justice practices is the fourth theme of the book. The justice philosophy and practices of the majority of the indigenous cultures in the United States differ markedly from the philosophy and practices of the nonindigenous peoples whose justice system is rooted in the British or other European law. Several of the authors explain that the European-based system is adversarial, punishment oriented, impersonal, and bureaucratic, whereas the indigenous systems were and are almost the opposite (see Melton 1995 and Dumont 1993 for excellent analyses of the conflicts between these systems). The Navajo Nation's isolation from non-Navajo society means that many of the peoples' expectations of justice are based on more traditional beliefs. European-based criminal justice seems alien and unjust. Several of the chapters in this book deal specifically with the issue of program effectiveness.

The *adaptability of Navajo practices* is the fifth theme. The Navajo people have always been adaptive to their surroundings. When they first arrived in the Southwest over seven hundred years ago, their culture was different than it is now (White 1983). They adopted parts of the culture and practices of their Pueblo and Hopi and eventually Spanish and American neighbors. This flexibility and adaptability continues to characterize Navajo society and extends to their justice system. Peacemaking as it is now is different from when it was an everyday part of traditional life. There are new problems and new spins on old problems, such as family violence, substance abuse, juvenile delinquency, and other crimes. There are also crimes involving non-Navajo individuals and large corporations. Traditional practices provide guidelines about how to handle these cases, but there are additional factors now that must be considered, such as options for resolution, and restrictions on jurisdiction and punishment. Whereas colonialism was on the whole an adverse and tragic process, it should be noted that Navajo people adopted many of the good aspects of European-based culture. Peacemaking is a dynamic process that has adapted to change and has borrowed from European-based justice as well, as seen throughout this book.

The final theme is the *importance of process in peacemaking*. Some of the chapters in this book describe the personal journey through which peace-making takes the parties in a dispute. This process is one of the keys to the success of peacemaking in resolving disputes. The purpose of peacemaking is not to fulfill some abstract notion of justice but to restore harmony so that the participants are returned to good relations. This means finding and dealing with the underlying causes of the dispute. Harmony must be regained not only between the two (or more) individuals intimately involved in the dispute, but also among their families, clans, and the community as a whole. Peacemaking does not end until a plan of action is agreed upon by all participants. The processes of peacemaking as presented in the chapters are logical, effective, and yet quite alien to most European-based models of justice.

About This Book

Because this is a compilation of writings, there are some oddities that need explaining. First, this book is not necessarily intended to be read in a linear fashion. There is repetition in some of the articles. As mentioned previously, scholars in the past have felt a need to explain and justify peacemaking. Certain concepts such as k'é, naat'áanii, and horizontal versus vertical justice, for example, are explained repeatedly. If removing the repetitive section did not detract from the argument, the article was modified. In other cases, we decided that the articles would be most useful if they remained whole because they have been cited frequently by scholars in the field. For the completist scholar, we recommend that you read the original articles. Sources are given at the beginning of each chapter's note section. Each section of the book is introduced by a short commentary that describes why each chapter was included, updates facts, and notes other points of particular interest.

A third point is terminology. The terms "Native American," "American Indian," and "indigenous peoples" are used in various chapters. In the Southwest, the term of preference by many people is "American Indian"; however, this term can be exclusive in that it refers to only one legally defined group; it leaves out a great many indigenous people. For example, over 60 percent of Native Americans live off reservations. Some of these people are enrolled members of specific nations; many are not but identify themselves as people "who trace their ancestry in this land to time immemorial" (Morse 1985, 1). In addition, the term "American Indian" leaves out Native Hawaiians, Inuit, and Aleutian Islanders. The term "indigenous peoples" is used by some authors when discussing Navajos and indigenous peoples from other countries, who are not Americans. In Canada, for example, the terms of preference are "Native Peoples," "First Nations," and "Aboriginal Peoples." Labels have been used in the past to divide indigenous peoples, to differentiate their interests and, therefore, make them less powerful than they would be if they worked together (Boldt 1993). Where appropriate, we have chosen the most inclusive term.

The term "Navajo" also needs explaining. The true name of the Navajo people is *"Dine'," "Dine'é,"* or *"Dineh."* The word "Navajo" was a term used by the early Spanish explorers and comes from "Apaches de Nabahu," or "strangers of the cultivated fields" (White 1983, 212). The term "Dine'" is complex in meaning but has been translated most often as "people" or "The People." There is a political change in progress so that more and more documents are now reading "Dine'"; however, "Navajo" is still the term in legal, scholarly, and popular usage.

Similarly, the chapters in this book have many names for non-Navajos: Anglos, westerners, Europeans, European Americans, dominant society members. All of these terms are in popular usage in the Southwest, although they may mean different things elsewhere in the country.

A fourth point is that the chapters use two terms for peacemakers. Until early 1996, the term "peacemaker courts" was used. This is a holdover from the days of needing to legitimize the existence of the peacemakers. Peacemaking, however, is not a court procedure, and the term "courts" is misleading about the purpose and procedures of peacemaking. As a result, the name is seldom used today.

A final point to notice is the style and tone of the articles. They range from legalistic writing to scholarly language to informal conversational pieces. These differences reflect the original purpose of each document. Because the majority of the articles were written by lawyers, judges, or legal scholars, the legalistic style predominates. In many chapters the majority of footnotes have been edited down to a few essential chapter endnotes, with references placed in the body of the text.

Notes

1. For readers interested in pursuing this background material, we recommend a number of basic readings. For a general history of Native American peoples, including the processes of colonialism and neocolonialism, we recommend Wright (1992); Nies (1996); Nichols (1998); and Trafzer (2000). For the history of the Navajo peoples, see Young (1978); White (1983); and Wilkins (1999). For the impact of colonial law and government policy, see Deloria (1985); Wilkinson (1987); and Pommersheim (1995). For overviews of colonial theory, see Mendelssohn (1975); Blaut (1993); Osterhammel (1997); and Ashcroft, Griffiths, and Tiffin (1998). For an overview of the state of indigenous peoples worldwide, see Burger (1987); Bodley (1988); and Wilmer (1993).

2. We thank Roberta Harris of the Office of the Chief Justice for some of the Navajo case law stories used in this section. Roberta worked hard to retrieve and write up the stories.

3. Many Navajo people had difficulties with the compensation program due to bureaucratic impediments. Since many claimants could not afford court proceedings for name changes, validations of marriage, or other status determinations, the doors of peacemaking were opened to them for such purposes.

References

Ashcroft, Bill, Gareth Griffiths, and Helen Tiffin. 1998. *Key Concepts in Post-Colonial Studies.* New York: Routledge.

Austin, Raymond D. 1993. Freedom, Responsibility and Duty: ADR and the Navajo Peacemaker Court. *The Judges' Journal* 32 (2): 8–11, 47, 48.

Blaut, J. M. 1993. *The Colonizer's Model of the World.* New York: Guilford Press.

Bluehouse, Philmer. 1996. The Ceremony of Making Peace: Excerpt from *People of the Seventh Fire,* edited by Dagmar Thorpe. *Native Americas* 13 (3): 54–57.

Bodley, John H. 1988. *Tribal Peoples and Development Issues: A Global Overview.* Mountain View, Calif.: Mayfield Publishing.

Boldt, Menno. 1993. *Surviving as Indians.* Toronto, ON: University of Toronto Press.

Burger, Julian. 1987. *Report from the Frontier.* London: Zed Books.

Deloria, Vine, Jr., ed. 1985. *American Indian Policy in the Twentieth Century.* Norman and Lincoln: University of Oklahoma Press.

Deloria, Vine, Jr., and Clifford M. Lytle. 1983. *American Indians, American Justice.* Austin: University of Texas Press.

Dumont, James. 1993. Justice and Aboriginal Peoples. In *Aboriginal Peoples and the Justice System: National Roundtable on Aboriginal Justice Issues,* ed. Royal Commission on Aboriginal Peoples, 42–85. Ottawa, ON: Ministry of Supply and Services.

Eichstaedt, Peter H. 1994. *If You Poison Us: Uranium and Native Americans.* Santa Fe, N.Mex.: Red Crane Books.

Goldberg, Carole E. 1997. Overextended Borrowing: Tribal Peacemaking Applied in Non-Indian Disputes. *Washington Law Review* 72: 1003–19.

Houston, Jean. 1995. *Manual for the Peacemaker.* Wheaton, Ill.: Quest Books.

Jennings, Francis. 1993. *The Founders of America.* New York: W.W. Norton.

Lednicer, Oliver. 1959. The Peacemaker Court in New York State. *New York University Intramural Law Review* 14: 188–95.

Melton, Ada Pecos. 1995. Indigenous Justice Systems and Tribal Society. *Judicature* 79 (3): 126–33.

Mendelssohn, Kurt. 1975. *The Secret of Western Domination.* New York: Praeger.

Mihesuah, Devon. 1996. *American Indians: Stereotypes and Realities.* Atlanta, Ga.: Clarity Press.

Morse, Bradford W. 1985. *Aboriginal Peoples and the Law.* Ottawa, ON: Carleton University Press.

Navajo Nation, Division of Community Development. 1995. *Navajo Nation Profile.* Window Rock: Navajo Nation.

Nichols, Roger L. 1998. *Indians in the United States and Canada: A Comparative History.* Lincoln: University of Nebraska Press.

Nielsen, Marianne O. 1998. A Comparison of Canadian Native Youth Justice Committees and Navajo Peacemakers: A Summary of Results. *Journal of Contemporary Criminal Justice* 14 (1): 6–25.

Nies, Judith. 1996. *Native American History.* New York: Ballantine.

O'Brien, Sharon. 1985. Federal Indian Policies and the International Protection of Human Rights. In *American Indian Policy in the Twentieth Century,* ed. Vine Deloria, Jr., 35–61. Norman: University of Oklahoma Press.

Osterhammel, Jurgen. 1997. *Colonialism: A Theoretical Overview.* Princeton, N.J.: Markus Wiener Publishers.

Pepinsky, Harold E., and Richard Quinney, eds. 1991. *Criminology as Peacemaking.* Bloomington: Indiana University Press.

Pommersheim, Frank. 1995. *Braid of Feathers: American Indian Law and Contemporary Tribal Life.* Berkeley: University of California Press.

Price, Richard T., and Cynthia Dunnigan. 1995. *Toward an Understanding of Aboriginal Peacemaking.* Victoria, B.C.: UVic Institute for Dispute Resolution.

Reno, Janet. 1999. Remarks of Honorable Janet Reno, Attorney General to the Department of the Navy, Office of General Counsel Conference, Arlington, Virginia, May 6, 1999.

Snipp, C. Matthew. 1989. *American Indians: The First of This Land.* New York: Russell Sage Foundation.

Stuart, Barry. 1997. *Building Community Justice Partnerships: Community Peacemaking Circles.* Ottawa, ON: Aboriginal Justice Directorate, Department of Justice, Canada.

Trafzer, Clifford E. 2000. *As Long as the Grass Shall Grow and the Rivers Flow.* Fort Worth, Tex.: Harcourt College Publishers.

Trigger, Bruce G. 1985. *Natives and Newcomers.* Kingston, ON: McGill-Queen's University Press.

UVic Institute for Dispute Resolution. 1997. Proceedings of Making Peace and Sharing Power: A National Gathering on Aboriginal Peoples and Dispute Resolution. Victoria, B.C.: UVic Institute for Dispute Resolution.

White, Richard. 1983. *The Roots of Dependency: Subsistence, Environment, and Social Change among the Choctaws, Pawnees, and Navajos.* Lincoln: University of Nebraska Press.

Wilkins, David E. 1999. *The Navajo Political Experience.* Tsaile, Ariz.: Dine College Press.

Wilkinson, Charles F. 1987. *American Indians, Time and the Law.* New Haven, Conn.: Yale University Press.

Wilmer, Franke. 1993. *The Indigenous Voice in World Politics.* Newbury Park, Calif.: Sage.

Wright, Ronald. 1992. *Stolen Continents.* Boston: Houghton-Mifflin.

Yazzie, Robert. 1993. Navajo Justice Experience — Yesterday and Today. In *Aboriginal Peoples and the Justice System: National Roundtable on Aboriginal Issues,* ed. the Royal Commission on Aboriginal Peoples, 407–14. Ottawa, ON: Supply and Services.

Young, Robert W. 1978. *A Political History of the Navajo Tribe.* Tsaile, Ariz.: Navajo Community College Press.

Zion, James W. 1999. Monster Slayer and Born for Water: The Intersection of Restorative and Indigenous Justice. *Contemporary Justice Review* 2 (4): 359–82.

Zucker, Lynn G. 1977. The Role of Institutionalization in Cultural Persistence. *American Sociological Review* 42: 726–43.

THE HISTORY OF PEACEMAKING

Commentary on Part 1

James W. Zion and Marianne O. Nielsen

We chose to introduce this part and this book with the chapter by Tom Tso, a former chief justice of the Navajo Nation, because it locates peacemaking within the larger framework of the Navajo justice system. It also incorporates many of the themes mentioned in the introduction, such as the importance of historical context, the effectiveness of Navajo justice methods, and the adaptability of the Navajo justice system. The chapter ties together modern developments in the Navajo court systems with a Navajo historical perspective, while emphasizing the relationship between the Navajo court system and Navajo values as found in the Navajo journey narratives. Furthermore, this chapter introduces many of the issues that are topics of other parts in this book.

This chapter by chief justice emeritus Tom Tso was one of the first—if not the first—law journal article by an Indian jurist telling the legal community his philosophy of law by describing his court system. Tso is not a law school graduate judge, but he has the wisdom of a traditional rearing and experience as a legal practitioner with DNA-People's Legal Services, Inc. He was a president of the Navajo Nation Bar Association before he took the bench, and he was greatly respected as a trial judge and later chief judge.

Chief justice Tso supported the revival of peacemaking as a trial judge in the Window Rock District Court, and he did the first formal referral of a case into peacemaking from his court on February 22, 1982. This case involved Nancy Allison asking the court for a "traditional conciliation" of her marriage with Frank Allison. Tso recognized the "longstanding custom and tradition" of Navajo judges appointing a community member, such as an elder, chapter official, or "other person of respect," to serve as a "community mediator," and he ordered Albert Ross, Jr., of the St. Michaels chapter to work with the couple "in mediating and conciliating their problems" (*In the Matter of Conciliation of the Marriage of Allison,* 3 *Navajo Rptr.,* 199 [Navajo Nation Sup. Ct. 1982]). The order also named interested individuals to participate in the process, ordered their cooperation, and asked Ross to "make an informal report of his work" to the court. That was the first reported peacemaking case as its revival began, and Judge Tso's order preceded adoption of the peacemaking rules by about two months. (Volume 3 of the *Navajo Reporter,* with Tso's order, does not relate what happened.)

As J. W. Zion points out in telling the early history of the revival of peacemaking, it almost failed (see chapter 3). The judges who met to consider the rules had at least three philosophies: a philosophy of commitment to the revival of traditional Navajo; a philosophy opposing traditionalism and advocating modernism, wherein the Navajo Nation courts would have the dignity of state courts; and a philosophy that traditional processes should be left in Navajo communities. Those competing views are still voiced in the Navajo Nation judiciary (although traditionalism is currently the prevailing philosophy). Judge Homer Bluehouse, a recognized traditionalist and former police officer, surprisingly opposed peacemaking and related some bad things he had seen with informal justice as a cop. At that point, Tso initiated a lengthy dialogue with Bluehouse—in Navajo—and when the two finished their side discussion and returned to speaking English to the group, Bluehouse had changed his mind. Unfortunately, what was said was not recorded, and Bluehouse and Tso did not tell the group what they said. However, there was a close bond of respect between Bluehouse, the older judge, and Tso, the younger, and Bluehouse's change of mind brought peacemaking into the Navajo Nation court system.

Chief Justice Tso became the first chief justice of the Navajo Nation Supreme Court when there were judicial reforms in 1985 to create a permanent court of last resort with three justices. A great deal of his work was administrative, and in 1990 he got a surprise call from a Bureau of Indian Affairs (BIA) official in Gallup, New Mexico, to tell him that "special tribal court" monies were available, and the judicial branch could get its share by submitting a proposal on how the courts intended to use the funds. Tso did not hesitate, given his long commitment to peacemaking. He proposed a special division of the court system to promote peacemaking, with a director and peacemaker liaisons to provide administrative support in the judicial districts. The Navajo Nation later assumed financial responsibility for the division and liaisons, and in 1991, the Navajo Nation Council gave the Peacemaker Division its first statutory authority.

Tso's chapter is important because it is the work of an Indian jurist explaining what his court did, but also because it tells us something about why he supported peacemaking and what it did. One of the shortcomings of writing in "Indian law" is that, until recently, the Indian voice was missing, and the stories were told by non-Indians and Indian academics. We hear a traditional voice in Tso's chapter.

Although this chapter was originally written in 1989, the structure and procedures of the courts as laid out by the Judicial Reform Act of 1985 are still in effect (see also Harris 1994). Tso also refers to the peacemaker "courts." This terminology has been changed since this article was written to better reflect the nonadversarial nature of peacemaking (see this book's introduction).

The second chapter, by chief justice emeritus Robert Yazzie, provides an excellent contrast between the Navajo and the European-based justice systems. His use of the concepts of vertical and horizontal justice highlights the difference between an adversarial system and a restorative system like Navajo peacemaking. The chapter also clearly illustrates the holistic and interconnected nature of the Navajo justice system. Navajo common law, as applied in the Navajo Nation courts, and Navajo peacemaking clearly operate on the basis of the same concepts.

Robert Yazzie became the chief justice of the Navajo Nation in January 1992, one hundred years after adjudication was imposed on Navajos. One of the problems J. W. Zion had in writing the rules mentioned in chapter 3 was that there was no model for conjoining a traditional method of Indian dispute resolution with a Western court system, so he used a court-annexed mediation scheme, in which cases would be channeled into peacemaking through judges. He did not recognize that these judges would then become gatekeepers, and that some would close and lock the gate because of their personal philosophies or perhaps feelings that they had to protect their turf. Chief Justice Yazzie confessed that he was hesitant about peacemaking as a trial judge because he didn't know much about it. Soon after he took his oath, invitations to tell the public about peacemaking started pouring in, and he studied it in discussions with staff, judges, peacemakers, and traditional wisdom keepers, such as medicine people.

Yazzie is a graduate of the University of New Mexico School of Law, and the editor of its law review asked Yazzie, as an alumnus and a chief judge, to contribute a piece outlining his philosophy of law as an Indian law school graduate. He put a lot of work into chapter 2 and asked a basic question before penning its title, "Life Comes from It": What is "law" from a Navajo point of view? Yazzie's voice is interesting because he developed a concept in the Navajo language and attempted to translate it into English. Yazzie's definition of law as something that life comes from demonstrates a linguistic and philosophical dilemma—the Navajo language is so sophisticated in conveying concepts that simple translations into English may confuse non–Navajo-speaking readers. Despite that, Yazzie attempted to explain Navajo legal thinking to law journal readers, and he introduced Navajo legal concepts underlying peacemaking that are now commonplace in usage. He attempted to explain the ideas that underlie Navajo substantive law, using both Navajo terms and analogous English legal concepts (many of which were drawn from legal anthropology), and he gave us a foundation to understand peacemaking as adjective, or procedural, law.

Chief Justice Yazzie's chapter is also a prologue to his later advocacy of peacemaking and his many public presentations and articles on it. (Many invited speeches were later published as articles.) His chapter gives his philosophy of Navajo law shortly after assuming office as chief justice, and he fine-tuned and built upon it throughout his tenure from 1992 through 2003. He continues to think it out in retirement.

Some authors in this book refer to a "peacemaker liaison," which is a very important position within the Peacemaker Division that frequently is ignored. Peacemaker liaisons are the administrative connection between the courts and the peacemakers. There are peacemaker liaisons located in each of the seven Navajo judicial districts. They move cases in and out of peacemaking and assist peacemakers in setting up sessions, giving notice, receiving reports, and handling other documentation. Their duties also include being community organizers, recruiting peacemakers, helping to train peacemakers, and encouraging support for peacemaking. They are salaried members of the Peacemaker Division.

As these chapters suggest, Navajo peacemaking is highly adaptable and involved in ongoing change, perhaps more so than the European-based court system. The Navajo court system, including peacemaking, has been changing in two directions, toward the incorporation of more Navajo cultural values and procedures as is communicated by this book, but also toward more professionalization, a trend that is addressed elsewhere in this book. For example, the *Navajo Nation Code of Judicial Conduct* was adopted by Navajo judges in 1991 (Tso 1992). This code, which also applies to peacemakers, contains eleven canons, or principles, based on both the American Bar Association's *Model Code* and traditional Navajo values. Examples of the professionally oriented canons include canon 4, "a Navajo judge shall assume administrative responsibility for the prompt, efficient, and careful exercise of court business," and canon 5, "a Navajo judge shall seek continuing education to achieve knowledge of the law, and promote the overall competency of the Navajo Nation judiciary" (Tso 1992, 20). A peacemaker-specific code of ethics eventually may be developed, but until then peacemakers, as officers of the court, are subject to judicial review and discipline if they do not follow this code.

An indication of a recent move toward more culturally based processes is the January 2000 amendment to the *Navajo Nation Criminal Code*. This amendment decriminalized a large number of offenses by providing for no jail sentences and no fines. In section 221, "Sentencing considerations," part C, it is stated, "The trial court may utilize the services of the Navajo Peacemaker Court to determine *nalyeeh* [restitution] and make a sentencing recommendation regarding that sentence, and the trial court may require the defendant to pay the fee of the peacemaker." These new sentencing considerations are applied to offenses such as threatening, unlawful imprisonment, contributing to the delinquency of a minor, weapons and explosives, and fifty-eight other charges. Peacemaking is not a sentencing consideration in the most serious offenses, such as arson and aggravated assault. This decriminalization is intended to encourage the court and individuals to make more use of peacemaking.

References

Harris, Al. 1994. An Overview of the Navajo Nation Court System. Paper presented at the Colorado University School of Law, Boulder, Colorado, December 4, 1994.

Tso, Tom. 1992. Moral Principles, Traditions, and Fairness in the *Navajo Nation Code of Judicial Conduct*. *Judicature* 76 (1): 15–21.

1 The Process of Decision Making in Tribal Courts

A Navajo Jurist's Perspective

Tom Tso

In this essay, I would like to discuss the process of decision making in tribal courts. I will speak about the Navajo tribal courts because that is what I know. It is difficult to discuss the process without first discussing the history and the background from which the Navajo courts developed.

Historical Perspective

The history of the Navajo Nation and of the Navajo tribal courts is one of many challenges. Today, we still face challenges to our sovereignty, our jurisdiction, and our right to exist as a people different from the dominant society. The ultimate challenge to the Navajos has always been survival. Those familiar with the history of the Navajos will recall that the Spanish and the United States Cavalry both attempted to exterminate us. In 1864, the United States Cavalry under Kit Carson succeeded in rounding up thousands of Navajos and driving them several hundred miles from their traditional homes in northern Arizona to Fort Sumner. The true objective of this mass removal, known as the "Long Walk," is unclear. What is known is that the cavalry engaged in the intentional, systematic destruction of Navajo villages and the herds and crops that supported the people. The starving Navajos were then forced to walk four hundred miles in inclement weather with inadequate food and clothing to their new "home"—a reservation surrounding Fort Sumner, which was to be shared with the Mescalero Apache. Once located on the reservation, the Navajos, numbering between eight and ten thousand, were forced onto farming land poorly suited to agriculture. Failure of crops and the unwillingness of the government to provide the tools, clothing, and food necessary to permit the people to survive resulted in the government's abandonment of the Fort Sumner reservation. In effect, four years after the disastrous Long Walk, the government threw up its hands, telling us to take our sheep and go home. The return of the Navajos to their ancestral home marked the beginning of the end of federal governmental efforts to terminate our physical existence.

Since that time, the challenges have been to our cultural identity and existence. These challenges reflect the false assumption on which relations between Indians and the Anglo world have always been conducted. The false assumption is that the dominant society operates from the vantage point of intellectual, moral, and spiritual superiority. The truth is that the dominant society became dominant because of military strength and power.

Examine this from the Navajo perspective. When people live in groups or communities, they develop rules or guidelines by which the affairs of the group may proceed in an orderly fashion and the peace and harmony of the group may be maintained. This is true for the Navajos. As far back as our history can be verified and further back into the oral traditions of our origins, there is a record of some degree of formal organization and leadership among the Navajos. In the earliest world, the Black World, which was the first phase of our existence, it is said that the beings knew the value of making plans and operating with the consent of all. In a later world, Changing Woman appointed four chiefs and assigned one to each of the four directions. These chiefs convened a council, established clans, and organized the world. The chiefs and councils of Navajo oral history made decisions for the larger group and regulated the clans. The oral traditions indicate that there was a separation of functions between war leaders and peace leaders. One of the major responsibilities of the Navajo headmen was offering advice and guidance.

The people chose the headmen from among those who possessed the necessary qualities. The headmen needed to be eloquent and persuasive, since they exerted power by persuasion rather than coercion. Teaching ethics and encouraging the people to live in peace and harmony were emphasized.

One of the important functions of a headman was dispute resolution. When a dispute or conflict arose in the community, the people would go to the headman for advice. If the matter involved what we today would call a criminal offense, the headman would meet with the wrongdoer, his or her family, the victim, and the victim's family to discuss how to handle the matter. The discussion usually involved two issues: how to compensate the victim or the victim's family for the wrong and how to deal with the wrongdoer. The discussion continued until everyone was in agreement as to what should be done (Tso 1986).

Prior to Kit Carson's arrival, we lived in communities. You might say we had a decentralized, grassroots government. We had our own mechanisms for resolving disputes. We had a profound respect for the separation of functions. Not only did we have various leaders for war and peace, we had our medicine men, who occupied a very important role in the operation of our society. The training and the teachings of the medicine men were respected, and no one interfered with their function. We had our own concepts of fairness in the way we handled disputes, seeking both to compensate the victim and to rehabilitate the wrongdoer.

After we returned to our land in 1868, the federal government began to tell us all the things we had to have. We had to have an organized government and a tribal council. We had to have courts. We had to have jails. We had to have separation of powers.[1] These things and many more have been instituted. They work very well in the Navajo Nation. I believe the main reason the Navajos have, by Anglo standards, the most sophisticated and the most complex tribal court system is that we were able to build upon concepts that were already present in our culture. Navajos are also flexible and adaptable people. We find there are many things that we can incorporate into our lives that do not change our concept of ourselves as Navajo.

The Navajo Court System

I regret that the outside world has never recognized that Navajos were functioning with sophisticated and workable legal and political concepts before the American Revolution. I regret even more that the ways in which we are different are neither known nor valued by the dominant society. Because we are viewed as having nothing to contribute, much time has been wasted. Let me be more specific. Anglo judicial systems now pay a great deal of attention to alternative forms of dispute resolution. Before 1868 the Navajos settled disputes by mediation. Today our peacemaker courts are studied by many people and governments.[2] Anglo justice systems are now interested in compensating victims of crime and searching for ways other than imprisonment to deal with criminal offenders. Before 1868 the Navajos did this. Now Anglo courts recognize the concept of joint custody of children and the role of the extended family in the rearing of children. Navajos have always understood these concepts. We could have taught the Anglos these things 150 years ago.

Today the Navajo courts are structured very much like the state and federal courts. We have seven judicial districts. The district courts are courts of general civil jurisdiction and of limited criminal jurisdiction. Civil jurisdiction extends to all persons residing within the Navajo Nation or those who cause an act to occur within the Nation (Navajo Trib. Code tit. 7, § 253 [Cum. Supp. 1984–1985]). The limitations on criminal jurisdiction are determined by the nature of the offense, the penalty to be imposed, where the crime occurred, and the status and residency of the individual charged with the offense.[3] Each district also has a children's court, which hears all matters concerning children except for custody, child support and visitation disputes arising from divorce proceedings, and probate matters.

The second tier of the Navajo court system is the Navajo Nation Supreme Court, composed of three justices. The supreme court hears appeals from final lower court decisions and from certain final administrative orders. The supreme court abolished trial de novo at the appellate level and now hears only issues of law raised in the lower court record. In addition, the peacemaker courts, established in each judicial district, use traditional mediation processes and are supported by the district courts' supervision and enforcement of the agreements reached through mediation.

The tribal government is rapidly developing an extensive network of administrative bodies with quasi-judicial functions. The final decisions of bodies such as the tax commission and board of election supervisors are appealable directly to the Navajo Supreme Court. Recourse from the decisions of other administrative bodies is sought through an original action in the trial court.[4] All opinions of the Navajo Supreme Court, and some opinions of the district courts, are published in the *Navajo Reporter*. Additionally, the Navajo courts have established rules of procedure for criminal, civil, probate, and appellate matters.

The Selection of Judges

Navajo judges and justices are chosen through a process designed to insulate them from politics. When a judge is to be selected, interested persons submit applications to the judiciary committee of the Navajo Tribal Council. The judiciary committee screens the applicants and draws up a list of the most highly qualified people according to the qualifications set forth in the *Navajo Tribal Code* (tit. 7, § 354, [Cum. Supp. 1984–1985]). This list is then sent to the tribal chair, who appoints a judge from the list for a two-year probationary period. Each appointment must be confirmed by the tribal council. During the probationary period, the judge receives training from carefully selected judicial education establishments, which offer a quality legal-judicial education. There are currently two such establishments: the National Judicial College in Reno, Nevada, and the National Indian Justice Center in Petaluma, California. The Navajo Nation Bar Association, the judiciary committee, and the chief justice all evaluate the probationary judge.

If the probationary judge receives an adequate performance evaluation and satisfactorily completes his or her course of training, the chief justice and the judiciary committee recommend the judge for permanent appointment. This permanent appointment must be confirmed by the tribal council. Thereafter, the judge remains in office until retirement or removal under procedures established in the tribal code (352–53). Permanent judges continue to be evaluated each year and receive training in areas where the evaluations show that knowledge and skills are lacking. Through its careful selection process, its vigorous educational programs, and its thorough evaluation procedures, the Navajo Nation maintains a high standard for its judiciary.

Substantive and Procedural Law in the Navajo Tribal Court System

Representation in Court

All parties may represent themselves in the courts. If a party chooses to be represented by counsel, a member of the Navajo Nation Bar Association must be chosen. Membership in the Navajo Nation Bar Association requires passing the Navajo bar examination, which is given twice a year. Both law school graduates and those who have not been to law school may practice in tribal courts. The practitioners who have not been to law school are called "advocates" and must complete either a certified Navajo bar training course or serve an apprenticeship.

The contribution of the advocates to the Navajo court system is beyond measure. Both our language and our traditions make Anglo court systems strange to us. In traditional Navajo culture, the concept of a disinterested, unbiased decision maker was unknown. Concepts of fairness and social harmony are basic to us; however, we achieve fairness and harmony in a manner different from the Anglo world. For the Navajo people, dispute settlement required the participation of the community elders and all those who either knew the parties or were familiar with the history of the problem. Everyone was permitted to speak. Private discussions with an elder who could resolve a problem were also acceptable. It was difficult for Navajos to participate in a system where fairness required the judge to have no prior knowledge of the case, and where who can speak and what they can say are closely regulated. The advocates helped the Navajos through this process, and the advocates continue to be an important link between the two cultures.

The Applicable Law

The law the Navajo courts must use consists of any applicable federal laws, tribal laws, and customs. The structure of our courts is based upon the Anglo court system, but generally the law we apply is our own.[5] When the Navajo tribal courts were established in 1959, the Navajo Nation did not have extensive laws of its own, and there were no reported opinions to guide the judges in the decision-making process. In 1959, the *Navajo Tribal Code* required the courts to apply the applicable laws of the United States, authorized regulations of the Interior Department, and any ordinances or customs of the tribe not prohibited by such federal laws. Any matters not covered by tribal or federal law had to be decided by the law of the state in which the case arose. Because the Navajo Nation encompasses land in three states, this sometimes led to confusion and the application of different laws in different parts of the reservation.

In 1985, the tribal code sections regarding applicable law were amended. Now, the courts are required to apply the appropriate law of the United States and laws or customs of the Navajo Nation that are not prohibited by federal law. If the matter is not covered by tribal or federal law, the courts may look to any state laws and decisions for guidance, *or* Navajo courts may fashion their own remedies (Navajo Trib. Code tit. 7, § 204a–204c [Cum. Supp. 1984–1985]) The Navajo Nation Supreme Court makes the ultimate decisions on these issues, thereby developing an internal body of law. As a result, many of the briefs filed in that court and many of the opinions issued by it cite only Navajo cases.

It is easy to understand that the *Navajo Tribal Code* contains the written law of the Navajo Nation, and that this law is available to anyone. When we speak of Navajo *custom* law, however, many people become uneasy and think it must be something strange. Custom law will sound less strange if I tell you it is also called "common law." Our common law comprises customs and long-used ways of doing things. It also includes court decisions recognizing and enforcing the customs or filling in the gaps in the written law. The common law of the Navajo Nation, then, consists of both custom law and court decisions. In a case decided in 1987, the Navajo Nation Supreme Court observed that:

> Because established Navajo customs and traditions have the force of law, this court agrees with the Window Rock District Court in announcing its preference for the term "Navajo Common Law" rather than "custom," as that term properly emphasizes the fact that Navajo custom and tradition *is* law, and more accurately reflects the similarity in the treatment of custom between Navajo and English common law. (*In re Estate of Belone,* 5 *Navajo Rptr.* [Navajo Nation Sup. Ct. 1987], 161–68)

The Navajo Nation Supreme Court is developing rules through case decisions for pleading and proving Navajo common law.

The Integrity and Independence of the Decision Makers

Once a court makes a decision, that decision is subject to change only through judicial processes. No other part of the tribal government has the authority to overrule that decision. The basis of the concept of a separate and independent judiciary is found in both Navajo common law and in the tribal code. The tribal code establishes the judicial branch as a separate branch of government (Navajo Trib. Code tit. 7, § 201 [Cum. Supp. 1984–1985]). The integrity of court decisions, however, has its basis in the respect given to the peacemakers as leaders who helped settle community disputes. In a case decided in 1978, the Navajo Supreme Court ruled that the respect given the peacemakers extends to the courts because Navajos have

> a traditional abiding respect for the impartial adjudicatory process. When all have been heard and the decision is made, it is respected. This has been the Navajo way since before the time of the present judicial system. The Navajo People did not learn this principle from the white man. They have carried it . . . through history. . . . Those appointed by the People to resolve their disputes were and are unquestioned in their power to do so. Whereas once the clan was the primary forum (and still is a powerful and respected instrument of justice), now the People through their Council have delegated the ultimate responsibility for this to their courts. (*Halona v. MacDonald,* 1 *Navajo Rptr.* [Navajo Nation Sup. Ct. 1978] 189, 205–6)

The Old and the New Way

A close look at the Navajo tribal government would reveal many characteristics that appear to be Anglo in nature. Actually, many concepts have their roots in our ancient heritage. Others are foreign to our culture but have been accommodated in such a way that they have become acceptable and useful to us. Ironically, the Navajo, whose governmental structure and operation are perhaps most like those of the Anglo world amongst United States Indian tribes, is the tribe that has no constitution. The Anglo world places much value on the written word, and there is a tendency to believe that if things are not written down, they do not exist.

Navajos have survived since before the time of Columbus as a separate and distinct people. What holds us together is a strong set of values and customs, not words on paper. I am speaking of a sense of community so strong that before the federal government imposed its system on us, we had no need to lock up wrongdoers. If a person injured another or disrupted the peace of the community, he was talked to, and often ceremonies were performed to restore him to harmony with his world. There were usually no repeat offenders. Only those who have been subjected to a Navajo "talking" session can understand why this worked.[6]

Today we have police, prosecutors, jails, and written laws and procedures. I am convinced that our Anglo-based system of law enforcement is no more effective than the ways we traditionally handled law enforcement problems. Our present system certainly requires more money, more facilities, more resources, and more manpower. But we have this system now, and it works as well as those of our brother and sister jurisdictions. My point is that the Anglo world has said to tribes, "Be like us. Have the same laws and institutions we have. When you have these things, perhaps we will leave you alone." Yet what the Anglo world has offered, at least as far as Navajos are concerned, is either something we already had or something that works no better than what we had.

The popular concept of tolerance in America is based upon its image as a melting pot, where everyone blends together to form an indistinguishable mixture. This is fine for people who come to this country and *want* to jump into the pot. The melting pot can, however, become a good place to hide people. When differences cause discomfort or problems, the pot can make everyone the same. The real measure of tolerance and respect for tribes may well be how successfully the outside world can coexist with tribes. We are part of the total environment of America and at least as important as the snail darter or the California condor. What a tragedy if fifty years from now a news commentator should report on how the government has set aside a preserve in the desert where nine Indians are being saved from extinction and how it is hoped they will reproduce in captivity.

As economic development plans progress, the Navajo Nation courts are likely to face a wide range of issues. The jurisdiction statutes of the Navajo Nation provide that the tribal courts have jurisdiction over all civil causes of action where the defendant resides within the Navajo Indian country or, regardless of residence, has caused an action to occur within the territorial jurisdiction of the Navajo Nation.[7] Future litigation involving the land and resources of the Navajo Nation will no doubt challenge tribal court jurisdiction. In light of the decisions in *National Farmers Union Insurance Co. v. Crow Tribe of Indians* and in *Iowa Mutual Insurance Co. v. LaPlante*, however, these questions will be decided in the Navajo Nation courts.[8]

Beyond the jurisdictional issues, questions of what law will be applied in civil disputes are likely to arise. Whether federal law will attach in a specific case will depend on the facts. In cases where federal law does not apply, tribal common law and statutes will be used. The *Navajo Uniform Commercial Code, Navajo Nation Corporation Code, Water Code,* and

Mining Code are examples of statutory provisions enacted to regulate on-reservation business ventures and the use of natural resources.

Non-Indians may have concerns about the impact of tradition and custom on case decisions. Navajo custom and tradition are unlikely to call for law entirely different from that expected in Anglo courts. They are more likely to supply additional factors to consider in an already familiar context. For example, the Anglo system is familiar with the concept of valuation and payment for the taking of land.[9] Compensation for the loss of use to the surface user of land is an accepted concept in both Anglo and Navajo law. The difference will be in the valuation. Land that may appear to have little value to a non-Indian may be very valuable to a Navajo. It may have spiritual or historical value that has little to do with the income it can produce. The difficulty will be in assigning a dollar figure to values that have no measure in the market. This is not an impossible task. It is done every day in tort cases, where damages are assessed for intangible harms like pain and suffering, intentional infliction of emotional distress, and loss of companionship.

Navajo courts will differ in the emphasis we place on the traditional relationship between Navajos and nature. We refer to the earth and sky as Mother Earth and Father Sky. These are not catchy titles; they represent our understanding of our place. The earth and sky are our relatives. Nature communicates with us through the wind and the water and the whispering pines. Our traditional prayers include prayers for the plants, the animals, the water, and the trees. A Navajo prayer is like a plant. The stem or the backbone of the prayer is always beauty. By this beauty, we mean harmony. Beauty brings peace and understanding. It brings youngsters who are mentally and physically healthy, and it brings long life. Beauty is people living peacefully with each other and with nature.

Just like our natural mother, our Mother Earth provides for us. It is not wrong to accept the things we need from the earth. It is wrong to treat the earth with disrespect. It is wrong if we fail to protect and defend the earth. It would be wrong for us to rob our natural mother of her valuable jewelry and to go away and leave her to take care of herself. It is just as wrong for us to rob Mother Earth of what is valuable and leave her unprotected and defenseless. If people can understand that the Navajos regard nature and the things in nature as relatives, then they will easily see that nature and the Navajos depend upon each other. Understanding this relationship is essential to understanding traditional Navajo concepts that may be applied in cases concerning natural resources and the environment.

We Navajos find it difficult to separate our lives into fragments or parts. Our ceremonies are religious, medical, social, and psychological. The seasons tell us how to live and what ceremonies to have. The earth gives us our food, the dyes for our rugs, and the necessities for our ceremonies. These may be seen as *everyday* things. Today, the earth gives us income and jobs from mining, from oil, and from the forests. Water and earth combine to give Navajo Agricultural Products, Inc., the ability to produce large amounts of food for the Navajo people. Snow and rain and proper runoff from the mountains give us lakes for fishing. These may be seen as *commercial* things.

We cannot separate our needs and our relationships in the same fashion. This is why our laws and judicial interpretations must accommodate *both* of these things. For example, our tribal law requires that persons who want to harvest or remove anything from the forests have a permit. An exception is made, however, for persons who need to gather plants and forest products for ceremonial purposes. In a recent Navajo Supreme Court probate case, the court held that any further division of the land would defeat the agricultural purposes of the land (*In re Estate of Wauneka*, 5 *Navajo Rptr.* [Navajo Nation Sup. Ct. 1986], 79–84). Under Navajo common law, the parcel went to the heir who was best able to use the land for agricultural purposes. The other heirs were given setoffs in other items of the decedent's property. This case illustrates the Navajo Tribal Court system's ability to accommodate traditional values.

Conclusion

I have tried to give you a brief overview of the judicial decision-making process in the Navajo tribal courts, and to indicate some of the ways we attempt to accommodate the best from two cultures so that the Navajo Nation may proceed to develop within a framework that is familiar to us. We, the people, are a natural resource. Our culture and our history are natural resources. We are so related to the earth and the sky that we cannot be separated without harm. The protection and defense of both must be preserved. On the other hand, the dominant society views things in terms of separateness, of compartmentalization. For this reason, the Navajo Nation is best able to make the laws and decisions regarding its own preservation and development.

I have spoken of the Navajo experience, but I believe that much of what I have said applies to all Indian tribes. Understanding the challenges facing tribes is the first step toward meeting them. The process of making judicial decisions in the Navajo Nation reflects our response to these challenges.

Notes

This chapter is an edited version of Tom Tso, "The Process of Decision Making in Tribal Courts," *Arizona Law Review,* 31: 225–35, 1989. Reprinted with permission of the *Arizona Law Review.*

1. Government regulation of Indian tribes has been anything but consistent. In the century since the Navajo return to the homeland, political philosophy and opinion have undergone dramatic changes, changes that resemble a pendulum swinging from one extreme to another. The overriding philosophy has been to assimilate Indians into the Anglo society and can be seen in most of the policy enactments. After assimilation as a stated policy failed, the new policy became allotment. After allotment, we saw the Indian Reorganization Act, which was followed by termination, which in turn was followed by self-determination. It was, however, the Indian Reorganization Act that dictated the structural changes in tribal organization referred to here. In so doing, the act imposed the Anglo model of government on Indian tribes and granted additional benefits and latitude in internal matters in return for compliance. See generally Deloria and Lytle (1984); Deloria and Lytle (1983); and Spicer (1962).

2. In 1982, the judges of the Navajo courts implemented a new court system that was designed to integrate traditional Navajo dispute resolution methods with traditional Anglo judicial methods. Called the "peacemaker court," it uses the traditional legal processes of mediation and arbitration to arrive at reasonable solutions to disputes while protecting the interests of the disputants.

The establishment of the peacemaker court represents a blending of the old with the new, with an eye toward accommodating needs that were simply not being met by the existing system. Recourse to the peacemaker court is voluntary; however, once the parties consent, the court has the authority to enforce attendance through subpoena power. The court also has authority to compel the participation of any other person involved in the dispute. The activities of the peacemaker court are coordinated by and through the district courts (Zion 1983).

3. The most important criminal law statutes are the Indian Country Crimes Act (18 U.S.C. § 1152), extending federal enclave jurisdiction to interracial crimes that take place in Indian country; the Major Crimes Act (18 U.S.C. §§ 1153, 3242), punishing Indian offenders for commission of seventeen articulated felonies in Indian country; and the Assimilative Crimes Act (18 U.S.C. § 13), permitting federal prosecutions for state law offenses. For a discussion of criminal jurisdiction in Indian country, see Clinton (1976).

4. In a decision upholding the power of the Navajo Nation to tax mineral lessees on tribal lands, the United States Supreme Court said: "The Navajo Government has been called 'probably the most elaborate' among tribes. The legitimacy of the Navajo Tribal council, the freely elected governing body of the Navajos, is beyond question" (*Kerr-McGee Corp. v. Navajo Tribe,* 471 U.S. 195, 201 (1985), citations omitted). Clearly the thrust of this decision is to uphold the exercise of substantial autonomy in governing the internal affairs of the Navajo Nation.

5. See *Williams v. Lee,* 358 U.S. 217 (1959): 221–22, footnotes omitted. On June 1, 1868, a treaty was signed between General William T. Sherman, for the United States, and numerous chiefs and headmen of the "Navajo nation or tribe of Indians." "Implicit in . . . [the] treaty terms . . . was the understanding that the internal affairs of the Indians remained exclusively within the jurisdiction of whatever tribal government existed"

(Williams v. Lee). Today the Navajo Court of Indian Offenses exercises broad criminal and civil jurisdiction, which covers suits by outsiders against Indian defendants.

6. See Shepardson and Hammond (1970) for a discussion of social control methods among the Navajos. For a description of traditional legal practices among other tribes, see Llewellyn and Hoebel (1941).

7. Navajo Trib. Code tit. 7, § 253 (Cum. Supp. 1984–1985). The definition of Navajo Indian country is consistent with the federal definition:

> The Territorial jurisdiction of the Navajo Nation shall extend to Navajo Indian Country, defined as all land within the exterior boundaries of the Navajo Indian Reservation or of the Eastern Navajo Agency, all land within the limits of dependent Navajo Indian communities, all Navajo Indian allotments, and all other land held in trust for, owned in fee by, or leased by the United States to the Navajo Tribe or any Band of Navajo Indians. (Section 254) [and] Except as otherwise provided . . . the term "Indian Country" . . . means (a) all land within the limits of any Indian reservation under the jurisdiction of the United States Government, notwithstanding the issuance of any patent, and, including rights-of-way running through the reservation, (b) all dependent Indian communities within the borders of the United States whether within the original or subsequently acquired territory thereof, and whether within or without the limits of a state, and (c) all Indian allotments, the Indian titles to which have not been extinguished, including rights-of-way running through the same.

8. 471 U.S. 845 (1985); 480 U.S. 9 (1987). In the latter, the Court held that exhaustion of tribal court remedies, required in determinations of federal-question jurisdiction under National Farmers Union, is also required in determination of diversity of citizenship jurisdiction. Justice Marshall wrote:

> In diversity, as well as federal-question cases, unconditional access to the federal forum would place it in direct competition with the tribal courts, thereby impairing the latter's authority over reservation affairs . . . The federal policy of promoting tribal self-government encompasses the development of the entire tribal court system, including appellate courts. At a minimum, exhaustion of tribal remedies means that tribal appellate courts must have the opportunity to review the determinations of the lower tribal courts.

9. The fifth amendment of the United States Constitution provides that "no person shall be . . . deprived of life, liberty or property, without due process of law; nor shall private property be taken for public use, without just compensation."

References

Clinton, Robert N. 1976. Criminal Jurisdiction over Indian Lands: A Journey through a Jurisdictional Maze. *Arizona Law Review* 18 (3): 503–83.

Deloria, Vine, Jr., and Clifford Lytle. 1983. *American Indians, American Justice*. Austin: University of Texas Press.

———. 1984. *The Nations Within*. New York: Pantheon Books.

Llewellyn, Karl N., and E. Hoebel. 1941. *The Cheyenne Way: Conflict and Case Law in Primitive Jurisprudence*. Norman: University of Oklahoma Press.

Shepardson, Mary, and Blodwen Hammond. 1970. *The Navajo Mountain Community*. Berkeley: University of California Press.

Spicer, Edward H. 1962. *Cycles of Conquest: The Impact of Spain, Mexico, and the*

United States on the Indians of the Southwest, 1533–1960. Tucson: University of Arizona Press.

Tso, Tom. 1986. The Tribal Court Survives in America. *Judges' Journal* 25 (2): 22–25, 52–56.

Zion, James W. 1983. The Navajo Peacemaker Court: Deference to the Old and Accommodation to the New. *American Indian Law Review* 11: 89–109.

2 "Life Comes from It"

Navajo Justice Concepts

Robert Yazzie

Navajo justice is unique because it is the product of the experience of the Navajo people. Prior to contact with European cultures, Navajos developed their ways of approaching life through many centuries of dealing with obstacles to their survival. Likewise, Navajo concepts of justice are a product of the experience we have gained from dealing with problems. To understand these concepts fully, the essential character of Anglo-European law must be compared to that of Navajo law.

Law, in Anglo definitions and practice, is written rules that are enforced by authority figures. It is human-made. Its essence is power and force. The legislatures, courts, or administrative agencies who make the rules are made up of strangers to the actual problems or conflicts that prompted their development. When the rules are applied to people in conflict, other strangers stand in judgment, and police and prisons serve to enforce those judgments (Barsh and Henderson 1978). America is a secular society, where law is characterized as rules laid down by human elites for the good of society.

The Navajo word for "law" is *beehaz'áanii*. It means something fundamental, and something that is absolute and exists from the beginning of time (*Bennett v Navajo Board of Election Supervisors,* 6 Navajo Rptr. [Navajo Nation Sup. Ct. 1990], 201–3). Navajos believe that the Holy People "put it there for use from the time of beginning" for better thinking, planning, and guidance. It is the source of a healthy, meaningful life, and thus "life comes from it."[1] Navajos say that "life comes from beehaz'áanii" because it is the essence of life. The precepts of beehaz'áanii are stated in prayers and ceremonies that tell us of *hózhó*—"the perfect state." Through these prayers and ceremonies, we are taught what ought to be and what ought not to be.

Our religious leaders and elders say that human-made law is not true "law." Law comes from the Holy People who gave the Navajo people the ceremonies, songs, prayers, and teachings to know it. If we lose our prayers and ceremonies, we will lose the foundations of life. Our religious leaders also say that if we lose those teachings, we will have broken the law.

These contrasts show that while Anglo-European law is concerned with social control by humans, Navajo law comes from creation. It concerns life itself and the means to live successfully. The way to a meaningful life can be learned in teachings that are fundamental and absolute.

Navajo justice is also pragmatic, and to explain how that is so, I will describe the problems Navajos address, contrast Navajo thinking with the major concepts of Anglo-European law, outline Navajo dispute resolution processes, and discuss the practical, problem-solving emphasis of Navajo law.

The Social Problems Navajos Face

The core of Navajo justice is problem solving. Navajo legal thinking requires a careful examination of each aspect of a given problem to reach conclusions about how best to address it (Yazzie 1993). Navajos have faced different problems as they have learned the ways of survival in a sometimes hostile environment. In the times of legend, Navajos slew monsters. Today, Navajos face new monsters:

Domestic violence, involving abuse to spouses, elders, and children (Zion and Zion 1993).
Gang violence, when Navajo youth do what they please and refuse to listen.
Alcohol-related crime, such as driving while intoxicated (DWI), with resulting loss of productive lives, and disorderly conduct and fighting among neighbors and families in communities.[2]
Child abuse and neglect (Hauswald 1988).
The breakup of families in divorce and separation, with lasting effects upon children.

These problems are today's monsters; they are problems that get in the way of a successful life. The element common to all of the stated problems, including widespread alcohol abuse, is a loss of hope. A disease of the spirit infects too many Navajos and leads to increased court caseloads.[3] What do modern systems of justice offer to deal with these problems? Have the courts been effective in addressing them? Perhaps the very nature of these problems, grounded in a loss of self-respect and hope, gives us clues about how to address them effectively.

The Adversarial System: Vertical Justice

The first modern courts were introduced to the Navajo Nation in 1892 (BIA 1982; Aberle 1982). Today's Navajo Nation courts were created in 1959 (1958 Navajo Nation Council Resolution Nos. CO-69-58 and CJA 5-59, codified at Navajo Trib. Code tit. 7, § 101 [1978]) and reconstituted in 1985 (1985 Navajo Nation Council Resolution No. CD-94-85, codified at Navajo Trib. Code tit. 7, § 101 [1978]). The courts of the Navajo Nation use the state model of adjudication, that is, the adversarial system. There are obvious conflicts between Anglo-European justice methods and those of Navajo tradition. In trying to resolve these conflicts, Navajo Nation justice planners sometimes use models to help analyze the differences between the Anglo-European and Navajo legal systems. One useful model describes the Anglo-European legal system as "vertical" and the Navajo legal system as "horizontal" (Barkun 1968; Falk 1959).

A "vertical" system of justice relies upon hierarchies and power (Barkun 1968). That is, judges sit above the parties, lawyers, jurors, and other participants in court proceedings. The Anglo-European justice system uses rank, and the coercive power that goes with rank, to address conflicts. Power is the active element in the process. Judges have the power to affect the lives of the disputants directly for better or worse. Parties to a dispute have limited power and control over the process. A decision is dictated from on high by the judge, and that decision is an order or judgment that parties must obey or else face a penalty. The goal of the vertical system, or adversarial law, is to punish wrongdoers and teach them a lesson. For example, defendants in criminal cases are punished by jail and fines. In civil cases, one party wins and the other party is punished with a loss. Adversarial law offers only a win-lose solution; it is a zero-sum game. The Navajo justice system, on the other hand, prefers a win-win solution.

A fundamental aspect of the vertical system is the adjudicatory process. Adjudication makes one party the "bad guy" and the other "the good guy"; one of them is "wrong" and the other is "right." The vertical system is so concerned with winning and losing that when parties come to the end of the case, little or nothing is done to solve the underlying problems that caused the dispute in the first place.

For centuries, the focus of English and American criminal law has been punishment by the "state." The needs and feelings of the victims are ignored, and as a result, no real justice is done. There are many victims of any crime. They include the direct recipients of the harm and those who depend on them—family members, relatives, and the community. These are people who are affected by both the dispute and the legal decision. Often, the perpetrator is a victim as well, caught in a climate of lost hope, alcohol dependency, and other means of escape.

The victims, or subjects of the adjudication, have little or no opportunity to participate in the outcome of a case. Their needs and feelings are generally not considered, and thus are not addressed. They leave the courtroom feeling ignored and empty handed. The adversarial system is all or nothing, in which strangers with power decide the future of people who have become objects rather than participants.

Money is a driving force in modern American society. Lawyers operate the adversarial system, and money buys lawyers. The best lawyers cost the most. Legal procedures are costly, and only the most wealthy litigants can afford them. Money for justice turns it into a commodity to be bought and sold (Cahn 1960). Many people in our wage- and money-driven industrial society cannot afford redress, so they sometimes turn to extralegal methods for a remedy. For instance, the verdict in the Rodney King case sparked angry outbursts in Los Angeles because the adversarial trial of police ignored systemic violence and racism.

What do consumers of law get from the adversarial adjudication process of the vertical system? This is a difficult question to answer since its methods do not repair damaged relationships, families, communities, and society; instead this process promotes further conflict and disharmony.

Another element of the vertical system is a preoccupation with "the truth." The adversarial system dictates that there must be a winner and a loser. The side that represents the truth as it is perceived by the court wins, while the other side loses. "Truth" becomes a game where people attempt to manipulate the process, or undermine it where it does not suit their advantage. Each person has a version of "the truth," which represents that individual's understanding or perception of what happened.

People have strong feelings about truth, yet the vertical system does not allow the individual an opportunity to express his or her version of the truth in court. This role is taken from the individual and given to a power figure who is a stranger, both to the participants and to the situation in question. Individual perceptions of the truth are based upon one's perspective; the "rules" of the vertical system prevent the parties from presenting their perspectives. As a result, the parties feel disappointed and cheated because they each know what they think happened and the conclusions which should be drawn from that perspective.

When there must be a winner and a loser, truth is important. However, not all situations are best resolved through the adversarial determination of winner and loser. Sometimes solving the problem presented by a situation is more important than determining right and wrong and imposing penalties. Truth is irrelevant to a method of law that emphasizes problem solving.

For example, in a divorce, husbands and wives fight over property, child custody, and hurt feelings. Each party views the situation from his or her perspective of the truth. Based on that "truth," each feels that he or she should win and that the other party should lose. The adversarial system calls upon a husband and wife to make important decisions about their future—and those of their children—at a time when they are not emotionally prepared to look wisely to the future. The couple is not allowed a means to express their hurt and anger, and because there is no opportunity to deal with emotions, lawyers and judges make unpalatable decisions for the couple. In the process, children are wounded, and the separated couple often fight more after the divorce than before. The process is alien to Navajo thought. In the Navajo tradition, there is a greater concern with the well-being of children and the ability of people to go on with life without hurt feelings.

Vertical justice looks back in time, to find out what happened and assess punishment for it. We may never know what really happened. Vertical justice does not look to the future. It does not try to find out what went wrong in order to restore the mind, physical well-being, the spirit, and emotional stability. I insist that any definition of "law" must contain an emotional element: one of spirit and feelings. Where the feelings of parties are separated from the process and the decision does not address them, dissatisfaction follows. Where the legal system ignores the emotions of the parties, there can be no restoration of relationships.

Vertical adversarial adjudication relies upon power, force, and coercion. When powerful figures abuse their authority, there is authoritarianism and tyranny (Sagan 1985). Navajo thought recognizes the danger of hierarchical, or vertical, systems. There is a Navajo maxim that one must "beware of powerful beings." Likewise, coercion is so feared in Navajo ethics that the invocation of powerful beings (e.g., calling upon them to use their force against another)—a form of coercion—is considered to be witchcraft. The inappropriateness of the vertical system, as imposed upon Indian nations in modern systems of law and courts, becomes more obvious when it is compared to the horizontal Navajo approach.

The Navajo System: Horizontal Justice

The "horizontal" model of justice is in clear contrast to the vertical system of justice (Barkun 1968; Falk 1959). The horizontal justice model uses a horizontal line to portray equality: no person is above another. A better description of the horizontal model, and one often used by Indians to portray their thought, is a circle. In a circle, there is no right or left, nor is there a beginning or an end; every point (or person) on the line of a circle looks to the same center as the focus. The circle is the symbol of Navajo justice because it is perfect, unbroken, and a metaphor of unity and oneness. It conveys the image of people gathering together for discussion.

Imagine a system of law that permits anyone to say anything during the course of a dispute, a system in which no authority figure has to determine what is "true." Think of a system with an end goal of restorative justice, which uses equality and the full participation of disputants in a final decision.

If we say of law that "life comes from it," then where there is hurt, there must be healing.

Navajo concepts of justice are related to healing because many of the principles are the same. When a Navajo becomes ill, he or she will consult a medicine man or woman. Patients consult Navajo healers to summon outside healing forces and to marshal what they have inside them for healing. A Navajo healer examines the patient to determine the illness, its cause, and what ceremony matches the illness to cure it.[4] The cure must be related to the exact cause of the illness, because Navajo healing works through two processes: First, it drives away or removes the cause of illness; and second, it restores the person to good relations in solidarity with his or her surroundings and self.

The term "solidarity" is essential to an understanding of both Navajo healing and justice.[5] Language is a key to law, and those who share common understandings of the values and emotions that are conveyed in words are bonded through them (Sagan 1985). Words are signs that also convey feelings. The Navajo understanding of "solidarity" is difficult to translate into English, but it carries connotations that help the individual to reconcile self with family, community, nature, and the cosmos—all reality. The sense of oneness with one's surroundings, and the reconciliation of the individual with everyone and everything, makes an alternative to vertical justice work. Navajo justice rejects simply convicting a person and putting him or her in prison; instead it favors methods that use solidarity to restore good relations among people. Most important, it restores good relations with self.

Navajo justice is a sophisticated system of egalitarian relationships, where group solidarity takes the place of force and coercion. In it, humans are not in ranks or status classifications from top to bottom. Instead, all humans are equals and make decisions as a group. The process—which we call "peacemaking" in English—is a system of relationships where there is no need for force, coercion, or control.[6] There are no plaintiffs or defendants; no "good guy" or "bad guy." These labels are irrelevant.[7] "Equal justice" and "equality before the law" mean precisely what they say.[8] As Navajos, we do not think of equality as treating people equal *before* the law; they are equal *in* it.[9] Again our Navajo language points this out in practical terms.

Under the vertical justice system, when a Navajo is charged with a crime, the judge asks (in English): "Are you guilty or not guilty?" A Navajo cannot respond because there is no precise term for "guilty" in the Navajo language.[10] The word "guilt" implies a moral fault that commands retribution. It is a nonsense word in Navajo law due to the focus on healing, integration with the group, and the end goal of nourishing ongoing relationships with the immediate and extended family, relatives, neighbors, and community.

Clanship—*dooneeike'*—is a part of the Navajo legal system. There are approximately 210 Navajo clans.[11] The clan institution establishes relationships among individual Navajos by tracing them to a common mother; some clans are related to each other in the same way. The clan is a method of establishing relationships, expressed by the individual calling other clan members "my relative." Within a clan, every person is equal, because rank, status, and power have no place among relatives.

The clan system fosters deep, learned emotional feelings, which we call *k'é*. The term means a wide range of deeply felt emotions that create solidarity of the individual with his or her clan. When Navajos meet, they introduce themselves to each other by clan: "I am of the [name] clan, born for the [name] clan, and my grandparents' clans are [name]." The Navajo encounter ritual is in fact a legal ceremony, where those who meet can establish their relationships and obligations to each other. The Navajo language reinforces those bonds by maxims that require duties and mutual (or reciprocal) relationships. Obviously, one must treat his or her relatives well, and we say: "Always treat people as if they were your relative." That is also k'é.

Navajo justice uses k'é to achieve restorative justice. When there is a dispute, the procedure, which we call "talking things out," works like this: Every person concerned with or affected by the dispute or problem receives notice of a gathering to talk things out.[12] At the gathering, everyone has the opportunity to be heard. In the vertical legal system, the "zone of dispute" is defined as being only between the people who are directly involved in the problem (*Association of Data Processing Serv. Orgs. V. Camp,* 397 U.S. 150, 153 [1970]). On the other hand, as a Navajo, if my relative is hurt, that concerns me; if my relative hurts another, I am responsible to the injured person. In addition, if something happens in my community, I am also affected. I am entitled to know what happened, and I have the right to participate in discussions of what to do about it. I am within the zone of a dispute involving a relative. In the horizontal system, the zone is wider because problems between people also affect their relatives.

The parties and their relatives come together in a relaxed atmosphere to resolve the dispute. There are no fixed rules of procedure or evidence to limit or control the process. Formal rules are unnecessary. Free communication without rules encourages people to talk with each other to reach a consensus.[13] Truth is largely irrelevant because the focus of the gathering is to discuss a problem. Anyone present at the gathering may speak freely about his or her feelings or offer solutions to the problem. Because of the relationship and obligation that clan members have with and to each other, relatives of the parties are involved in the process. They can speak for, or speak in support of, relatives who are more directly involved in the dispute.

The involvement of relatives assures that the weak will not be abused and that silent or passive participants will be protected. An abused victim may be afraid to speak; his or her relatives will assert and protect that person's interests. The process also deals with the phenomenon of denial, when people refuse to face their own behavior. For instance, a perpetrator may feel shame for an act done and therefore be hesitant to speak. Relatives may speak to show mitigation for the act and to try to make the situation right. For example, Judge Irene M. Toledo of the Navajo Nation Ramah Judicial District has recounted a story in which the family helped a man confront the results of his actions.

The actions of this particular man commenced as an adversarial paternity proceeding familiar to today's child support enforcement efforts. The alleged father denied paternity while the mother asserted it. Judge Toledo sent the case to the district's Navajo Peacemaker Court for resolution. The parents of the couple were present for talking things out in peacemaking. It is difficult for a man and a woman to have a relationship in a small community without people knowing what is going on. The couple's family and everyone else who was present at the peacemaking were well aware of the activities of the couple. In light of the presence of family, the man admitted that he was the father of the child, and the parties negotiated paternity and child support as a group.[14] The participation of a wider circle of relations is an effective means to address denial and get directly to a resolution of a problem rather than get sidetracked in a search for "the truth."

The absence of coercion or punishment is an important Navajo justice concept because there are differences in the way people are treated when force is a consideration. If, as in the vertical system, a decision will lead to coercion or punishment, there are procedural controls to prevent unfair decisions and state power. These safeguards include burdens of proof on the state, a high degree of certainty (e.g., proof beyond a reasonable doubt), the right of the accused to remain silent, and many other procedural limitations. If, however, the focus of a decision is problem solving and not punishment, then parties are free to discuss problems. Thus, another dynamic we may see in Judge Toledo's example is that if we choose to deal with a dispute as a problem to be solved through discussion, rather than an act that deserves punishment, the parties are more likely to address their dispute openly.

Traditional Navajo civil procedure uses language and ceremony to promote the process of talking things out. Navajo values are expressed in prayers and teachings—using the powerful connotative force of our language—to bring people back to community in solidarity. Navajo values convey the positive forces of *hózhǫ́ǫ́jí,* which aims toward a perfect state. The focus is on doing things in a "good way," and to avoid *hashkéji naat'àa,* "the bad or evil way of speaking."

The process has been described as a ceremony (Bluehouse and Zion

1993). Outside the Navajo perspective, a "ceremony" is seen as a gathering of people to use ritual to promote human activity. To Navajos, a ceremony is a means of involving supernatural assistance in the larger community of reality. People gather in a circle to resolve problems but include supernatural forces within the circle's membership. Ceremonies use knowledge that is fundamental and that none of us can deny. Traditional Navajo procedure invokes that which Navajos respect (i.e., the teaching of the Holy People or tradition) and touches their souls. Put in a more secular way, it reaches out to their basic feelings.

For example, traditional Navajo tort law is based on *nalyeeh,* which is a demand by a victim to be made whole for an injury. In the law of nalyeeh, one who is hurt is not concerned with intent, causation, fault, or negligence. If I am hurt, all I know is that I hurt; that makes me feel bad and makes those around me feel bad too. I want the hurt to stop, and I want others to acknowledge that I am in pain. The maxim for nalyeeh is that there must be compensation so that there will be no hard feelings. This is restorative justice. Returning people to good relations with each other in a community is an important focus. Before good relations can be restored, the community must arrive at a consensus about the problem.

Consensus makes the process work. It helps people heal and abandon hurt in favor of plans of action to restore relationships. The dispute process brings people together to talk out a problem, then plan ways to deal with it. The nature of the dispute becomes secondary (as does "truth") when the process leads to a plan framed by consensus. Consensus requires participants to deal with feelings, and the ceremonial aspects of the justice gathering directly address those feelings. If, for any reason, consensus is not reached (due to the human weaknesses of trickery, withholding information, or coercion), it will prevent a final decision from being reached or will void one that stronger speakers may force on others.[15]

Another Navajo justice concept we must understand for a better comprehension of Navajo justice is distributive justice. Navajo case outcomes are often a kind of absolute liability, in which helping a victim is more important than determining fault. Distributive justice is concerned with the well-being of everyone in a community. For instance, if I see a hungry person, it does not matter whether I am responsible for the hunger. If someone is injured, it is irrelevant that I did not hurt that person. I have a responsibility, as a Navajo, to treat everyone as if he or she were my relative and therefore to help that hungry or injured person. I am responsible for all my relatives. This value, which translates itself into law under the Navajo system of justice, is that everyone is part of a community, and the resources of the community must be shared with all.[16] Distributive justice abandons fault and adequate compensation (a fetish of personal injury lawyers) in favor of assuring well-being for everyone. This affects the legal norms surrounding wrongdoing and elevates restoration over punishment.

Another aspect of distributive justice is that in determining compensation, the victim's feelings and the perpetrator's ability to pay are more important than damages determined using a precise measure of actual losses. In addition, relatives of the party causing the injury are responsible for compensating the injured party, and relatives of the injured party are entitled to the benefit of the compensation.

These are the factors that Navajo justice planners have used in the development of a modern Navajo legal institution—the Navajo Peacemaker Court. Before the development of the peacemaker court, Navajos experienced the vertical system of justice in the Navajo Court of Indian Offenses (1892–1959) and the courts of the Navajo Nation (1959-present). Over that one-hundred-year period, Navajos have either adapted the vertical system to their own ways or expressed their dissatisfaction with a system that made no sense (Vicenti et al. 1972). In 1982, however, the Judicial Conference of the Navajo Nation created the Navajo Peacemaker Court (Zion and McCabe 1982). This court is a modern legal institution that ties traditional community dispute resolution to a court based on the vertical justice model. It is a means of reconciling horizontal (or circle) justice to vertical justice by using traditional Navajo legal values, such as those described above.

The Navajo Peacemaker Court makes it possible for judges to avoid adjudication and avoid the discontent adjudication causes by referring cases to local communities to be resolved by talking things out. Once a decision is reached, it may (if necessary) be capped with a formal court judgment for future use.

The Navajo Peacemaker Court takes advantage of the talents of a naat'áanii (peacemaker).[17] A naat'áanii is a traditional Navajo civil leader whose authority comes from his or her selection by the community. The naat'áanii is chosen based on demonstrated abilities, wisdom, integrity, good character, and respect of the community. The civil authority of a naat'áanii is not coercive or commanding; he or she is a leader in the truest sense of the word. A peacemaker is a person who thinks well, who speaks well, who shows a strong reverence for the basic teachings of life, and who has respect for himself or herself and others in personal conduct.

A naat'áanii acts as a guide, and in a peacemaker's eyes, everyone—rich or poor, high or low, educated or not—is treated as an equal. The vertical system also attempts to treat everyone as an equal before the law, but judges in that system must single out someone for punishment. The act of judgment denies equality, and in that sense, "equality" means something different from the Navajo concept. The Navajo justice system does not impose a judgment, thereby allowing everyone the chance to participate in the final judgment, which everyone agrees to and which benefits all.

Finally, naat'áanii is chosen for knowledge, and knowledge is power that creates the ability to persuade others. There is a form of distributive justice in the sharing of knowledge by a naat'áanii. He or she offers it to the disputants so that they can use it to achieve consensus.[18]

Today's consumers of justice in the Navajo system have a choice of using the peacemaking process or the Navajo Nation version of the adversarial system (Tso 1992). The Navajo justice system, similar to contemporary trends in American law, seeks alternatives to adjudication in adversarial litigation. The Navajo Nation alternative is to go "back to the future" by using traditional law (Austin 1993).

Navajo Justice Thinking

The contrast between vertical and horizontal (or circle) justice is only one approach, or model, to see how Navajos have been developing law and justice. We, as Navajo judges, have only recently begun to articulate on paper and in English what we think and do. Navajo concepts of justice are simple, but our traditional teaching, which we use to make peace, may sound complicated.[19] Peacemaking—Navajo justice—incorporates traditional Navajo concepts, or Navajo common law, into modern legal institutions. Navajo common law is not about rules that are enforced by authority; it deals with correcting self to restore life to solidarity. Navajo justice is a product of the Navajo way of thinking. Peacemakers use Navajo thought and traditional teachings. They apply the values of spiritual teachings to bond disputants together and restore them to good relations.

This chapter uses English ways of saying things and English language concepts. It uses "paper knowledge" (in the words of a Navajo academic and lawyer, Elsie B. Zion) to try to teach you some of the things that go on in a Navajo judge's mind. To give a flavor of Navajo language thinking, consider the following:

Never let the sun catch you sleeping. Rise before the sun comes up. Why? You must not be dependent. You must do things with energy and do things for yourself. You must be diligent, or poverty will destroy you.

Watch your words. Watch what you say. Remember, words are very powerful. The Holy People gave them to us, and they created you to communicate. That is why you must think and speak in a positive way. Be gentle with your words. Do not gossip. Gossip has a name. It has a mind, eyes, and a voice. It can cause as much trouble as you make by calling it, so do not call it to you. It causes disharmony and creates conflict among people. It is a living monster because it gets in the way of a successful life. So, as we and our young Anglo friends say, "What goes around comes around." Remember that there are consequences to everything you say and do.

Know your clan. Do not commit incest. You cannot court or marry within your own clan. If you do, you will destroy yourself; you will jump in the fire. Incest is something so evil that it will make you crazy and destroy you.

You have duties and responsibilities to your spouse and children. If you are capable and perform them, you will keep your spouse and children in a good way. If not, you will leave them scattered behind. You will not be a worthy man or woman. If you act as if you have no relatives, that may come to you.[20]

The Holy People created human beings. Due to that fact, each must respect others. You cannot harm another. If so, harm will come back on you. There are always consequences from wrongful acts, just as good comes from good. Like begets like; harm must be repaired through restitution (nalyeeh) so that there will be no hard feelings, and victims will be whole again.

These teachings, and many others, are spoken from the beginning of childhood. Navajo judges are beginning to look at familiar childhood experiences as legal events. For example, when a baby first becomes aware of surroundings and shows that in a laugh, there is a ceremony—the "Baby's First Laugh Ceremony." Family and friends gather around the baby, sharing food and kinship, to celebrate with the child. What better way can we use to initiate babies into a world of good relationships and teach them the legal institution that is the clan?

These learned values serve as a guide in later years. As a child grows, he or she will act according to the teachings. Elderly Navajos tell us that we must always talk to our children so that they can learn these Navajo values and beliefs. If we do not, there will be disorder in the family and among relatives. The children will not listen, and they will have no responsibility to live by. We have youth violence because parents failed to talk to their children (Hauswald 1998).

Conclusion

Traditional peacemaking is being revived in the Navajo Nation with the goal of nourishing local justice in local communities. The reason is obvious: Life comes from it. Communities can resolve their own legal problems using the resources they have. Local decisions are the traditional Navajo way, in place of central control. Everyone must have access to justice that is inexpensive and readily available, and that does not require expensive legal representation. Peacemaking does not need police, prosecutors, judges, defenders, social workers, or the other agents of adversarial adjudication. Peacemaking is people making their own decisions, not others forcing decisions upon them. There are 110 chapters, or local governmental units, in the Navajo Nation. As of this writing, there are 210 peacemakers in 89 chapters, and we will extend the Navajo Peacemaker Court to every community.

This revival assures that Navajo justice will remain *Navajo* justice and not be an imported or imposed system (Austin 1993). Navajo peacemaking is not a method of alternative dispute resolution; it is a traditional justice method Navajos have used from time immemorial.

Author's Note

I adapted this chapter from an instructional outline I developed for presentations to non-Navajo lawyers and judges. It evolved in my thinking since January 20, 1992, when I assumed responsibilities as the chief justice of the Navajo Nation and chose Navajo common law and the Navajo Peacemaker Court as personal priorities. These ideas will continue to grow as I discover more about my culture, language, and traditions.

I draw upon two sources as I attempt to reconcile Navajo justice thinking with Anglo-European thought. I am a product of Bureau of Indian Affairs (BIA) boarding-school education, the type of education that was so destructive of the Navajo culture (Hauswald 1988). When I got out of boarding school, I was given a ticket to California to learn a manual skill in an electronics school. They told me I could not go to college, so I went to college. I was fascinated with the power, authority, and (as I thought then) money that went with being a lawyer, so I went to law school. When I got my law degree, I put it to use as a trial judge in the courts of the Navajo Nation. That returned me to another school—the school of Navajo life. Now, I seek to reconcile my paper knowledge with the vast knowledge that is held by my elders—"the keepers of the tribal encyclopedia" (in the words of Canadian philosopher Marshall McLuhan).

Sometimes I get impatient when I consider how traditional wisdom has so much value that has been forgotten. Sometimes I get angry about how Anglo law has overcome Navajo law, to the harm of Navajos. I read an evaluation of my talk on Navajo common law, after a conference with state judges and lawyers, which said, "Yazzie is bashing Anglo justice systems again." That is not my intent.

Emotions are important to me. The stereotype of the stoic, passive, or unemotional Indian is false, and emotions are an important part of Indian life. Navajos have a lot of pride, and when used in a good way, pride is a very positive emotion. How else could I have thrown away a ticket to an electronics school and insisted that I was capable of getting a college degree? It took a lot of drive and a little angry pride to tough it through law school in a time when non-Indians assumed that Indians were not capable of understanding the mysteries of "the law."

To me and too many other Navajos, law is something that "just is." To explain it in my own mind and to you, I need a basis for comparison. That basis is the shortcoming of modern American adjudication, and I am not alone in decrying its destructive elements. I share a fondness for centuries of English-American common law traditions, but changing circumstances now require us to take a new look at that indefinable quality we call "justice." As we of the Navajo Nation discuss the traditional knowledge that gives us power to survive in modern times, I find a property that is immensely valuable. I want to share it with you out of respect and to honor Navajo distributive justice. You, who have taken an interest to read this, are like a relative. This relationship will help us grow together in a good way, because life comes from it.

Notes

This chapter is an edited version of Robert Yazzie's "'Life Comes from It': Navajo Justice Concepts," *New Mexico Law Review,* 14 (1): 175–84, 1994. Reprinted with permission of the *New Mexico Law Review* and the author.

1. The term "Holy People" refers to divine personages or spirit forces that were instrumental in the creation of the world. Following creation and the exodus of the Navajo people to their present place in this world, the Holy People went into the rocks and earth, where they still help. "Put there from the beginning of time" is a well-known Navajo phrase that means the Holy People established certain fundamentals as part of creation. "Life comes from it" refers to the fact that law is basic and that a meaningful life is one of its products.

2. We estimate that of our current criminal caseload (cases brought forward plus new filings), approximately 90,000 matters, or 70 percent of the offenses, are related to or the product of alcohol use. This leads us to wonder whether criminal law is the best tool to address crime and alcohol (Barsh and Henderson 1978). Driving while intoxicated is a problem all jurisdictions in the Southwest share. Alcohol-related mortality (deaths that are the product of alcohol consumption) is high in New Mexico. It has the highest motor vehicle–accident fatality rate in the United States. Blood alcohol levels are present in 51 percent of auto crash deaths, 49 percent of homicide victims, and 42 percent of suicides (Chavez et al. 1993). Disorderly conduct and fighting is our greatest category of criminal offenses. Navajo Nation trial judges agree that disorderly conduct most often involves drinking and fighting in family and community settings.

3. Over 85,000 criminal and civil cases were pending in FY 1992, and 93,000 in FY 1993.

4. In Navajo thought, like begets like.

5. Note that one dictionary definition of the word "solidarity" recognizes Native thought as "a union of interests, purposes, or sympathies among members of a group;

fellowship of responsibilities and interests: *'The savage depends upon the group . . . for practical cooperation and mental solidarity'* (Bronislaw Malinwski)" (Morris 1981).

6. Again, forcing a person to do something against his or her will is a form of witch-craft, something that is considered horrible in Navajo thought.

7. Navajo Nation associate justice Raymond D. Austin recently told an audience of lawyers at a conference that we must not use bad words to accuse others because the Holy People gave us our language and told us we must not abuse others with it. I cannot call another a "bad guy," and when Navajos are called upon to do so in adjudication, that goes against their ethical values.

8. Navajos sometimes appear to be literal because the Navajo language is very precise. The maxim is that "words are very powerful" because we use them with precision, and they mean what they say.

9. In Anglo thought everyone is equal *procedurally* within the judicial system. Yet there are still glaring inequalities among the poor, women, AIDS victims, and others who are distinguished by gender, class, race, or sexual orientation. In Navajo thought, all people are genuinely equal in status and outcomes; equality is not limited to an individual's involvement with the judicial process.

10. Judges of other Indian nations point out the same conclusion for their languages. As in the state and federal courts, guilty plea rates are high in tribal courts. Is it because of the overwhelming power of the "state"? Is it because (as we believe) Indians are essentially honest and tell the truth? Is it because those who are charged in our courts have a different concept of fault? Is it because our traditional law disregards "guilt" and "innocence" in place of problem solving?

11. There are four original clans. As Navajo women married people from other Indian nations, or women from other nations became clan mothers, the number of clans grew. However, the exact number of clans that resulted from this process is a point of some controversy among the Navajo people. A Navajo is a member of his or her mother's clan and "born for" his or her father's clan; the use of grandparent clans establishes even more extended relationships so that most Navajos are relatives of most others.

12. Disputes commonly involve matters such as land squabbles, divorce, probate, or contract. Navajo "notice" need not be in writing, and it is not concerned with a specific written statement of an accusation or proposed punishment. There is a right to participate in a gathering to solve problems because it affects everyone. Navajo due process requires notice to a wider circle of people than is required by general American due process.

13. There are some unspoken limitations, of course, such as the prohibition against abusing each other with words.

14. Judge Toledo also saw a creative use of services, such as supplying firewood in place of money, which the father did not have.

15. The Navajo language tells us a lot about Navajo attitudes toward Anglo justice. A lawyer, *'agha'diit'aahii,* is one who takes away with words. This definition describes someone who uses words for coercion. Someone who "takes away with words" is a pushy bossyboots.

16. One study of Navajo witchcraft directly relates the beliefs and practices to sharing and group survival (Kluckhohn 1944).

17. The word "naat'áanii" refers to someone who speaks well and whose words reflect good guidance. Sometime around the year 1832, Chinle area Navajos attacked the Hopi village of Oraibi because of the killing of a Navajo leader, Darts at the Enemy, by a Hopi. The death was particularly harmful to the man's Towering House Clan, because

when he delivered speeches, "he would 'talk in' all kinds of goods from every side (i.e., he would bring prosperity to his people by saying they were to receive it)" (Preston 1954). The respect for Darts at the Enemy shows that successful planning is the aspect of "speaking well" that Navajos respect in a leader.

18. I have often said that "knowledge is power." To Navajos, knowledge is a form of wealth or property. Sharing it with those who do not have it is distributive justice and assumes that those the naat'áanii helps are entitled to a fair share of that power.

19. As Navajo judges and their staff discuss law, history, religion, and philosophy to improve their system, language barriers and conceptual differences become more obvious — that is, there are difficulties when we discuss such things in English and write them down. Mary White Shirley, a Navajo lawyer, once complained to a non-Navajo lawyer: "You silly Anglos; you always have reasons for everything. Don't you know that some things just *are*?"

20. Navajo says of a wrongdoer, "He acts as if he has no relatives." It is horrible to think that such a thing could happen. Homer Bluehouse once said that when a person did something very evil, or was a repeat offender, the community would shun him or her. That often leads to suicide because being without relatives is the worst thing that can happen.

References

Aberle, David. 1982. *The Peyote Religion among the Navaho.* Chicago: University of Chicago Press.

Austin, Raymond D. 1993. Freedom, Responsibility and Duty: ADR and the Navajo Peacemaker Court. *Judges Journal* 32 (2): 8–11.

Barkun, Michael. 1968. *Law without Sanctions: Order in Primitive Societies and the World Community.* New Haven, Conn.: Yale University Press.

Barsh, Russel L., and J. Youngblood Henderson. 1978. Tribal Courts, the Model Code, and the Police Idea. *American Indians and the Law,* ed. Lawrence Rosen, 25–60. New Brunswick, N.J.: Transaction Books.

BIA [Bureau of Indian Affairs]. 1982. *Sixty-First Annual Report of the Commission of Indian Affairs to the Secretary of the Interior.* Washington, D.C.: Bureau of Indian Affairs, U.S. Department of the Interior.

Bluehouse, Philmer, and James W. Zion. 1993. *Hozhooji Naat'aanii:* The Navajo Justice and Harmony Ceremony. *Mediation Quarterly* 10 (4): 327–37.

Cahn, Edmond. 1960. The Consumers of Injustice. In *The World of Law,* vol. 2, 3rd ed., ed. Ephraim London, 574–90. New York: Simon and Schuster.

Chavez, Liza D., Thomas M. Becker, Charles L. Wiggins, Charles R. Key, and Jonathan M. Samet. 1993. Alcohol-Related Mortality. In *Racial and Ethnic Patterns of Mortality in New Mexico,* ed. Thomas M. Becker, Charles L. Wiggins, Rita S. Elliott, Charles R. Key, and Jonathan M. Smart, 108–17. Albuquerque: University of New Mexico Press.

Falk, Richard A. 1959. International Jurisdiction: Horizontal and Vertical Conceptions of Legal Order. *Temple Law Quarterly* 32: 295–320.

Hauswald, Lizabeth. 1988. Child Abuse and Child Neglect: Navajo Families in Crisis. *Dine' Be'iina': A Journal of Navajo Life* 1: 37–53.

Kluckhohn, Clyde. 1944. *Navaho Witchcraft.* Boston: Beacon Press.

Morris, William, ed. 1981. *The American Heritage Dictionary of the English Language.* Boston: Houghton-Mifflin.

Preston, Scott. 1954. The Oraibi Massacre. In *Navajo Historical Selections,* ed. Robert W. Young and William Morgan. Phoenix, Ariz.: Phoenix Indian School Print Shop.

Sagan, Eli. 1985. *At the Dawn of Tyranny: The Origins of Individualism, Political Oppression, and the State.* New York: Knopf.

Tso, Tom. 1992. Moral Principles, Traditions, and Fairness in the *Navajo Nation Code of Judicial Conduct. Judicature* 76 (1): 15–21.

Vicenti, Dan, Keonard B. Jimson, Stephen Conn, and M. J. L. Kellog. 1972. *The Law of the People—Dine' Bibee Hazaanii.* Vol. 2. Ramah, N.Mex.: Ramah High School Press.

Yazzie, Robert. 1993. Tribal, State, and Federal Relationships in Our Future Society. Address at Building on Common Ground: A Leadership Conference to Develop a National Agenda to Reduce Jurisdictional Disputes between Tribal, State, and Federal Courts, Santa Fe, New Mexico, September 8–22.

Zion, James W., and Nelson McCabe. 1982. *The Navajo Peacemaker Court Manual.* Window Rock: Judicial Branch of the Navajo Nation.

Zion, James W., and Elsie B. Zion. 1993. Hozho's Sokee' [Hozho Sokee']– Stay Nicely Together: Domestic Violence under Navajo Common Law. *Arizona State Law Journal* 25 (2): 407–26.

PEACEMAKING CONCEPTS AND PRACTICES

Commentary on Part 2

James W. Zion and Marianne O. Nielsen

This section presents peacemaking in action. The concepts, principles, and processes are described and shown in a variety of contexts. Although peacemaking has been more or less the strategy of choice for handling civil and family cases, its appropriateness and growing use in criminal cases is also demonstrated here. All three chapters are written by James W. Zion, who was one of the principals involved in developing the current form of peacemaking. He has both an insider's and an outsider's point of view, making him a unique observer of the history, structure, and dynamics of peacemaking. Even though he has retired from his previous position as solicitor to the judicial branch of the Navajo Nation, he is still active in peacemaking. He is now using his many years of administrative and scholarly knowledge as a frontline worker; he was appointed as special domestic violence commissioner for the Crownpoint Judicial District family court in January of 2004.

The opening chapter in this part is probably the most cited piece of work that exists on peacemaking. Editing of this chapter has been kept to a minimum, with a change in format being the only difference. Zion's chapter will seem repetitious of other works included in this book, but that is only because they are quoting *it*. This chapter provides a detailed history of the personalities involved, the meetings, the disagreements and consensuses, the challenges, and the solutions of beginning the "new" program. Zion emphasizes the challenge of overcoming pressures to assimilate and the efforts needed to prove the legitimacy of Navajo justice values and procedures.

This article is part of a trilogy of writings—the April 1982 court rules; a May 1982 manual on peacemaking, with legalistic rules, plain language rules, guidance on each section, and forms; and this article, which sought to explain that peacemaking was a means of giving deference to the traditional, or "old," while accommodating the "new," namely, the modern, imposed court system. The article was written for the 1983 symposium of the Commission on Folk Law and Legal Pluralism held in Vancouver, British Columbia. That was the first occasion when peacemaking was showcased to academics outside the Navajo Nation, and it began a tradition of Navajo Nation justices, judges, peacemakers, and staff traveling outside the Navajo Nation to explain peacemaking to the outside world.

Despite the intended audience of outsiders, the article was also intended to play a role at home. Public officials outside the court system were slow to embrace peacemaking. Although tribal chairman Peter MacDonald, Sr., members of the judiciary committee of the Navajo Nation Council, and others directed chief justice Nelson J. McCabe to take steps to reintegrate traditional Navajo law in the court system in 1981, politicians were hesitant to embrace it. The system was set up using court rulemaking power rather than legislation, and it was intentionally funded by payments from users to avoid having to approach the council for funding. When Peterson Zah assumed power as the chairman of the council in 1982, he held public hearings to ask for input into his policies and priorities, and peacemaking was received well when it was presented. Zion's paper was designed to give policy makers a philosophy and approach to the novel process (nationally and internationally) of recognizing and reviving a traditional Indian legal system, which operated out of public view for decades following the introduction of adjudication to the Navajo Nation in 1892.

Chapter 4 describes the social-psychological processes that operate within peacemaking. Zion explains how and why peacemaking brings forth the underlying issues that led to a particular dispute. He shows how European-based psychological concepts can be used to describe the peacemaking processes. This chapter was originally an attempt to answer a question that Chief Justice Yazzie kept asking before going to or after coming from conferences and discussions of peacemaking: "How does it work?" (The associated question "Does it work?" is addressed in other chapters of this book.) Yazzie attempted to answer his own question from a Navajo point of view in "Life Comes from It" (chapter 2). When Zion was the solicitor (chief lawyer) for the judicial system, he liked to write think pieces and policy explorations. Chapter 4 is an attempt to use social psychology to try to explain peacemaking.

Another recurring problem with peacemaking is the question of whether its processes and procedures can be replicated in other societies. Zion takes the point of view that although there are many things that are unique to Navajos as a matter of culture (in their language and world view), the processes that inform peacemaking and make it work have a great deal to do with basic human drives. He attempted to construct a model to both explain peacemaking and examine its processes in action. As the peacemakers began to talk about what they did, Zion examined what they said in light of the psychological dynamics he explored.

Chapter 5, "When People Act as if They Have No Relatives," is a continuation of a piece that is not republished in this book, "Hozho' Sokee'—Stay Together Nicely: Domestic Violence under Navajo Common Law" (Zion and Zion 1993). The original article was written in 1992, as Navajo Nation domestic violence law was being developed. The Navajo Nation Council's judiciary, public safety, and health and social services committees sponsored a public hearing on domestic violence in the fall of 1991, and that energized the Navajo Nation legal community to think about the content and procedure of a domestic violence code. The original article was another think piece designed to help guide legal policy development based upon research of Navajo traditions.

The original article, the court rules adopted in August 1992 (after the draft was written), and the Domestic Abuse Protection Act of July 1993 were controversial because they advocated and provided for peacemaking in domestic violence cases. A decade of public debate—sometimes heated—followed as DNA-People's Legal Services lawyers, victim advocates, anti–domestic violence program staff, and others insisted that peacemaking could not—and should not—be used to address domestic violence because it is mediation, and victims of violence are revictimized in a mediation process because of a power imbalance.

In chapter 5, Zion reports his initial conclusions on the longstanding controversy over peacemaking and domestic violence, based upon hearing cases between February 6, 2004, and July 9, 2004 (the cutoff point to meet the deadline for the chapter), using both his take on Navajo peacemaking and his experience as an adjudicating commissioner. The chapter attempts to resolve the longstanding debate of whether or not we can use peacemaking in domestic violence cases by redefining the term and applying his theories in actual case settings to address factors to decide when it may or may not "work." Our understanding of the issue is advanced by this original work, but further exploration is needed.

References

Zion, James W., and Elsie B. Zion. 1993. Hozho' Sokee' —Stay Together Nicely: Domestic Violence under Navajo Common Law. *Arizona State Law Journal* 25 (2): 407–26.

3 The Navajo Peacemaker Court

Deference to the Old and Accommodation to the New

James W. Zion

There is a body of Navajo law that has survived the occupation of Spanish, Mexican, and American military forces; the domination of the government of the United States; and the intrusion of the European and American industrial revolution into the life of the Navajo people, the *Dine'*. The traditions, customs, and usages of the Navajos, more properly identified as Navajo common law, survived sixty-seven years of attempts by the Bureau of Indian Affairs (BIA) to "educate" and "civilize" the Navajos through an imposed Navajo Court of Indian Offenses, which required Navajo judges to use foreign law. Navajo common law has also remained alive for twenty-five years in a court system controlled by the Navajo government, but it was born of fears of a state takeover and a forced adoption of methods used by American state courts. The Navajo common law has survived through the demands of the Navajo people and their elected leaders.

The Navajo Peacemaker Court is an experiment in blending the procedures of the Navajo common law with Anglo methods, and it is an attempt to see whether the best means of using Indian custom law is through the development of procedures for its use rather than through cataloging its substantive rules. This chapter presents the history of the beginning of the Navajo Peacemaker Court and a discussion of why it came into being. The Navajo judges who established the peacemaker court hoped to find an alternative to Anglo judicial methods by accommodating demands for the use of custom law.

In April of 1982, the judges of the Navajo courts adopted a new kind of court system that blended traditional Navajo methods of mediating disputes with regular court operations. The existing Navajo court system is modeled after the state courts of the United States, and in many ways it is as alien to traditional Navajo ways as are the other courts of the United States (Brakel 1978; Fahey 1975; Conn 1978; Keon-Cohen 1981; Barsh 1973).[1] The peacemaker court was adopted partly because of a desire to soften the impact of an alien system. In forming the new court the judges appealed to the longstanding tradition of the Navajos that provides for headmen and women or community leaders to mediate and arbitrate local problems. The rules adopted by the judges carefully stated that the old method had been used continually until the present time, particularly in the courts (Zion and McCabe 1982).

The Reason for the Court:
The Persistence of Navajo Legal Culture

Studies of Indian religions show a persistence in traditional religious ways. Some of those practices may have been modified from ancient times, but many are in fact modern and a response to Anglo pressures (Aberle 1966; Dusenberry 1962; Jorgensen 1972; Kluckhohn and Leighton 1974; Hult-krantz 1976).

Many modern religious and ceremonial practices are a product of Indian people feeling threatened and trapped by outside institutions, and many res-ervation Indians respond to the pressures of a materialistic and discrimina-tory America by attempting to reach back to old values and ways (Kluck-hohn 1944). Ceremonial and religious practices are not the only aspects of Indian life that are affected by outside pressures. The need to resolve conflicts or disagreements usually addressed by law has also been affected by a desire to use old values and ways of self-protection.

If any division of the Navajo people by acculturation or values can be made, then there are three groups of Navajos (Gilbreath 1973; Shepardson 1963). The first group, which could be called the "traditionals," generally live in isolated rural areas, and they live simply, using the older ways of the Navajos. The second is a large group of people who are in a transitional status between traditional Navajo ways and the ways of modern America. These "caught-in-the-middles" are the largest and most visible group. Of-ten they were reared in traditional ways and sent to boarding schools at an early age, where they acquired Anglo educations and values. Now they feel uneasy in both worlds. The third group is the "moderns," made up of young people who speak Navajo poorly or not at all. These people are more attuned to the outside culture because of education, employment, and the ever-increasing presence of television.

Using Navajo common law appeals to all three of these groups, but for different reasons. The traditionals want custom law used in the courts be-cause they feel comfortable with it; they understand it, and they have more control when using it. The caught-in-the-middles feel more comfortable with the ideas associated with their upbringing, and they feel the use of custom can provide a tool for protection from the white outsiders who discriminate against them. Often the moderns feel they have an obligation to return to their roots. They know enough about the mechanics of the dominant society (e.g., widespread prejudice and the impact of the capitalist ethic) to desire a legal system they will be able to influence. The problem for the courts is how to accommodate all three groups and serve their needs.

Some Navajos oppose the use of Navajo customary ways. Navajo history has as one of its central themes the conflict between the traditionals and the moderns on the issue of returning to the traditional ways or becoming assimilated. The proposed adoption of a Navajo constitution, livestock control, and the distribution of mineral income have all been political issues in this fight, and the fight continues (Young 1978; Iverson 1981).

The conflict between the traditionals and the moderns has also reached the Navajo courts, and its judges find themselves "in a dilemma of traditional versus professional authority." (Barsh 1973). When the Navajo courts were founded, the pressures from outside the tribe were to fill the judgeships with Navajos who were highly educated and highly trained in Anglo methods. Despite these pressures, both the Navajo Tribal Council and the judges expressed their desire to use traditional Navajo thinking, methods, and customs (Conn 1978).

Today the acquired Anglo professionalism of the judges, engendered by the climate in which the Navajo courts were founded, has secured their continued functioning on an American state court model. The judges are, however, responding to the dilemma of blending traditional values with their professional authority. They recognize the utility of the American court system, but at the same time they are searching for ways to give lasting legitimacy to the persistence of Navajo common law by bringing it into the court system.

Navajo history is full of illustrations of strong cultural survival complemented by a canny pragmatism. This has led to the adoption of features from the outside that are desirable and the rejection of those that do not fit Navajo values. The use of Spanish weaving and silversmith techniques and a passion for education show a selective adoption of other ways. The rejection of an imposed constitution and governmental structure shows the tough rejection of methods that do not fit. The persistence of Navajo legal culture and the rejection of harsh rules of law are but another example of that pragmatism.

Events Leading to the Adoption of the Peacemaker Court

On April 2, 1981, Nelson J. McCabe, the chief justice of the Navajo courts, gave instructions to begin a study of how Navajo customs could be used in the courts as law. He stated that the chairman of the Navajo Tribal Council, the judiciary committee of the council, and some of the judges had made repeated requests for a study of custom law, and McCabe wanted the study to be made by the courts (Nelson McCabe, pers. comm., April 2, 1981). Tribal chairman Peter MacDonald expressed a great interest in finding a system for using Navajo customs. There was a place for them because the courts are permitted to use Navajo "customs and usages" in civil litigation (Navajo Trib. Code tit. 7, § 204 [1978]).[2] Chairman MacDonald asked a noted non-Indian legal expert and a tribal attorney to research the possibilities for the use of Navajo custom law (Jean Cahn, pers. comm., June 24, 1982).[3] The combined insistence of the executive and legislative leaders of Navajo government led to an organized effort within the courts (Lee Be-Gaye, pers. comm., April 23, 1982).

The court's efforts had barely begun, having produced only an internal discussion paper of some of the possibilities for research and the outline of a proposal for funding the project, when Chairman MacDonald formed a nine-member task force on the Navajo judiciary to examine the "structure and functioning of the Judiciary System," including "ways in which great emphasis on and utilization of traditional Navajo customs and methods of resolving disputes can be incorporated into the court system as the preferred method and set of values" (MacDonald 1981).

The task force began its work, but there were disputes among its members, and its demands for funding were ignored. After only a few meetings were held to agree upon the goals of the task force and to hear initial reports from the participant organizations, the work of the task force was brought to an end.[4]

During the initial months of the court initiative, there was little concrete progress because of an assumption that funds would be needed to conduct a comprehensive study of Navajo substantive law. There were many informal discussions with the judges, the judiciary committee, the president of the Navajo Nation Bar Association, and others.[5] These led to an agreement that Navajo customs, traditions, and usages must be legitimized as law and used in the courts. There were, however, few concrete ideas on *how* that would be done. The talks centered on codifying custom laws through tribal council action, on preparing a restatement of Navajo common law in the modern American common law manner, or developing a method of using Navajo common law in the same manner as English and American common law. No ideas were implemented, however.

In December 1981, two simple questions resulted in the idea that became the foundation for the Navajo Peacemaker Court. Tribal council delegate Albert Ross, Jr., of the St. Michaels Chapter, near Window Rock, the Navajo capital, came to the office of Chief Justice McCabe to ask a few simple legal questions.[6] The chief justice called his attorney to answer them.

The main concern was, "If a Navajo judge appoints someone to work with people in the community, can the person be sued?" After some discussion, another question was, "Can the person appointed by the judge force the Navajo police to carry out his orders?"

These questions were asked because of a court custom that had been in existence for a long time. The custom was not found in any Navajo legal writings, and it was little used in modern times. The court custom was that a judge could call in a respected member from the local community to work with litigants on problems for which mediation, rather than the American adversarial system, was more appropriate. These disputes were usually over family matters, such as divorce or drinking problems, or over everyday problems. Both Chief Justice McCabe and council delegate Ross confirmed that this custom had existed from the times of the Navajo Court of Indian Offenses, 1892 to 1959. The idea that there was a customary mechanism already in use for resolving disputes was exciting. It quickly became the foundation idea for the court's custom law project.

The first task of the project was to verify the custom as stated by Chief Justice McCabe and council delegate Ross. An important authority was consulted: retired judge Alfred Hardy, Sr., who had served as a judge in the former Navajo Court of Indian Offenses from 1939 through 1958. Judge Hardy confirmed that there was such a custom. He stated that he often used it successfully in divorce matters and other domestic actions (Alfred Hardy, pers. comm., March 1, 1982). Judge Hardy's validation of the custom was important because he was a highly respected judge during his years on the bench, and he continues to be consulted and acknowledged as a wise man.

Another source for verifying the custom was judge Homer Bluehouse of the Chinle Judicial District. He was widely acknowledged as the sitting Navajo judge most knowledgeable in the area of Navajo custom law.[7] Judge Bluehouse also confirmed the use of the mediation method in the Navajo Court of Indian Offenses and in the Navajo-controlled courts from 1959. He stated that he had used the system, but that he preferred to act as the mediator himself. He told of assault cases in which an individual came before the court charged with a crime. On closer examination, the judge discovered that the criminal case was in reality a dispute between neighbors. When the neighbors were brought into court for an informal discussion of the case, the judge sometimes found underlying disputes, for example, over grazing rights or fences, or other problems that had turned neighbors against each other. Judge Bluehouse often persuaded the parties to reach an agreement on the underlying dispute, and he had them shake hands and agree to be enemies no longer. He often induced agreement through lectures on the law, particularly through lectures on Navajo traditional values. This process turned a criminal case under American legal principles into a Navajo civil action.[8]

Informal discussion with the Navajo judges in private, along with questions asked of those who knew the custom, confirmed that the courts had frequently used people outside the regular court structure on cases. The older judges and practitioners outlined the custom and told of its harmony with the thinking of the Navajos. Navajo judges and practitioners confirmed there was a strong desire for an alternative to the American adversarial method of presenting cases. The problem was how to devise a method that would combine the identified custom with normal court operation.[9]

Since a method of mediation had been identified, a short search of the literature was made to see if there were any systems of mediation that would be useful. One item of interest was a Pennsylvania colonial experiment, which grew out of the religious practice of the Quakers (Society of Friends) of resolving their disputes within their local communities (the meetings), rather than resorting to the common law court (Scott 1982). In 1683 the Quaker-dominated Pennsylvania General Assembly "provided an institutional alternative to court action by appointing common peacemakers who would arbitrate disputes. The law stated that 'the judgment of the peacemakers, shall be as Conclusive, as a sentence given by the County Court'" (Scott 1982, 9). The Quaker idea arose from its practice of localizing authority within small religious communities. This localization is probably the result of the English persecution of dissenters, which produced small, independent, and self-reliant religious bodies that protected themselves through methods of regulating their own members. The Quakers may have taken the name or the practice of their court from the Seneca Indian Nation, which had a peacemaker court (*In re Jimerson,* 4 Misc. 2d 1028, 225 N.Y.S.2d 627 [N.Y. Sup. Ct. 1963], *aff'd,* 22 A.D.2d 417, 255 N.Y.S.2d 959 [N.Y. App. Div. 1965]; Lednicer 1959). Internal disciplinary systems born of persecution by a dominant force are a dynamic that is found in Indian cultures as well.

The contemporary American legal community has been looking to mediation and arbitration as an alternative means of handling disputes and diverting cases from the congested dockets of American courts, and the Navajo courts examined some of the experiments that use those methods.[10] The small-claims court system was also considered.[11]

The Navajo mediation custom had been identified, and it was strong enough on its own to use as a basis for a court system. However, outside examples and authorities were used not only as suggestions for a mechanism to be installed in an adversarial system, but as a justification for a formal mediation court operated by members of Navajo communities. In a speech to the annual meeting of the Navajo Nation Bar Association, chairman Peter MacDonald summed up the feeling of independence and the assertion that the Navajos already had a better answer. MacDonald pointed out that there was a traditional Navajo way of settling disputes using mediation and agreement. He pointed to the fact that under Navajo tradition, offenders would be required to undo the harm they did through community service, with the use of gentle coercion and persuasion. MacDonald made two propositions to the Navajo bar. First, in dealing with the law, they should not throw out the old, and second, "justice" for the Navajo means self-protection against the outside and taking care of matters internally.[12]

Contemporary recollections of the Navajo mediation system were collected, and a cursory search was made of legal, anthropological, and sociological literature for accounts of Navajo legal practices. Contemporary legal literature gave some suggestions for a mechanism to use and justify the Navajo custom, but there was little to be found of much practical use in either social science works or works on Navajo practices.[13] Based upon this information, a draft of some proposed Navajo court rules was prepared.

The Debate on the Rules

The Navajo courts follow the practice of most American jurisdictions of exercising the power to adopt court rules to regulate and define court operations.[14] After a great deal of discussion, the chief justice decided to use the rulemaking authority of the courts to create the peacemaker court, rather than apply to the Navajo Tribal Council for legislation authorizing it. The reasoning for the decision was that legislation would delay putting a custom court into operation, and that the courts should exercise their authority to structure themselves, just as state courts freely create court divisions, departments, and small-claims courts by court rule.

The standard practice of the Navajo Tribal Council and its committees, as well as the chapters, is to use the resolution format for making laws and setting policies. The resolutions normally contain a preamble explaining the legal authority and reasons for the enactment, and contain enacting language setting forth the actual laws or policies adopted. This format was used by the Navajo court for the adoption of the peacemaker court rules (Zion and McCabe 1982).

The Navajo judges meet frequently, and when they act to adopt rules of court they meet as the Navajo Nation Judicial Conference. The judges considered the proposed peacemaker court rules on April 23, 1982. On that early spring day, the judges felt a spirit of progress because of the dedication of a new multimillion-dollar tribal office building that afternoon, and they considered the proposed rules with enthusiasm. Their enthusiasm was restrained by caution, however.

A report outlining the origin, purpose, and structure of the new court was presented to the judges along with a draft resolution and the actual rules (Zion and McCabe 1982). The rules were explained, and many questions about their specifics were answered.

Judge Bluehouse led the discussion, opposing adoption of the rules. He stated his support for Navajo tradition but expressed his strong feeling that the civil rights of individual Navajos would be violated by a sanctioned return to old, abusive ways. He mentioned examples of violence and coercion, and he asked how these could be prevented under the proposed system. His objections and questions were answered and discussed, and he finally shifted his stand to one of support.

Judge James Atcitty also opposed the rules.[15] He felt that the use of traditional procedure was completely out of step with modern times and contemporary needs. He felt that the existing system was the only way to handle disputes. Judge Atcitty is from Shiprock, and his arguments echoed those raised by earlier Shiprock leaders in the battles over oil revenues, livestock control, and a Navajo constitution.

Judge Tom Tso entered the argument, and at first he was mildly critical of the rules.[16] However, his views shifted as the discussion and the arguments progressed. He stressed the reasonableness of the system, the protections built into it, and, most of all, the demand for and the need to use Navajo traditional legal processes. He was the strongest proponent of the rules. Judge Harry Brown gave his cautious endorsement to the rules, as did Judge Henry Whitehair.[17] Judge Marie F. Neswood was hesitant about the rules. She wondered if it was possible to blend a custom that was in little use with regular court operations, but after lengthy exchanges with the other judges, she gave her tentative support for the plan.[18]

Chief Justice McCabe backed the plan and reported the demands he had received for the use of custom law. However, since the tribal code provides that a majority of judges must agree to adopt court rules (approved by the chief justice and a tribal attorney), the chief justice left most of the argument to the trial judges (Navajo Trib. Code tit. 7, § 601 [1978]).

A majority agreed to back the experiment, and the rules were enacted by a vote of five in favor and one opposed. One judge was absent.

The judges left their conference feeling optimistic about this experiment in Navajo custom law. Now it had to be acceptable to the Navajo government and to their people.

The Structure of the Navajo Peacemaker Court

The informal agreement within the court was that the Navajo customary method should be protected, preserved, and encouraged, but it should not be regulated. The Navajo courts did not have the funds to hire individuals to conduct mediation in local communities nor to conduct training programs in modern methods of mediation and arbitration. More important, there was a feeling that the chapters were so independent that they would not respond well to instruction and Anglicized methods for using their traditional mediation mechanism. Navajo traditional mediation involves respect for the mediator, lectures on religious and traditional values, and an awareness of the dynamics of the local community. The judges and staff developing an outline for the new court recognized this and decided that the Navajo tradition should not be influenced in its actual operation.[19] Navajo pragmatism and independence were recognized as forces to be accommodated.

The theoretical basis of the court consisted of four elements.[20] At the core of the court, the Navajo mediation tradition was to be left untouched. It would be surrounded by a formal court system that would act as clearinghouse and referral mechanism. The formal court system would be based on the elements of structure, protection, choice, and enforcement.[21]

The element of structure gave authority to the tradition. The tradition would now have existence as a formal court with a name, and it would have status as an official body of Navajo government, as a division of the Navajo courts. The courts would provide clerical assistance, such as record keeping, because these resources are not readily available on the chapter level. An important part of the element of structure was that the regularly constituted courts would enforce decisions produced through mediation or arbitration.

The element of protection was necessary in order to bring the new method into existence because of problems and abuses that had occurred in the past. Judge Bluehouse and council delegate Ross told of instances in which community members, sometimes with the assistance of Navajo police officers, would take an offender or troublemaker to the local chapter house, lock the doors, and then mentally and physically abuse the person. The suggestion that the system would not work because of such abuses led to the decision that the appointed judges must be given overall supervisory powers over the peacemaker court. They would be able to issue speedy protective orders to guard against abusive conduct.

When informed of the plan, some persons asked what would happen if someone did not want to be bound by the decision of a person who was not an appointed judge. There was often the misunderstanding that those in the community appointed to serve in the new court would be judges in the same sense as the Navajo judges who made decisions in the adversarial setting. This issue was addressed in the third element of the court, expressed as choice. The normal method used would be mediation, in which the appointed official would only be authorized to encourage individuals to talk out their dispute. If an individual did not recognize the legitimacy of the process or the mediator, then he or she could not be forced to agree to a particular resolution to the dispute. Quasi-judicial decision making in the form of arbitration was provided, but the protection of requiring a written agreement to arbitration was required.

The choice element was made available to the judges by providing for the transfer of pending civil and criminal cases to the peacemaker court for mediation. This was what the judges had been doing all along. Individuals then had the right to refuse to cooperate with mediation and return to adversarial litigation in the trial court.

There was no reason to provide a formal structure in the Navajo courts if the goal was simply to recognize what had been taking place for a long time. The idea, however, was to support and encourage the tradition by giving it legitimacy in a structured setting, through encouraging its operation and enforcing its decisions. The element of enforcement provided for a judgment to be entered in the local district court representing the results of a mediated agreement or an arbitrated decision. Thus entered, the judgment carried all the authority of any judgment of the Navajo court and could be similarly enforced. Since any judgment on a mediated settlement or an arbitrated decision would be one of the district court, the Navajo police could be required to enforce the community decision. Such a judgment could also be appealed to the Navajo Court of Appeals and be given full faith and credit in other jurisdictions. Questions about enforcement powers were resolved by making it mandatory that individuals participate in mediation sessions, once this method was chosen, and requiring participants to come to those sessions under formal court subpoenas. Once the theoretical outline was made, the procedures to be used fell into place.

The rules are intended to be simple, and they are only ten pages long. The general rules state the authority of the peacemaker court and indicate the kinds of matters that can be addressed by it.[22] They also provide for compulsory participation in mediation and the voluntary participation of non-Indians as parties. Non-Indians are compelled to cooperate as witnesses or participants but not as parties (peacemaker court rule [PCR] 1.5; Zion and McCabe 1982, 102).[23] Given the independence and pragmatism of the Navajos, the general provisions allow for an informal application and a liberal construction of the rules, and state that the "rules will be used and applied in as close to accordance with Navajo tradition and custom as is possible." (PCR 1.7, p. 102). This is intended to be an escape clause in the event the formal rules are not compatible with traditional practices or with what the parties want. Members of the Navajo bar are forbidden to participate in peacemaker court proceedings (with the exception of some matters to be handled in the district court; PCR 1.6, p. 102). Judges are eliminated from the heart of the court's operations.

The persons who actually conduct mediation and arbitration are called "peacemakers." They are selected because of their "ability to work with chapter members, reputation for integrity, honesty, humanity and . . . ability to resolve local problems" (PCR 2.1, pp. 102–3). This rule is an enshrinement of the Navajo tradition of selecting peace leaders. The peacemakers are to be chosen by the Navajo judges in the absence of community action. The chapters are, however, encouraged to make their own selections of peacemakers at chapter meetings (PCR 2.1 [6], p. 102). In response to commentary that the peacemakers chosen by the chapters or judges might not have the respect of the community, or might be closely related to a party, or might favor one side of a dispute, the judges included a provision in the rules that the parties to a dispute can agree to any individual as a peacemaker (PCR 2.1[d], p. 103). This is also designed to accommodate the three levels of Navajo society (the traditionals, the caught-in-the-middles, and the moderns), because they should have the ability to choose their own respected mediators. These mediators can be traditional medicine men or women, non-Indian clergy or counselors, traders, lawyers, Native American Church leaders, or other trusted figures of authority.

The peacemaker is given the authority to mediate disputes, but there are few requirements on the form the mediation is to take (PCR 2.2[e], p. 103). They clearly are not to act as judges, but they must have the specific authority to arbitrate if the parties agree to that process (PCR 2.3, pp. 103–4). The duties of the peacemaker are to assemble the disputants and participants (anyone who has a role in the dispute) for mediation (peacemaking) and to coordinate activities with the district court (PCR 2.4 and 2.5, p. 104).

The clerical and referral system places the burden for paperwork and referrals upon the district court staff, particularly the clerk of the court. The clerks prepare written requests for use of the peacemaker court, make reports to a centralized records office, notify the peacemakers of their appointment, receive and transmit user fees, assist in preparing necessary paperwork, and generally act as an information and assistance resource (PCR 3.1 and 3.4–3.8, pp. 104–6). Because many Navajos have problems dealing with bureaucratic systems and paperwork, Navajo clerks of court act as public scribes and information resources in order to serve people who must travel many miles to attend to their business.[24]

The hope is to provide a simple system in which an individual Navajo need see only a clerk of court for a referral to a peacemaker. After the rules were adopted, a manual was written for the judges, chapters, peacemakers, and clerks of court, with instructions for each of these officials. The manual also contains forms that can be photocopied. The clerks are instructed that they may fill out the forms in their own handwriting and can keep the papers for requests in simple ring binders (Zion and McCabe 1982), thus dispensing with most of the formal record keeping of regular court systems.[25]

The sitting judges appoint peacemakers in individual cases, issue simple protective orders when abuses are brought to their attention, and issue formal written judgments on mediated or arbitrated decisions (PCR 4.1–4.6, pp. 107–8). The judges are also given the authority to halt formal litigation before them and transfer civil cases and some kinds of criminal prosecutions to a peacemaker for community action (PCR 6.1–6.5, pp. 109–10). This procedure acknowledges that the adversarial system does not adequately serve the participants in many kinds of civil and criminal litigation. Family cases are often aggravated by the emotions and personalities of the parties, and the rules provide a cooling-off process in those situations. The historical practice of Navajo judges turning criminal prosecutions under American court procedures into Navajo civil matters is now followed by the referral system. The judges (particularly Chief Justice McCabe and Judges Bluehouse and Tso) stated that parents or spouses had often requested the judge give a lecture to an erring family member, and that these requests had to be denied because of the adversarial practices of the court system. The judges also received requests from the families of criminal defendants that a prosecution be stopped in favor of a stern lecture from the bench, but the criminal processes of the courts were not designed for this.[26] The referral and transfer provisions were designed especially to serve these needs. Judge Bluehouse particularly stressed the effectiveness of lectures based upon legal standards, moral guidelines, and traditional religious principles.

A controversial problem was how the peacemakers would be paid for their services. The judges had the option of presenting legislation to the Navajo Tribal Council to fund peacemaker court operations or to make the system rely upon user payment. The option of going to the council was rejected because of the experimental nature of the peacemaker court and the small likelihood that funds could be obtained to pay the peacemakers. The thinking was that people would be able to pay a fee to the peacemaker because they would not have to pay a court filing fee or the attorney's fees required in regular court litigation. There was also a feeling that the users of the peacemaker court system would respect the court more if they had to pay for it. This view acknowledged a practical "you don't get something for nothing" attitude.[27]

Because the new court is experimental, it is believed wise to put a system in place that has as many options as possible, and then see what modifications will have to be made after mistakes occur or suggestions are received. The predictions for the future were that the system would be accepted with modifications, or totally rejected, but in either event, it would be influenced by the forces of Navajo pragmatism and the persistence of Navajo tradition. Since the system is experimental, the peacemaker court rules were written in formal legal language for use by the judges and the lawyers, as well as in plain language (or what is hoped will be seen as plain language) for local leaders.[28]

The Justification for the Peacemaker Court under Navajo Common Law

The Navajo courts have inherent and statutory authority to adopt rules of court pleading, practice, and procedure (Zion and McCabe 1982), and they must use Navajo customs and usages where they are not preempted by United States law (Navajo Trib. Code tit. 7, § 204 [1978]). In creating the peacemaker court, the judges exercised their powers to create a new division of the trial court, and they also followed established Navajo custom and usage in creating it.

The twentieth-century Navajo judicial custom was well established, and it was reinforced by available oral tradition and established literature. As it is with most Indian nations, there are few published works on the legal customs of the Navajos, although some materials can be found that, though brief, are excellent.[29]

There were sufficient published materials available to justify the custom and trace its origins to pre-Hispanic and pre-Anglo times. From the earliest times to the modern period, the Navajos have had headmen, or naat'áanii. These are local leaders who function without the coercive authority found in other governmental structures, and they are individuals of prestige who govern by persuasion (Young 1978). The Navajo leaders were (and are) chosen in a democratic fashion, because of their ability (Van Valkenburgh 1936), and by canvassing community opinion (Shepardson 1963). Men and women had an equal voice in the selection of these leaders, and the ideal was to make a unanimous selection (Shepardson 1963).

Leadership was required for the purpose of conducting war and for supervising a peacetime economy based upon agriculture, livestock, and hunting. War chiefs, or leaders, were chosen for their military abilities, and peace chiefs, or leaders, were chosen for their eloquence and discrimination (Van Valkenburgh 1936; Young 1978). Most important for the peacemaker court's authority, the naat'áanii, who was also a peace chief *(hózhǫ́ǫ́jí naat'ááh),* held power only because of eloquence and achievement (Van Valkenburgh 1936), and his or her role was nonauthoritarian, noncoercive, and used only in the interests of the group (Shepardson 1963). The naat'áanii arbitrated disputes, mediated quarrels, resolved family problems, and tried to correct wrongdoers (Shepardson 1963; Young 1978). If this leader overstepped the bounds of authority, the basis for his or her legitimacy was destroyed. Obedience to the naat'áanii was lost, then, due to a lack of community respect and confidence (Shepardson 1963).

This democratic form of leadership, which had a built-in kind of recall mechanism, was carried over into the period of relations with the United States. The same tradition flowed into the operations of the Navajo legislative and judicial bodies (Shepardson 1963; Young 1978). Although judges are not selected in the same manner as the naat'áanii and have more than simple persuasive powers, the important fact for the peacemaker court is that those chosen to mediate and arbitrate disputes must have the respect of the people and can only exercise persuasive and not coercive powers. Although the Navajo common law supporting the new procedure was firmly established, the judges looked to other precedent in order to command recognition of the new court by the United States and the states.

Outside Recognition of Navajo Common Law

When the *Navajo Judicial Code* containing the authority to use custom law in civil cases was enacted by the Navajo Tribal Council, the code was approved by the secretary of the Interior. This made the recognition of custom law obligatory upon the BIA (*Oliver v. Udall,* 306 F.2d 819, 822 [D.C. Cir. 1962]; *In re Tsosie,* 3 *Navajo Rptr.* 182, 186–87 [D. Chinle 1981]; *Estate of Descheeny,* No. WR-CV-565-82 [D. Window Rock, Navajo Tribal Court 1983]). This policy follows the general legal policy of the United States that Indian customs are to be accorded respect by the United States government as law (See *Ex parte Crow Dog,* 109 U.S. 556 [1883]; *Frank v. State,* 604 P.2d 1068 [Alaska 1979]; *In re Sah Quah,* 31 F. 327 [D. Alaska 1886]; *People v. Woody,* 40 *Cal. Rptr.* 69, 394 P.2d 813 [1964]; Indian Child Welfare Act, 25 U.S.C. §§ 1901 *et seq.* [1978]; Resolution on American Indian Religious Freedom, Pub. L. 95-341 [1978]).

Legal recognition of Navajo custom by federal and state authorities is important because the peacemaker court rules make it possible for the individual Navajo to obtain a judgment under a customary procedure and turn it into a judgment of the Navajo courts of record. That means that the traditional court judgment will be recognized by the states. The state of New Mexico recognizes Navajo law under the full faith and credit doctrine (*Jim V. CIT Fin. Serv. Corp.*, 87 N.M. 362, 533 P.2d 751 [1975]), and Arizona will recognize it (unless it is found to be contrary to Arizona public policy) under the doctrine of comity (*Brown v. Babbitt Ford, Inc.*, 117 Ariz. 192, 571 P.2d 689, 695 [1977]; *Begay v. Miller*, 70 Ariz. 380, 822 P.2d 624 [1950]).

The Navajo judges also looked to other American legal principles for support in rejecting the adversarial system of resolving disputes. The Navajo courts looked to an 1829 United States Supreme Court ruling rejecting unacceptable rules of English law. In the case, the Supreme Court noted: "The common law of England is not to be taken in all respects to be that of America. Our ancestors brought with them its general principles, and claimed it as their birthright; but they brought with them and adopted only that portion which was applicable to their situation" (*Van Ness v. Pacard*, 27 U.S. [2 Pet.] 137, 144 [1829]).[30] Indian attorneys have concluded that the law used for Indian peoples must be private, inexpensive, and accessible, and it must fit the ends of compensation and reconciliation (Barsh and Henderson 1978). The noted Indian writer and attorney Vine Deloria, Jr., has reminded the United States Congress of the American political doctrine that the states are to be left alone to become laboratories for political change, and he claimed the same role for Indian nations, saying, "tribes are not vestiges of the past, but laboratories for the future" (Barsh and Henderson 1978). The general American philosophy that local governments are to be left alone to develop systems based upon local needs was claimed by the Navajo judges for their own government, and they pointed to basic American legal and political doctrines for support.

Validation and Acceptance of the Court

The success or failure of the peacemaker court will be recorded or forgotten some time in the future, and its full history to date cannot be recited in a short article. After the peacemaker court rules were adopted, however, there were attempts to inform Navajo leaders and the chapters of the new system. Contacts were also made with individuals and organizations outside the Navajo Nation to find more ideas.

A public informational conference was held for tribal council delegates and chapter leaders in June of 1982, and judges and court personnel visited local chapter meetings and Navajo conferences to educate the public on the new idea.[31] Because of the size of the Navajo Nation, communications with the rural chapters are very difficult. Financial shortcomings have made educational visits to the chapters in the various areas impossible, but efforts to gain acceptance of the peacemaker court continue to be made.

Representatives of other Indian governments have been contacted in order to share information and exchange ideas. The Navajos have been in contact with representatives of the Chippewa-Cree, the White River Apache, the Salt River Pima-Maricopa, the Blackfeet, and the Salish-Kootenai tribal governments in the United States in an effort to develop rational systems of custom law more fully. The contacts have extended to Canada, with visits to the Federation of Saskatchewan Indians and the Native Law Center of Saskatoon, Saskatchewan. In December 1981, the Navajo court hosted a conference of the National American Indian Court Judges Association and made a presentation to the tribal court representatives gathered at Gallup, New Mexico, in order to obtain comment on the peacemaker court. In the international arena, visiting African judges and representatives of the Australian Laws Commission have discussed procedural mechanisms for the use of custom law.

These contacts between Navajo leaders and people from the outside have led to the conclusion that the process chosen to use Navajo custom law is valid and acceptable. The courts find that the biggest problem they have in using the peacemaker court is in educating local Navajo leaders about it, and that will be difficult without obtaining the resources to reach out to the chapter level of Navajo government.

Conclusion

The Navajo judges are as pragmatic as the communities they represent. They know the peacemaker court will work only if it is accepted by the people who are to make it work, and the judges expect changes in the peacemaker court as the experiment progresses. The important result thus far is that the Navajos who have heard of the peacemaker court praise it.[32]

The Navajos accept what they find useful to them and reject what they do not. The peacemaker court was founded upon demands that are a product of the persistence of the Navajo culture, and the Navajo judges believe they have chosen the correct method of blending Navajo common law into an American-style court system.

Notes

This chapter is an edited version of James W. Zion's "The Navajo Peacemaker Court: Deference to the Old and Accommodation to the New," *American Indian Law Review*, 11: 89–109, 1983. Reprinted with permission of the publisher. A version of this article was also presented before the Commission on Folk Law and Legal Pluralism, Eleventh International Congress of Anthropological and Ethnological Sciences, Vancouver, British Columbia, August 19–23, 1983.

1. Though the form of the Navajo courts may be alien to the Navajos, that the judges are Navajo and are responsive to their communities is reassuring.

2. This is also permitted in the courts of Indian offenses operated by the federal government (25 C.F.R. § 11.23 1981).

3. Chairman MacDonald commissioned attorney William Reordon of the Navajo Tribe's legal division to research and draft arbitration procedures.

4. The task force was composed of three members each from the judiciary committee, the Navajo courts, and the Supreme Judicial Council. The Supreme Judicial Council was a highly political quasi-judicial body, composed of the chief justice, retired judges of the Navajo courts, and tribal council members. The personal and political dynamics of the judicial council's creation led to strong clashes with the legitimate courts and others. Infighting coupled with a failure of the chairman to support funding for the project led to the task force's rapid dissolution. The Supreme Judicial Council expired in September 1981, when the Navajo Tribal Council did not further fund its operations.

5. The Navajo Nation Bar Association is a lively organization of approximately 250 Navajo and non-Navajo members, most of whom did not attend law school. It is becoming a strong force in the development of the Navajo courts and Navajo law.

6. A chapter is a form of local Navajo government. It is conducted much like the town meeting form of local government of New England, and like that form, the people of an area meet to discuss and vote upon matters of local interest. The chapter resolution has a great deal of influence upon the central Navajo government's operations and programs (Bingham and Bingham 1976).

7. Comments of court officials, Navajo practitioners, and opinion of the author. Judge Harry Brown is another sitting judge known to have an excellent knowledge of custom law; retired Chief Justice Murray Lincoln and retired Judge Tom B. Becenti are also acknowledged as experts in this area. An excellent interview with Judge Becenti that exemplifies Navajo judicial thinking is found at Vicenti et al. (1972).

8. Other observers have also seen this. See Barsh (1973) and Conn (1978).

9. Discussions with Judge Bluehouse, for example, held in December 1981 and January 1982. Judge Bluehouse was a continuing source for finding customary legal procedures and principles. The Navajo judges hold frequent meetings to discuss court operations, and those meetings are a good opportunity to gather information. Albert Hale, president of the Navajo Nation Bar Association, acted as an informant and critic, and Benjamin Curley, the Window Rock District prosecutor, served as a sounding board and idea man during this period.

10. The experiences of the American Arbitration Association (AAA) and its community mediation and arbitration centers in Philadelphia, Pennsylvania, and Hartford, Connecticut, were considered (AAA 1971). The courts of conciliation of California and Montana, which use mental health professionals, counselors, and clergy in divorce and

child custody cases, were held out as justifications for a mediation system. *The Mediator's Handbook*, by Beer, Stief, and Walker (1982), was also used.

11. The experiences considered were those of Connecticut, Montana, and the Blackfeet Tribal Court small-claims courts.

12. Keynote speech of chairman Peter MacDonald to the annual meeting of the Navajo Nation Bar Association at Gallup, New Mexico, April 3, 1982. The speech was made after a draft of the peacemaker court rules had been written, but before they were announced for public comment. MacDonald probably did not know of them.

13. Few materials are readily available to the contemporary researcher in the field of Indian custom law. Perhaps this is better, because it makes modern tribal experiments in the use of Indian common law more self-reliant.

14. *Navajo Tribal Code* tit. 7, § 601 (1978) permits a majority of the trial judges to adopt rules of "pleading, practice and procedure." The legislative history of the rule is reviewed in the Navajo Court of Appeals case *In re Practice of Battles* (3 *Navajo Rptr.*, 92 Ct. App., Navajo Nation, 1982).

15. Judge Atcitty was one of the first Indians elected to the New Mexico House of Representatives (Vogel 1974).

16. Judge Tso is a product of the Navajo Nation Bar Association. Prior to becoming a judge, he was an attorney (i.e., a member of the Navajo bar but not a law school graduate) with DNA-People's Legal Services and a president of the bar association. He is considered to be a brilliant judge and a well-known Navajo leader.

17. Like Judge Tso, Judge Whitehair is a former practitioner.

18. Judge Neswood, who is the highest-ranking female Navajo official, is a senior judge. She is a former clerk of court and a former acting chief justice.

19. Consensus of Chief Justice McCabe, Judges Tso and Bluehouse, council delegate Ross, and others (to my knowledge).

20. Navajo tradition gives great weight to the concept of four elements. There are four sacred directions, with four sacred mountains. The coincidence of this tradition with the four elements comprising the theoretical structure of the court was later found helpful in taking the peacemaker court idea to local leaders.

21. The system has been diagrammed as a circle (representing tradition) surrounded by a square formed by the four elements of the court. The diagram is used as an instructional device in explaining the peacemaker court.

22. The peacemaker court's ultimate authority is the ability to use Navajo customs and traditions, as authorized by *Navajo Tribal Code* tit. 7, § 204a (1978), and almost any kind of community or personal dispute can be addressed (Peacemaker court rules 1.2 and 1.4 as found in the *Navajo Peacemaker Court Manual* [Zion and McCabe 1982].) Although the intent was to provide only for simple community disputes, Navajo practitioners and government workers quickly thought of using the court for divorces and child welfare cases.

23. The policy choice of not requiring non-Indians to participate as parties was made because of the state of the law of jurisdiction over non-Indians at the time the rules were adopted.

24. The use of thumbprint signatures by elders on checks and documents is still common, and many people have to hitchhike long distances to get to Navajo governmental offices.

25. The rules were adopted in April 1982, and the manual was prepared in May 1982.

26. Both Conn (1978) and Barsh (1973) give excellent explanations of the dynamics of traditional Navajo ways of taking care of "criminal" matters.

27. The views of Benjamin Curley, the Window Rock District prosecutor, were particularly helpful and persuasive on the fee issue.

28. PCR 7.2., as found in Zion and McCabe (1982, 110). See also Zion and McCabe (1982, 111–211). Previously the chief justice issued an order forbidding the use of legalese and requiring the use of understandable English in the courts (Administrative Order, May 4, 1981).

29. *The Navajo Bibliography with Subject Index, and 1973 Supplement* (Corell, Watson, and Brugge 1969 and 1973) is illustrative; of the twenty-eight entries under the topic of law, only a few relate to Navajo custom law. The only comprehensive work is the multivolume *The Law of the People—Dine' Bibee Hazaanii* (Vicenti et al. 1972).

30. This case is cited and quoted in Zion and McCabe (1982, 5).

31. These visits have included presentations to a conference on Indian child welfare sponsored by the Navajo Division of Social Services, a chapter leader program of the Navajo Community College, and presentations to the Kinlichee, Hogback, Shiprock, Houck, and Ramah chapters. The Navajo judges presented the peacemaker court concept to the advisory board of DNA-People's Legal Services, and the court carried out a program of informational news releases and interviews with the press and radio.

32. Participants in the June 1982 public presentation commented that they liked the idea and that they did not realize custom law could be used in such a fashion. There has been enthusiastic commentary from various chapter leaders. A citizens' advisory group to the new executive administration under chairman Peterson Zah fully supported the peacemaker court idea when they were briefed on it at a January 4, 1983, meeting.

References

AAA [American Arbitration Association]. 1971. Presentation to the Hartford County Bar Association, Hartford, Connecticut, September 15 (approx.).

Aberle, David. 1966. *The Peyote Religion among the Navaho.* 2nd ed. Viking Fund Publications in Anthropology, No. 42. Chicago: Aldine.

Barsh, Russel L. 1973. The Formative Period of Navajo Law: Probate 1940-72. Unpublished manuscript.

Barsh, Russel L., and J. Youngblood Henderson. 1978. Tribal Courts, the Model Code, and the Police Idea. In *American Indians and the Law,* ed. Lawrence Rosen, 26–60. New Brunswick, N.J.: Transaction Books.

Beer, Jennifer, Eileen Stief, and C. Walker. 1982. *Mediator's Handbook.* Philadelphia: Friends Conflict Resolution Programs.

Bingham, Sam, and Janet Bingham. 1976. *Navajo Chapter Government Handbook.* Rock Point, Ariz.: Rock Point Community School.

Brakel, Samuel. 1978. *American Indian Tribal Courts: The Costs of Separate Justice.* Chicago: American Bar Association.

Conn, Stephen. 1978. Mid-Passage—The Navajo Tribe and Its First Legal Revolution. *American Indian Law Review* 21: 329–70.

Correll, Lee, Editha L. Watson, and David M. Brugge, eds. 1969 and 1973. *Navajo Bibliography with Subject Index, and 1973 Supplement.* Window Rock: Museum and Recreation Department, Navajo Nation.

Dusenberry, Verne. 1962. *The Montana Cree.* Uppsala, Sweden: Almquist and Wiksells Bogtryckeri.

Fahey, Richard P. 1975. Native American Justice: The Courts of the Navajo Nation. *Judicature* 59: 10–17.

Gilbreath, Ken. 1973. *Red Capitalism: Analysis of the Navajo Economy*. Norman: University of Oklahoma.

Hultkrantz, Alice. 1976. *The Religions of the American Indians*. Berkeley: University of California Press.

Iverson, Peter. 1981. *The Navajo Nation*. Westport, Conn.: Greenwood Press.

Jorgensen, J. 1972. *The Sun Dance Religion*. Chicago: University of Chicago Press.

Keon-Cohen, B. 1981. Native Justice in Australia, Canada and the U.S.A.: A Comparative Analysis. *Monash University Law Review* 7: 250–325.

Kluckhohn, Clyde. 1944. *Navaho Witchcraft*. Boston, Mass.: Beacon Press.

Kluckhohn, Clyde, and Dorothea Leighton. 1974. *The Navaho*. 4th ed. Cambridge, Mass.: Harvard University Press.

Lednicer, Oliver. 1959. The Peacemaker Court in New York State. *New York University Intramural Law Review* 14: 188–95.

MacDonald, Peter, letter to chief justice Nelson J. McCabe, June 5, 1981.

Scott, Anne F. 1982. Fishing in Troubled Waters. *Friends Journal* 1 (15): 8–11.

Shepardson, Mary. 1963. *Navajo Ways in Government: A Study of the Political Process*. Washington D.C.: American Anthropological Association.

Van Valkenburgh, Richard. 1936. Navajo Common Law I: Notes on Political Organizations, Property and Inheritance. *Museum Notes* [Museum of Northern Arizona] 9 (4): 17–22.

Vicenti, Dan, Keonard B. Jimson, Stephen Conn, and M. J. L. Kellogg. 1972. *The Law of the People—Dine' Bibee Hazaanii*. Vol. 2. Ramah, N.Mex.: Ramah High School Press.

Vogel, Virgil J. 1974. *This Country Was Ours*. New York: Harper and Row.

Young, Robert W. 1978. *The Political History of the Navajo Tribe*. Tsaile, Ariz.: Navajo Community College Press.

Zion, James W., and Nelson McCabe. 1982. *Navajo Peacemaker Court Manual*. Window Rock, Ariz.: Navajo Nation Judicial Branch.

4 The Dynamics of Navajo Peacemaking

Social Psychology of an American Indian Method of Dispute Resolution

James W. Zion

Peacemaking is an indigenous Native American form of dispute resolution and a leading example of restorative justice. Restorative justice, unlike adjudication and the prevailing patterns of world criminal justice systems, views crime and offending as a conflict between individuals that results in injuries to victims, with a process that seeks to reconcile parties and repair the injury caused by a dispute through the active participation of victims, offenders, and communities to find solutions to conflict (Hudson and Galaway 1996). Although American politicians are moving toward more mandatory sentencing, "truth in sentencing," "three strikes and you're out," charging juvenile offenders as adults, and other repressive measures, there is some hope for alternatives to punitive criminal law through restorative justice, "which views crime as an act against another person and the community" (Bazemore and Day 1996; Wallace 1996). The proponents of new alternatives, which Indian nation justice leaders point out are very old Indian ideas of justice, seek something more effective in place of retribution and punishment.

The Navajo Nation court system gets many visitors from across North America and around the world, and the Navajo justices and court staff have had international invitations to describe peacemaking. The questions they get are often the same: What is the recidivism rate in peacemaking? What happens if someone does not agree with a decision reached during the process? What punishment does peacemaking have? What do you do with offenders who are amoral or sociopaths? For some reason, our British Commonwealth lawyer friends are fascinated with homicide and say, "Well, surely, you can't handle murder in peacemaking." When Chief Justice Robert Yazzie was at the Justice Department's Restorative Justice Conference in January 1996, he was asked, "How does peacemaking work?" (Wallace 1996). He was also asked whether peacemaking is culturally specific to the Navajo culture or whether there are certain universals in the process.

This chapter attempts to answer those questions. It will examine the nature of offenders, some of the group dynamics or problems that are associated with crime, and individual psychological barriers or excuses usually offered by offenders; and it will describe how Navajo peacemaking addresses those problems. This is not a chapter on social psychology, but it does address many of the common excuses offered by offenders, which can be described using the approaches of social psychology.

Offenders and Their Excuses

The courts of the Navajo Nation handle many kinds of offenses in a misdemeanor criminal justice system. There are large numbers of domestic violence cases in the criminal justice system and in civil restraining-order proceedings. Most crimes are associated with alcohol use, and most violent offenses involve people who are related by a family or Navajo clan relationship (Reiss and Roth 1993). Ron Zimmerman, a clerk of court from Austin, Texas, offered a summary of the kinds of offenders that are found in his court (Zimmerman 1996). They are also the kinds of offenders found in most state and Indian nation courts. They include the following:

The Norman Rockwellians: These individuals are straight off the canvas of the vaunted chronicler of America. They have jobs, families, cars, and cats, and they roast a turkey on Thanksgiving Day. Generally, when a judgment is entered against them, they pay.

The down-and-outers: This group runs the gamut from casualties of corporate downsizing to homelessness at the extreme. The jobs and cars are gone, the turkey is unaffordable, and the fate of the cat is—well—unknown. They would dearly love to pay but cannot.

The institutional refugees: Since 1986, we have purged our mental health facilities of large numbers of hapless persons who have gone to the streets. They are a dismal underclass who shuffle, unwashed and forlorn, from the jail, to arraignment, to the street, and back to jail in a perpetual cycle of despair broken only by death.

The truly mean: Our socioeconomic structure produces, quite predictably, a growing polity of permanently alienated, sociopathic personalities who commit regular, episodic, or one-time violence of some sort. They are contemptuous of sanctions.

The anesthetized: Nothing is more important before consuming a quart of liquor and nothing is painful afterwards. Booze and other drugs are the shields that deflect any hope of changing their behavior. Jail simply defines the greater or lesser periods of lucidity in their lives.

The stupidly obstinate: This small group consists of people who never once obeyed a teacher and who take perverse delight in power failures.

Although that is perhaps a flippant overview of what courts see, it summarizes a gross psychological makeup of many offenders in all American legal systems, including those of America's Indian nations. We can argue over their numbers in the criminal justice system, but they are there. They are present in the Navajo Nation. The "truly mean" of the Navajo Nation are repeat offenders who drink and fight, and they are also the spouse and child abusers (Hauswald 1988). The Navajo Nation courts see many of the "anesthetized," who are primarily dependent on alcohol. The "stupidly obstinate" are generally brought before the court in criminal or civil domestic violence cases. The nature of offenders in their reaction to judicial process is one element in the picture of peacemaking and restorative justice.

Another element of any discussion of how peacemaking works is the rise in the various *excuse* defenses to criminal charges, which are most often based on the specific intent required for a criminal conviction or mitigating factors (Winkelman 1996). Modern sentencing trends, which tend to be increasingly punitive, drive criminal defense attorneys to offer new excuses for criminal behavior: involuntariness, reasonable deficiency, and nonresponsibility in defenses such as brainwashing, "rotten social background," the battered-spouse defense, the Vietnam veteran defense (i.e., post-traumatic stress disorder [PTSD]), and the culture defense. The culture defense "exempts an accused person from criminal liability when it is shown that the reason for the criminal act was that it was required to be done by the norms of a culture to which the accused belonged, that is, by a folk law to which the accused was subject" (Woodman 1993, 46).

Such defenses make us uncomfortable because they seem to run against common sense and our feelings of outrage when there is a victim—particularly of acts of violence. Defendants offer excuses for their conduct—more often alcoholism or drug dependency—and we cannot adequately deal with them in adjudication. The self-incrimination privilege (although it is vital to civil liberties in an authority-based system), high caseloads, and formalized court procedures make it difficult to confront offenders, elicit their explanations for behavior, and deal with the underlying causes of their conduct.

Whether or not such defenses are asserted by criminal defense counsel, the Navajo Nation judges recognize them: The Honorable Irene Toledo of the Ramah (now Crownpoint) Judicial District had her probation officer look for the existence of PTSD in Vietnam veterans and found that it is associated with assault offenses among adult offenders. She also found that adults with PTSD are teaching its suspicious and violent behaviors to their children (Holm 1996). The growing concept of restorative justice gives an opportunity to deal with the dynamics that underlie those kinds of offenders, hear their excuses, and deal with them in context. That is why Navajo peacemaking works.

Group Dynamics

American Indian crime rates are generally higher than average American crime and violence incidence. Bachman (1992) places a great deal of confidence in crime statistics in painting her picture of Indian nation crime, but given the lack of decent databases in Indian country (due to a lack of federal support), her figures cannot be viewed with confidence. Despite the unreliability of Bachman's statistics, we can agree that Indian country crime rates are high (Silverman 1996). Why? An important (and ignored) report of the National Minority Advisory Council on Criminal Justice (1982) sums up the causes well:

> The displacement of Indian sovereignty by the encroaching Anglo-European system of laws and values has had pernicious, debilitating effects to the present. The legacy of this dispossession is graphically revealed in current criminal justice statistics. American Indians have, by far, the highest arrest rate of any ethnic group. Their arrest rate is consistently three times that of blacks and ten times that of whites. As many as 80 percent of Indian prisoners are incarcerated for alcohol-related offenses, a rate of twelve times greater than the national average. The major crime rate is 50 percent higher on reservations than in rural America. The violent crime rate is eight times the rural rate, murder is three times the rural rate, and assault is nine times as high. Furthermore, the percentage of unreported crime on reservations is higher than anywhere else; thus the situation is actually worse than the statistics portray, according to a 1975 Task Force Report on Indian Matters by the Department of Justice. (13)

The crime picture is the product of the internal colonialism of American Indian policy, which produced social disorganization, culture conflict, a subculture of violence, economic deprivation, and alcohol dependence (Bachman 1992). Such pressures on distinct peoples create anomie, or the lawlessness that is the product of extreme stress and the disruption of traditional life. One study of Navajo crime patterns concluded that anomie does not explain the crime rate (which was low compared to general American crime; Levy and Kunitz 1971), but past comparisons based on inadequate criminal arrest and prosecution data are unreliable, and the contemporary pattern may be described as anomie. Indian nations and their members suffer from mass PTSD, also described as intergenerational post-traumatic stress (Duran, Guillory, and Tingley 1995).

Whether we use the terminology of "anomie" or "mass PTSD" to summarize the effects of centuries of oppressor behavior and internal colonization in Indian country, its effects are obvious: Indians of North America fall at the bottom of every indicator of socioeconomic well-being (Zion 1992), and those conditions create group dynamics that underlie crime and social disruption. Individual Indians, as members of the affected group, are conditioned to individual behaviors of disruption and conflict, with associated individual rationales or excuses for their conduct.

Describing Individual Excuses

Navajos have particular ways of looking at the world, including excuses for behavior, but the Western world has important insights too. One Western elder, Aristotle, said this in his *Politics* (328 BCE):

> Man is by nature a social animal; an individual who is unsocial naturally and not accidentally is either beneath our notice or more than human. Society is something in nature that precedes the individual. Anyone who either cannot lead the common life or is so self-sufficient as not to need to, and therefore does not partake of society, is either a beast or a god. (quoted in Aronson 1995, xvix)

Humans are not beasts, nor are they gods. Each human has a tendency to believe that he or she is "good," but when someone does an act that hurts another, there must be some way to live with what was done. The mental mechanism to deal with that conflict is called "cognitive dissonance."

> Basically, cognitive dissonance is a state of tension that occurs whenever an individual simultaneously holds two cognitions (ideas, attitudes, beliefs, opinions) that are psychologically inconsistent. Stated differently, two cognitions are dissonant if, considering these two cognitions alone, the opposite of one follows from the other. Because the occurrence of cognitive dissonance is unpleasant, people are motivated to reduce it; this is highly analogous to the processes involved in the induction and reduction of such drives as hunger or thirst—except that, here, the driving force arises from cognitive discomfort rather than physiological needs. (Aronson 1995, 178)

When someone hurts another—performs a "bad" act—cognitive dissonance results. The individual must rationalize his or her behavior—to self and to community. It leads to many kinds of excuses or explanations for behavior. They may include denial, minimalization, or externalization. Denial is one of the most frequent excuses offered by offenders: Judges often complain about the defendant who pleads guilty but who refuses, when prompted, to explain or justify conduct. Minimalization often exploits stereotypes of age or gender, that "boys will be boys" or "it's just a man thing." That is where machismo seeks recognition as a justification (Shepardson 1982). Externalization also uses stereotypes and blaming: That it was the woman's fault that she was beaten or raped, that men "just can't help themselves," or "he's just a poor drunk."

Cognitive dissonance appears in other forms: the ignorant person who needs value clarification because he or she did not think the conduct was wrong, those who are supposedly amoral or have no values because they were never taught them or were taught false values, those with antisocial attitudes, and sociopaths. Finally, there is "hooliganism," which is a popular term used to describe young men and women who act out, such as vandals, fighting drunks at public events, and others who use their age (and alcohol) as an excuse for acting out.

Another reaction to cognitive dissonance is shame, and the emotion of shame is the primary or ultimate cause of all violence, whether toward others or toward self. Violence is designed to diminish the intensity of shame and replace it with pride, to prevent the individual from being overwhelmed by the feeling of shame. Thus, violence itself can be a result of the conflict between what one believes and what one does: When an individual feels shame, one reaction can be violent conduct toward others.

One classic study of prejudice (Allport 1979) found that the suffering it induces through the frustration caused by discrimination and disparagement can lead to positive and negative personality reactions: If an individual is basically extropunitive, that can lead to behaviors such as obsessive concern and suspicion, slyness and cunning, strengthening in-group ties, prejudice against other groups, aggression and revolt, stealing, competitiveness, rebellion, or enhanced striving. The results for those who are basically intropunitive can include denial of membership in their own group, withdrawal and passivity, clowning, self-hate, in-group aggression, sympathy with all victims, symbolic status striving, or neuroticism. Prejudice that is directed against a group, such as Indians, can fuel both positive and negative behaviors—severely enhanced by alcohol or other mind-changing drugs. Indians, as the target of a great deal of prejudice over the centuries, are forced to cope with both positive and negative behaviors, many of which they seek to discover (and thus the popularity of contemporary Indian movements, primarily among women, to "re-traditionalize" for strength and identity of self and the group).

Those are individual reactions. They are expressed in the modern excuse defenses and sometimes by individual defendants at the time of sentencing, when asked to explain their behavior. Most often, judges hear, "I was drunk," or some other justification. Sometimes, defendants get away with it, and some individual Indians do rely on stereotypes to get a lighter sentence. More often, however, the excuses are used to complicate adjudication or the sentence, and the privilege against self-incrimination allows a defendant to escape confrontation over personal responsibility. A criminal defendant can go through the system without once having to confront his or her conduct or be called on to explain it. The excuses may come out when there is such an opportunity for explanation in peacemaking, and the actors in that process know how to deal with it.

The Excuses in Peacemaking

Navajo peacemaking is a forum that not only permits expression of those excuses but encourages them. The phenomenon of cognitive dissonance is a part of the process because traditional Navajo legal procedure recognizes it. Traditional Navajo thought uses cognitive dissonance in a way that permits people in communities to confront it and make it part of the dispute resolution process.

Navajos are empiricists. Many of their values are based on centuries of tradition and experience, which are preserved in chants, stories, and, most important, creation scripture. Associated with that experience is the belief that "'talking it over' is the way to 'straighten out troubles'" (disputes of one type or another). "Way back there, the Navajo people didn't have any kind of law. They used to just talking it together, and the things straightened up by talking together—maybe three or four people talking together" (Ladd 1957, 204). That methodology is reflected in Navajo tradition, and the spoken word is a form of compulsion that dissuades a person from doing something wrong. The experiences of the ancient creator beings and spirit forces, taught in the creation scripture, create the context for Navajo dispute resolution.

Peacemaking Process and the Excuses

Navajo peacemaking is unique, and it is not mediation as practiced in the United States. That is, the person who presides is not neutral in the sense of a "mediator neutral." Navajo peacemakers are naat'áanii in Navajo tradition, a term sometimes inaccurately translated as "peace chief." Instead a naat'áanii is a community leader whose leadership depends on respect and persuasion and not on a position of power and authority. Words are powerful in the Navajo language, and the dispute resolution procedure is "talking things out." The word "naat'áanii" has a word root that relates to speaking. A naat'áanii is someone who speaks wisely and well, with the content of the speech being based in Navajo tradition, often the creation of scripture and associated songs and stories. A naat'áanii has an opinion about the dispute, but it is not expressed as a command. A naat'áanii peacemaker is a teacher whom participants in peacemaking respect, because the person is chosen by the community based on his or her reputation.

The Navajo process is also unique because of the participants: They are not only the immediate disputants but their relatives as well. The relatives include persons who are related by clan affiliation or by blood. They participate in the process and have significant input in the form of expressing an opinion about both the facts and the effects of the dispute, the parties' conformity to Navajo values, and the proper outcome of the dispute.

One way of looking at peacemaking is the notion that the people make the law. In peacemaking, the participants enter the process with all the values and attitudes that are the product of their rearing and socialization. Values are norms, which are the foundation of law, and attitudes are emotional ways of expressing norms. The "talking out" process permits the group to decide what the applicable law happens to be. In most instances, people will not express their values and attitudes to discuss law as the Western world knows it. There are no discussions of rules or "principles of law" to be applied to the dispute, but instead there is an interactive discussion of the problem and what the group feels about how it should be resolved.

One of the most important studies of Navajo peacemaking was done by Laurie Melchin Grohowski (1995), who visited the Navajo Nation courts to study peacemaking. She had extensive discussions about it with Philmer Bluehouse (former director of the Peacemaker Division), court-attached peacemaker liaisons, and peacemakers. She did participant observation of peacemaking. The product of her visit was a master's thesis that reviews mediation literature to find its approaches and theories of process and outcome, the literature of social psychology as applied to disputes, and theories of a cognitive-affective model of reconciliation applied to peacemaking (Grohowski 1995).

The goal of mediation and of Navajo peacemaking is reconciliation of the parties in dispute (and their relatives in the Navajo context), which is "a process of social interaction that generates a cognitive and affective synergy for the participants. Reconciliation as a process results in the participants co-creating a new shared reality or perception about the conflict and each other that allows them to move forward in their lives" (Grohowski 1995, 1). Grohowski sees peacemaking as a system "where mediation techniques during this social interaction can lead to perceptual shifts or a cognitive-affective (head to heart) transition that clears the path to reconciliation" (8). A key to the process is social cognition, which is important for understanding the excuses offered by offenders, with the important addition that the perceptions of all who are a part of or affected by the dispute are important (Grohowski 1995).

Moving from cognition theory to Native American practice, Grohowski identifies traditional "consensus processes," which implement the shift from cognitive or "head thinking" to affective or "heart thinking" among parties, and the efficacy of storytelling and prayer in traditional processes. Traditional justice methods work because they move people away from "head thinking" so that they can identify attributional errors, to overcome them and get to causes of conflict caused by assumptions about the other party. A naat'áanii facilitates the process by guiding the parties in a move from the head to the heart to achieve reconciliation. "Reconciliation is the product of a mutually sculpted reality where skepticism and rejection are replaced with acceptance" (Grohowski 1995, 34).

Traditional Navajo peacemaking procedure and cognitive-affective process are very close. They use different language to describe what is going on, but the general dynamics are the same. The question of the cultural specificity or universality of Navajo peacemaking may be resolved in matching linguistics and perceptions in deep cross-cultural discussion and examination.

In Navajo, where there is a dispute, there is *hóxhó*. The concept eludes accurate translation into English, but it refers to a state of conflict in which people are not in right relations with their surroundings, or environment (the universe). The situation is one of *anahoti'*, which is a state of conflict and the opposite of hózhó, an ideal situation where everyone and everything relates to each other as they and it should. Given the state of conflict, the process often begins with prayer.

Navajos view their justice method as a ceremony (Bluehouse and Zion 1993). Prayer is very powerful in Navajo thinking, because it summons supernatural beings to take part in the process. It brings them to the gathering, to participate and to help with the outcome. Put in a more secular way, prayer helps focus the attitudes of the participants to get them to commit to the process. Another way to describe it is "priming," where the peacemaker starts "the process of bringing certain things, typically behaviors or personal characteristics to mind, activating them" (Grohowski 1995, 35). Navajos tend to be empiricists, and empiricism recognizes the role of prayer from tradition. It is a cement that commits even those with cognitive dissonance to the process. Prayer prepares the parties for the "talking out" to come, commits them to engage in that process sincerely and "in a good way," and starts them on the beginning of the process of reconciliation to achieve hózhó through consensus.[1]

The next state is the actual process of talking things out, and that is where the excuses become important. The peacemaker may acknowledge the victim or the person who wishes to relate what happened. The victim has an opportunity to relate the event and how he or she feels about it. Sometimes, the person will be a concerned relative, as with a mother of a child in an abusive relationship with a spouse, or a parent who is concerned about a child's drinking or acting out.[2] Venting is encouraged, where the parties relate not only what happened but also its effects. They express their feelings about the event and how it affected them.[3]

An offender has the opportunity to listen to the charges and description of the impact of conduct on the person complaining. He or she will most likely have the benefit of the victim's family's reactions before speaking. When the accused offender has had the opportunity to hear those things and the feelings associated with them, then he or she has an opportunity to respond. That is the point at which the excuses are likely to come out: "It was *her* fault"; "It's no big deal"; "I couldn't help it—I'm just a hopeless alcoholic"; "I was drunk"; and so on. One of the difficulties with excuses, which are cognitive dissonance, is that they are often not grounded in reality. An offender believes the excuses, because they are what helps reconcile conduct with feelings toward them. An offender may not listen to an authority figure such as a judge, probation officer, or social worker. Often, Navajos perceive those representatives of state power as simply "powerful beings." A powerful being is an external force that controls or punishes another, often without regard for the individual; that is, powerful beings do not respect individuality. Navajos know the "them versus us" of authority in court systems and do not allow them to overcome the internal barrier of cognitive dissonance.[4]

In peacemaking, in contrast, the people who hear the excuses are relatives, community members, and a peacemaker chosen for having the respect of the community. They are people whose message is likely to overcome the barrier of the excuse and have their observations sink in. They are the people who know the offender best and who are able to deal with excuses such as "I don't really have a drinking problem." In one peacemaking case, a batterer laid out the usual domestic violence excuses of "I don't have a drinking problem," "It's her fault," and so on. His sister listened to his story and confronted him. This is the process of internalization, where the relationship of the speaker to the person giving the excuses may be more important than the content of the message.

Another advantage of the process is that it deals with emotional barriers. Although an offender may have internal barriers that are unrealistic and the product of cognitive dissonance, others have them as well. Victims have barriers too, and many in the field of domestic violence are puzzled about the seeming ignorance or unreality of a victim of family violence. Victims have many defense mechanisms, which are also a product of cognitive dissonance. The same holds true for groups such as families, whose denial of the misdeeds or problems of a loved offender often reinforces bad behavior.

Talking out to expose excuses, respond to them, and clarify values is perception sharing, where people are called on to reflect on their own behavior and to see its impact on others. It then leads to verification of who did what to whom and why and clarification of attributional errors (Grohowski 1995).

The next phase of peacemaking is called "the lecture" in English. It is another unfortunate translation of a Navajo concept, because the lecture is not an abstract sermon but a form of teaching. A naat'áanii peacemaker knows traditional Navajo values and will most often express them by relating what happened in creation times to the problem at hand. The teaching is in fact a kind of case law in which the naat'áanii can point to similar disputes or problems in the past, relate who went through them, and show how the situation was resolved. Often, Navajo precedent speaks to mutual respect or the well-being of the group and community. What takes place is called "attribution reassignment" (Grohowski 1995). This is the phase where people move from "head thinking" to "heart thinking" to have empathy for others. It is a process of communication through which an offender learns the inaccuracy of the given excuse and begins to change attitudes toward others. It is also a process through which others learn more about the offender's motivations and why the excuses are offered. The same holds true of other participants who believe false attributions about what motivated the offender. The process is guided by traditional teachings that tap the internal learned values of everyone in the group.

The next and final phase is reconciliation (Grohowski 1995). If the parties have committed themselves in prayer, vented their perceptions and feelings, talked out the problem and relationships, and received the guidance of the naat'áanii, reconciliation is the final phase, when people have moved to the end of the cognitive-affective, head to heart, process. At this stage, parties in peacemaking reach consensus on what should be done to resolve the problem. The primary consensus is about relationships—where people stand with each other at the end of the process. There may also be consensus about restitution or reparation to a victim (which can be symbolic only, often in the form of a payment of cattle or jewelry) or what needs to be done to prevent past bad actions from happening in the future. In the traditional context, that can mean that a family will watch over an offender or make certain that person keeps his or her promises. In more modern contexts, it can commit people to Western therapy, counseling, or treatment, or other kinds of action to follow up on the realization that cognitive dissonance has led to false thinking. Sometimes, Navajo curing ceremonies can be a plan reached by consensus. A plan is a major Navajo justice concept. It is associated with *naat'ááh,* or planning, which is a practical process of turning intuition reached through prayer and reflection into talk, and the talking out of peacemaking into a concrete plan of action.

At the end of the process, hózhó should be achieved, and people will describe it with the phrase *hózhó nahasdlii* (or *hózh náshdleeh*). The translation is to the effect that now that the process has been completed, the individuals involved in it are in good relations and, indeed, all reality is in good relationship, with everything in its proper place and relating well with each other in hózhó. Navajo dispute resolution is process oriented, and the process is itself important. It builds on relationships and solidarity. The parties make their commitment to the process in the opening prayer, and if successful, the process concludes with new relationships of respect, where excuses are exposed as being false and there is a new commitment to an ongoing relationship. The process does not involve coercion or punishment. Navajo thought rejects force and ordering others around. Navajo thought is highly individualistic, with great respect for individual integrity and freedom, yet the process guides people to realize that freedom is exercised in the context of the group and relationships with others. The Navajo maxim is "He acts as if he had no relatives." At the end of the process, the value of relatives and relationships leads both victim and offender to leave off seeing the world with the head and to see it with the heart instead. One of the biggest misunderstandings of Indian thought is that Indians are stoic and have no emotions. The opposite is true, and justice process uses human emotions, along with all other faculties, to adjust relationships.

Conclusion

This review attempts to answer some of the questions posed at the beginning. Peacemaking depends on consensus and will not work without it, so if someone does not agree with the group's decision, that person need not go along with it, and peacemaking will fail. Courts are available as a backup in the event of failure.

The question of what to do about people who are amoral or sociopaths is too often put in a snide or a flip way. No one is completely amoral. As long as someone is a member of a community, that person will adhere to its values to some extent. Internalization, which relies on respect for the group and socialization, will always take place to some extent. In traditional Navajo lore, an individual who refuses to work with the group would be ostracized after attempts to get that offender to comply. The term "sociopath" assumes that someone is outside the group's common values. Peacemaking will either lead the person to comply through group teaching and the wisdom of a naat'áanii or, again, the individual may be locked out of the community. In the Navajo way of thinking, the most horrible punishment or thing that could happen would be to be excluded from relationships with relatives.

Can you handle murder in peacemaking? It is done. Just as offenses such as rape or other sexual insults can be and are dealt with in peacemaking, a wide variety of disputes can be resolved using it. Rather than attempt to establish categories of the kinds of cases that can or cannot be handled, peacemaker rule revisions assume that anything can be dealt with in peacemaking, and if it does not work, the usual adjudication methods are available.

A great deal of peacemaking may be culturally specific to Navajos. However, to the extent that social psychology literature and analysis can be used to explain the dynamics of peacemaking, it should be translatable. It is a matter of context, where the individuals who exhibit excuses (and believe them) can be moved, depending on individual socialization and the lingering authority of the group, to help people internalize the values of the group and act using them.

At the end, the success of peacemaking is not in its concrete result or the actual remedy given. It is in an adjustment of the attitudes of the parties. Both offenders and victims begin with cognitive dissonance or related emotions that are based on assumptions and unreality, and the process leads them to common understandings. The parties frame the understandings themselves; they are not guided by abstract rules in the law, which are imposed by outsiders. The parties talk out their problem and how they feel about it to gain empathy and, at the end, consensus on how to realign their relationships in a meaningful way.

Notes

This chapter is an edited version of James W. Zion's "The Dynamics of Navajo Peacemaking," *Journal of Contemporary Criminal Justice,* 14 (1): 58–74, 1998. Reprinted with permission of the journal and the author.

1. When this chapter was being written, the Navajo Nation judicial branch was in the process of revising the peacemaker rules to incorporate more Navajo traditional values. This process of committing the parties or starting them down the path to reconciliation and hózhó is, according to Philmer Bluehouse, called *"hózhó nahodoodleel,"* or the beginning of the path. This is a place where it is difficult to reconcile Navajo understandings with English discourse. In preparing this chapter, I spoke with Dan Vicenti of the

court staff, who is an experienced educator and wise adviser. Dan stressed the importance of Navajo spirituality as a key to peacemaking. That is genuinely a Navajo perspective, but it is a difficult one to relate in secular discourse. One of the communication barriers we have in American society is the inability to discuss spirituality without the clouds of suspicion, distrust, and even hostility toward religion and spirituality getting in the way. We must find a way for things such as religion, spirituality, and morality to be discussed without the lens of distrust, hostility, insecurity, and perhaps even guilt getting in the way of understanding. That is the whole point of Grohowski's (1995) thesis, where she states that cognitive attitudes are often the cause of conflict.

2. In the experience of the Peacemaker Division, many cases brought to peacemaking involve relatives who are concerned about poor marital relationships in a common home or the drinking and acting out of children or other relatives. There are many land dispute cases that come to a head because of violent confrontations or arguments that trigger strong pride or self-esteem emotions. Vincent Craig, Navajo Nation judicial branch chief probation officer and a noted Navajo humorist, identifies the problem in a very Navajo way: A woman says, "Officer, arrest that man! He's looking at me somehow." Many Navajo disputes are framed in very vague ways, and accusers have a difficult time expressing the wrong. Outsiders are often confused by the vague way in which a dispute is expressed, with minimal description. That is part of the Navajo discourse, in which emotional reactions to harm are vented but details are missing.

3. Philmer Bluehouse explains that the most important piece of paper in peacemaking is the tissue. Peacemakers keep boxes of tissue on hand, which again reinforces the importance of emotions in Navajo thought. A further illustration of the difference in thinking is the fact that chief justice Robert Yazzie will often react to my analysis of a problem by saying, "Chicago, Illinois!" That is a pun on "shi cago" (phonetic spelling), which means "over my head" or "Huh?" He will also sometimes rag me (as do other Navajos) about relying too heavily on "paper knowledge."

4. There are three kinds of responses to social influence: compliance, identification, and internalization. Compliance is the force of sanctions—of police and other authority figures—on behavior where compliance is the product of the threat of force. When the force is not present, it does not compel behavior. Identification is listening to a respected figure, such as a parent or loved relative, where the response is geared to respect for that person. Such is not the case with authority figures—strangers—who act on people. The third response, internalization, is where the person wants to listen to the speaker and responds out of respect for that person or the desire to listen to and acknowledge what is said. That is why authority-figure lectures to offenders do not work, particularly when they are simply authoritarian and cannot "reach" the offender. (See Aronson 1995, 34–40, n. 30.)

References

Allport, Gordon W. 1979. *The Nature of Prejudice*. Reading, Mass.: Addison-Wesley.

Aronson, E. 1995. *The Social Animal*. 7th ed. New York: Freeman.

Bachman, Ronet. 1992. *Death and Violence on the Reservation*. New York: Auburn House.

Bazemore, Gordon, and Susan E. Day. 1996. Restoring the Balance: Juvenile and Community Justice. *Juvenile Justice* 3 (1) http://www.ncjrs.org/txtfiles/jjjd96.txt (accessed August 24, 2004).

Bluehouse, Philmer, and James W. Zion. 1993. *Hozhooji Naat'aanii*: The Navajo Justice and Harmony Ceremony. *Mediation Quarterly* 10 (4): 327–37.

Duran, E., B. Guillory, and P. Tingley. 1995. Domestic Violence in Native American Communities: The Effect of Intergenerational Post Traumatic Stress. Unpublished manuscript.

Grohowski, Laurie M. 1995. Cognitive-Affective Model of Reconciliation (CAMR). Master's thesis, Antioch University of Ohio.

Hauswald, Lizbeth. 1988. Child Abuse and Child Neglect: Navajo Families in Crisis. *Dine' Be'iina'* 1 (2): 37–53.

Holm, Tom. 1996. *Strong Hearts, Wounded Souls: Native American Veterans of the Vietnam War*. Austin: University of Texas Press.

Hudson, Joe, and Burt Galaway. 1996. Introduction. In *Restorative Justice: International Perspectives,* ed. Joe Hudson and Burt Galaway, 1–14. Monsey, N.Y.: Criminal Justice Press.

Ladd, John. 1957. *The Structure of Moral Code: A Philosophical Analysis of Ethical Discourse Applied to the Ethics of the Navajo Indians*. Cambridge, Mass.: Harvard University Press.

Levy, Jerrold E., and S. J. Kunitz. 1971. Indian Reservations, Anomie, and Social Pathologies. *Southwestern Journal of Anthropology* 27: 97–128.

National Minority Advisory Council on Criminal Justice. 1982. *The Inequality of Justice: A Report on Crime and the Administration of Justice in the Minority Community*. Washington, D.C.: Government Printing Office.

Reiss, A. J., and J. A. Roth. 1993. The National Research Council's Panel of the Understanding and Control of Violent Behavior Concluded: Intoxicated Navajo Fight Almost Exclusively with Family Members. In *Understanding and Preventing Violence,* ed. A. J. Reiss and J. A. Roth, 198. Washington: National Academy Press.

Shepardson, Mary. 1982. The Status of Navajo Women. *American Indian Quarterly* 149: 161–62.

Silverman, Robert A. 1996. Patterns of Native American Crime. In *Native Americans, Crime, and Justice,* ed. Marianne O. Nielsen and Robert A. Silverman, 58–74. Boulder, Colo.: Westview.

Wallace, S. 1996. Alternative Sentencing Goes Mainstream. *NLADA Cornerstone* 1 (18): 3.

Winkelman, M. 1996. Cultural Factors in Criminal Defense Proceedings. *Human Organization* 55 (2): 154–59.

Woodman, Gordon. 1993. Culture and Culpability: The Potential of the Culture Defense. *Commission on Folk Law and Legal Pluralism Newsletter* 23 (October): 46–50.

Zimmerman, R. 1996. The Sanction Paradox. *Center Court* 1 (2): 3.

Zion, James W. 1992. North American Perspectives on Human Rights. In *Human Rights in Cross-Culture Perspectives,* ed. A. A. An-Na'im, 191–220. Philadelphia: University of Pennsylvania Press.

5

When People Act as if They Have No Relatives

Domestic Abuse Cases in the Crownpoint Family Court

James W. Zion

When Elsie B. Zion and I wrote "Hozho' Sokee'—Stay To-gether Nicely: Domestic Violence under Navajo Common Law" (Zion and Zion 1993), the Navajo Nation was aware from public hearings held in late October 1991 of severe domestic violence. The article was written after the hearings but before 1992 domestic violence court rules and the adoption of the Navajo Nation Domestic Abuse Protection Act of 1993. It was written as background research and a policy guide, based upon literature on domestic violence and how it was handled in Navajo tradition. One of its most contro-versial conclusions was that hózhǫ́ǫ́jí naat'áanii, Navajo peacemaking, can be used to deal with domestic violence (called "domestic abuse" in Navajo Nation law). That recommendation was put in the court rules and legisla-tion, and there has been debate about that for over a decade. Some anti–do-mestic violence advocates have repeatedly (and hotly) asserted that Navajo women are revictimized in peacemaking (without presenting evidence of any specific instance) and say that you can't "mediate" domestic violence. The usual response is that Navajo peacemaking isn't "mediation" because peacemakers are not "neutrals," and the process involves family members to protect petitioners. That theoretical answer has not been satisfactory.

In January 2004, Judges Irene M. Toledo and Angela Keahanie-Sanford of the Navajo Nation Crownpoint Judicial District in northwest New Mexi-co appointed me as a domestic abuse commissioner in the family court, and I began hearing cases on Fridays starting on February 6, 2004. Based on data I gathered, this chapter revisits some of the conclusions in "Hozho' So-kee'" that were based on theory and anecdotal evidence from peacemakers and support staff. It will (1) analyze the nature of domestic violence cases; (2) identify instances showing when peacemaking works and when it does not; and (3) show how a combined approach using peacemaking and quasi-judicial powers can be innovative. There are distinct differences between the procedures I use and "pure" peacemaking, and they will be addressed in more detail in future writing.

The Nature of Domestic Abuse in the Crownpoint Court

I assumed that there was a great deal of domestic violence in the Navajo Nation, in the sense of actual and severe violence, because of the high numbers of cases under that category in annual court reports. I saw several instances where no violence was present, or it was low-level violence, but I rarely encountered violence so severe as to require medical treatment or hospitalization. Court staff confirmed that they did not see many cases involving serious violence, and they were surprised because of statistics showing a high domestic violence caseload in the judicial district.

The Navajo Nation Domestic Abuse Protection Act is unique because it covers all relationships and not just individuals in marital, post-marital, affectionate or intimate, and post-relationship situations. There are ten classifications of conduct in the definition of "domestic abuse" in the law, including assault, battery, threatening, coercion, confinement, damage to property, emotional abuse, harassment, sexual abuse, and "other conduct," defined as any offense or tort under Navajo Nation law. The definitions of "emotional abuse" and "harassment" are detailed and broad, so they cover a wide range of harmful activity. Although "elder abuse" is not defined in the code, such cases are fairly frequent, and they call for a creative reading of the definitions and use of the standard-of-proof definition of preventing abuse in the future when it is based on neglect.

The act's broad coverage of relationships and all-inclusive definitions likely prompt a caseload that is different from caseloads in jurisdictions that have more restrictive definitions of covered relationships and the kinds of acts that are violent. That may make the climate of proceedings in the Crownpoint court different. Some petitioners are individuals (including non-Navajos) who are unable to get relief in the nearby New Mexico courts (because of differences in definition, covered actions, or relationships) and who file again in the Crownpoint court.

Crownpoint Cases

The ability to use peacemaking (or not) could be accounted for by the levels of violence and the attitudes of parties. Unlike peacemaking, domestic abuse hearings are summary in nature, and the Friday dockets are heavy, with many parties waiting in a hallway for their cases to be heard. I kept journal notes of hearings and recommended decisions, and they are full of "case" evidence (used in the legal anthropology sense of a "case" as an example). Unfortunately there is not sufficient space here to relate detailed case examples to prove the following conclusions.

I heard 104 cases between February 6, 2004, and July 9, 2004 (the period covered by this chapter), in thirteen days of hearings and three specially set hearings. "Case" means the total number of hearings where a party or parties appeared. Separate petition files were often consolidated for one hearing because of the identity of parties and issues, so the term does not mean the total number of files or docketed matters. There was only one hearing involving counsel on both sides with a full evidentiary hearing using strict rules of procedure and evidence.

Of the 104 total hearings, 80 were disposed of on the merits and 24 were interim procedural orders, most often when the matter had to be continued because the respondent was not served with process. Of the 80 disposed of on the merits, 64 had orders granted and 16 were dismissed. Of the 64 cases heard on the merits where orders were granted, 6 involved serious violence (requiring hospitalization or medical treatment for physical trauma), 9 involved low-level violence (slapping, pushing, etc.) and 49 involved various insults not involving physical violence. In order of frequency, the insults were verbal abuse or other harassment (15); home invasions (5); child custody, property damage, and elder abuse (4 each); pecking order abuse and theft (3 each); marital rape and threats (2 each); and a land dispute, act of hooliganism, a threatening letter, reconciliation after the entry of a "no-contact" order, contempt, sexual harassment, and a child in a lesbian relationship (1 each). The last was referred to peacemaking by consent of the parties.

Most cases involved conflicts between spouses or intimates (and individuals in post-intimate relationships), but there were also cases of conflict between parents and children or grandchildren, elder abuse, property damage, and land disputes. Cases that involved "hooliganism" were ones that went beyond conflicts between individuals and disturbed the public peace ("disorderly conduct" under Navajo Nation criminal law), such as public confrontations and fighting, obscene gestures, foul language, and so forth that was related to groups of young people going after each other in public. Although infrequent, there were indications of gang activity in some cases, although it was difficult to sort out whether gang affiliation was actual or the perception of a petitioner. Individuals did not appear in gang colors, wear clothing associated with gangs, or testify using gang terminology. Pecking order abuse is a situation where a woman in a prior relationship with a man will harass a woman in a subsequent relationship, in addition to or separate from harassment of the man.

When Peacemaking Works

What is the measure of success when the peacemaking process is used? The other chapters in this book speak of consensus and an affect shift to achieve it, but such a shift was infrequent, although there were a few instances where there was a complete affect shift and consensus that could be identified. Several couples negotiated voluntary reconciliation, with a "no abuse" order to assure protection. A combination of peacemaking style and adjudication was used in all cases, so there are no statistics to distinguish the two.

A peacemaking approach is often successful in situations where petitioners (most often women) ask the court to allow them to withdraw their petitions. They usually use a handwritten *pro se* motion form or a letter to ask that the petition be withdrawn or dismissed, and the usual practice is for the judge to deny the request and have the matter heard by a commissioner. There is often a high degree of petitioner minimalization, particularly when the respondent appears in court. That refers to a petitioner who does not fully articulate the facts to support the petition, and that could be associated with fear of confronting the respondent or with Navajo cultural values that blaming should be avoided. Petitioners are walked through the petition to discuss the nature of the abuse and the length of time it has been going on. The standard form petitions have a section for petitioners to give a history of abuse, showing other incidents and when they occurred. The parties are counseled that there should be at least a "no future abuse" order to assure protection, and to act as an incentive, and they usually agree. Some couples insist that the petition should be dismissed out of consideration of their right to privacy or noninterference by government. Their request is granted if the nature of the abuse, likelihood of future abuse, and effects on children indicate that a reconciliation could be successful. The practice, not addressed in the Navajo Nation domestic abuse law, is to issue a "contact" order, allowing reconciliation in the family home or a separation with communication between the couple.

Modern techniques can facilitate a peacemaking approach. The Campbell Danger Assessment is a useful tool to deal with minimalization and denial. It is a list of twenty questions about specific kinds of recent abuse, and its severity, that can be used to deal with minimalization, particularly when a petitioner asks for leave to withdraw the petition. The questions are asked simply and informally (often without an indication that an assessment is being done) to highlight abusive conduct. It can be used as a form of reality therapy to elicit the facts, point out the nature and extent of abuse to a petitioner, and show respondents the extent of their denial. It can be used to get parties who wish to reconcile to agree to a "no future abuse" order with court supervision, voluntary participation (as a couple or individually) in counseling programs recommended by the local domestic violence advocacy and treatment program, or alcohol treatment. Although the court can compel individuals to get counseling or treatment, there are specific efforts to get voluntary compliance by discussing the need for family support services. That approach prompts a specific agreement or consensus by a couple, or at least a tacit agreement if they do not object when such orders are proposed. The scope of consensus is broader when there is a suggestion of how to approach problems and the parties agree. They are told that I will not impose a decision on them and that they must tell me what relief I should propose in the orders I write for the presiding judge to approve.

Although their participation is irregular, victim and elder advocates are very helpful when they are involved in discussions with the parties. The McKinley County (New Mexico) Sheriff's Department has a federally funded victim advocate in Crownpoint; there is a Navajo Nation victim advocate; the Family Harmony Project (a private, nonprofit advocacy and counseling agency) has advocates; and there is a Navajo Nation elder abuse program advocate. They are Navajos; most have good advocacy skills; and they are very helpful by providing suggestions for the resolution of problems and by identifying resources. They give an additional dimension to peacemaking that is similar to situations where social service or other service providers are included in peacemaking sessions. They are very helpful in giving support and protection for petitioners when relatives are not present to perform that function.

Peacemaking is not always successful. Notably, it has not been successful where there has been severe violence. Respondents will not appear, and if they do, there is often a "she said, he said" situation where the respondent (usually male) will angrily deny the act or responsibility for it. When I see stonewalling, I switch to an adjudicator mode and resolve conflicts in testimony (I do not administer an oath) using "reliable" (a legal term) exceptions to the hearsay rule for domestic violence cases to corroborate a story, or I assess the credibility of the parties using "demeanor evidence" (the parties' bearing, body language, tone of voice, inconsistencies in statements, etc.). On occasion, I use literature on "the abusive personality" to detect attitudes of control and dominance to determine credibility. I attempt to use the techniques outlined in chapter 4 to get a respondent to at least agree to the entry of orders. Some other situations for which peacemaking was not suitable were when there was disruptive activity in the homes of elderly relatives, most often fueled by alcohol, and other relatives brought petitions to exclude children or relatives from a home or family outfit against the will of the elderly person. There is a Navajo value, expressed in the maxim "it's up to him," that prompts elderly Navajos to tolerate disruptive behavior, even when it is highly disruptive or dangerous. Exclusion orders are recommended to the presiding judge when there is a predictable danger to an elderly person.

One problem area that may prove to be a measure of a lack of success is rage, which is apparent in cases of severe violence and in some moderate violence situations, as well as in other forms of abuse, such as in extreme impulsive outbursts. Petitions will sometimes indicate behavior done in rage, and the body language and bearing of some respondents show present rage at various levels. Extreme rage cannot be addressed in a summary hearing. The process of internalization can be used to address anger that does not rise to the level of rage, where a respondent is asked what the proper response is to a situation that makes that person angry (e.g., adultery), and the respondent volunteers a socially acceptable answer (e.g., that adultery does not justify physical violence). Anger is often expressed when individuals use a self-defense justification, and I deal with it by pointing out that provocation is not a defense under our law or that the level of violence used to defend self was excessive and took the case out of self-defense. Rage is too deep an emotion to address in summary hearings where an affect shift would take a great deal of time, while other parties are waiting in the hallway for their cases to be heard.

There is one unique kind of case that is particularly difficult to address, but where peacemaking may be successful—land disputes. Most of the land within the Crownpoint Judicial District is in the "checkerboard area" of northwest New Mexico. The name comes from a pattern of ownership on grid maps that shows ownership in fee, trust lands held for individual Navajo families (allotments), land held by the Navajo Nation, federal land, and state land. Many Navajos live on allotments or leased lands in a traditional land-use pattern called an "outfit," where individuals who are related by blood, clan, or marriage share the same parcel. There are conflicts over entry, permissive use from relatives who "own" the allotment or hold the lease, and sharing use of the land. Such conflicts frequently lead to violent or abusive conflicts. There are situations where family members bully others to dominate in land use or exclude outfit members. The approach is to determine who has the ownership interest to get that person's (or, most often, several people's) say on who should be on the land or how it should be used, and to get the majority view of outfit members. I then make a suggestion of a proper outcome based on those considerations and attempt to get at least tacit agreement to it. The approach of eliciting a majority consensus when disputes involve neighbors is also usually successful. Land disputes are a unique form of domestic abuse, and it is worthwhile to address them to prevent future violence and frequent criminal charges that arise from them.

Innovation that Combines Peacemaking and Adjudication

Peacemaking and adjudication appear to be on opposite ends of the spectrum of justice, but that is not clearly the case. A great deal of the discourse about peacemaking is to the effect that peacemakers are teachers and bearers of traditional wisdom who do not make decisions for parties or coerce them in any way. Although the noninterfering discourse of peacemaking is largely true, and peacemakers use a peaceful and gently guiding style in their lectures, there is historical support for the notion that naat'áanii (peacemakers) were forceful in their lectures and would tell off offenders in no uncertain terms.

I attempt to lecture parties using traditional Navajo moral and ethical maxims and philosophy, as do peacemakers, but I also use modern law and domestic violence literature to prompt discussion and clarify values. The modern knowledge includes provisions of the Navajo Nation Domestic Abuse Protection Act, general principles of law, domestic abuse literature and techniques, clarifying facts using exceptions to the hearsay rule, and factors that determine the best interests of children under Navajo Nation case law. I use the Campbell Danger Assessment, literature on the emotional dynamics of divorce and separation, and literature on the abusive personality in discussions with the parties. Peacemakers get training in the principles of domestic violence so that they can use the same kinds of information in their lectures, and several peacemakers are social workers or counselors who also use modern techniques to supplement traditional approaches.

One of the debates over using peacemaking in domestic violence cases is the extent to which coercion is present. Some critics assume that families coerce women into reconciliation against their will, or against their best interests, but I have not seen that. There is a strong coercive element in the petitions brought to the court and the remedies sought in them. Great care must be taken to avoid coercion in the sense of forcing or compelling a given decision or outcome, but I can make suggestions, and use family input, to elicit specific or tacit consent to a proposed order. I often see tacit consent in the faces of parties or in their body language. Hearings are held in a large courtroom where the parties and the commissioner sit at two large conference tables, and relatives sit in rising spectator seating. Following the development of the facts of the case, there is a casual and open-ended discussion with the parties and the audience to draw out facts, feelings, the root causes of the incident, and suggestions for resolution. Navajo parties and their relatives are able to define their own problems well and suggest practical and concrete approaches to them.

I see family members nodding in approval as I suggest a traditional approach or explain what might work in a given situation. I watch for parties to nod approval as I suggest possible orders, and I will propose them again and again until I have a sense of approval. I close hearings by asking if anyone has anything else to say, and if a party or relative asks if they can speak one last time, I say, "Of course." Navajo perceptions of right relationships, family solidarity, respect, and other values or traditional elements identified in *"Hazho' Sokee'"* are expressed in hearings when relatives are present, and they do have an impact on the attitudes of the parties.

Conclusion

Does peacemaking work in domestic *abuse* cases? Yes and no. We have been misled by using the term "violence," when what we see in the Crownpoint family court is most often low-level violence (slapping, kicking, shoving, and the like) or insulting and harassing behavior.

The kinds of cases that are heard in Crownpoint may reflect shifts in Navajo culture and a degree of acculturation (to general American cultural perceptions) that are a product of language and culture loss. When respondents are accompanied by relatives, and they are involved in problem-solving discussions and explorations of the root causes of a particular conflict that manifests itself as abuse, peacemaking is more likely to work. When there is violence or insult between younger Navajo couples and they do not involve their family members and relatives, it is more likely a respondent will attempt to stonewall and use the excuses described in chapter 4. There are different generations of Navajos, ranging from traditionalists who do not speak English or who speak it well; individuals who are somewhat aware of their language and culture but not firm in them; and young Navajos whose high degree of language and culture loss are apparent.

The word "consensus" requires a more precise definition based upon both what I see and what Navajo peacemakers do. It is possible for parties to fail to reach complete consensus, identified as such, yet benefit from a "talking out" process where a commissioner suggests an outcome in terms of finding an act of "abuse" as defined in the code and recommending a range of proposed orders to the presiding judge. Consensus in the form of agreement to given orders can be specific, but it can also be tacit and revealed in body language or a kind of "going, going—sold" technique.

There is one final technique I use that I think has a peacemaking quality. I tell the parties and their relatives (when they are present) that I will not impose a given order by recommending it without their approval. When I get it, I write decisions that state findings of fact, conclusions of law, and specific orders so that the parties know the basis for the proposed decision. (When I do not get approval, I can act as an adjudicator and recommend orders.) The literature says that peacemakers are teachers, and written decisions are teaching tools. An explanation of the basis of a decision can be used to get compliance with the orders that issue.

This chapter overviews unfinished business in the debate over whether the Navajo Nation courts can or should use peacemaking as a form of "mediation" (which I insist it is not). The discourse of peacemaking has gone a long way since its inception in court rules in 1982 and the developments following a more formal program starting in 1991. Navajo peacemakers have done a great deal to articulate who they are, what they do, and why. A friend who has studied Navajo peacemaking for many years, Jon'a Meyer, kindly sat in to observe three days of hearings I held. She said that she has seen more than one hundred peacemaking sessions done by Navajos and that I use many of the same techniques they use. I cannot conduct hearings in Navajo, and my understanding of Navajo culture is limited because I cannot speak the language; however, to the extent that Navajo peacemaking reflects universal human values, and to the extent of my understanding of Navajo culture over many years, I can attempt to use peacemaking style to identify its dynamics (in practice rather than the theories I have proposed in the past) to further our understanding. Does it work? Yes, it does, but we need more actual case data to find out more about when and how.

References

Zion, James W., and Elsie B. Zion. 1993. Hozho' Sokee'—Stay Together Nicely: Domestic Violence under Navajo Common Law. *Arizona State Law Journal* 25 (2): 407–26.

Commentary on Part 3

James W. Zion and Marianne O. Nielsen

Aside from the question "How does peacemaking work?" one of the most important questions, initially posed by federal government grant-funding sources and by academics, has been "Does it work at all?" The Navajo Nation judicial system and its peacemaking program have benefited from alliances with academics who bring their skills to the Navajo Nation to answer that question.

Unfortunately, there has been little empirical research done, primarily because of its challenging nature. Despite the good will and enthusiastic support of the peacemakers, the peacemaker administration, and the judicial branch, there are still many obstacles a researcher must overcome, including long distances between communities, transience of participants, lack of telephones, poor literacy rates among older clients, poor record keeping at the inception of the program, and a lack of computer records. Added to these logistical problems are issues of developing culturally appropriate methods, avoiding cultural appropriation, ensuring Native American voice, and negotiating a fair exchange for cooperation (see Nielsen and Gould 1999; Nielsen 2000; Mihesuah 1996; Grenier 1998). It is because of these difficulties that the first two chapters are so important; they represent the first attempts to do rigorous research (as defined by Western social sciences) on peacemaking.

Chapter 6, Eric Ken Gross's study of peacemaking in the Chinle and Shiprock family courts, was the first empirical study to attempt to answer the "does it work?" question from the point of view of participant satisfaction. He investigated several aspects of the effectiveness of peacemaking, using family court cases as a comparison group. In this chapter he reports on how participants perceive peacemaking in terms of fairness. This is the only evaluation that has ever been done on peacemaking using a survey instrument, a comparison group, and quantitative statistics.

One of his findings was that Navajos preferred peacemaking over adjudication in the family court. He made other findings that are more subtle yet relevant to contemporary Navajo Nation justice planning: Have Navajo youths so lost their language, culture, and tradition that they are no longer "Navajo"? That problem was particularly relevant as the Navajo Nation judicial branch undertook a gang study, where problems of language and tradition loss and accompanying acculturation emerged. Gross found that most youths, when asked their religious beliefs, answered that they are "traditionalist." Given the importance of self-identity in justice planning from the standpoint of the relationships of violence and identity, that was an important finding. Gross was the first empirical examiner to report on whether peacemaking works, from the point of view of participant satisfaction, and he gave a positive answer.

Jon'a Meyer (chapter 7) is another academic who frequently visits the Navajo Nation. She and her associate, Richard Paul, have studied Navajo peacemaking for several years. Their methodologies include the case study, bolstered by statistics from case records; reviews of peacemaking case records to show the kinds of matters that are handled in peacemaking, their source (e.g., court referrals or self-selected "walk-ins"), and their outcomes; interviews with peacemakers and judges; literature reviews; observation of peacemaking sessions; and observing Zion as he hears cases using his take on peacemaking.

This chapter is the summary of an evaluation of the Yaa Da' Ya program (which is no longer in existence because of a lack of funding). It was a three-year pilot project that started in the community of Chinle and expanded to Shiprock. It provided peacemaking services to young people. This chapter emphasizes a number of important points that affect the success of a peacemaking project, including financial environment and the importance of commitment from participants and their families in making peacemaking work.

It is a statistical analysis of 108 case files in which the case had a conclusion. Dr. Meyer was able to demonstrate, by looking at actual cases, that peacemaking is a relatively successful form of intervention to address youthful offending and problems.

Marianne O. Nielsen, the coeditor of this work, has been a consistent friend and supporter of peacemaking. She has used her influence as a member of the Department of Criminal Justice at Northern Arizona University to integrate Navajo Nation law and government into the curriculum after meeting with Navajo Nation justice leaders to elicit what should be in that curriculum.

Chapter 8 is based upon a literature review and interviews with actors within the Navajo Nation legal system who were most closely associated with peacemaking and the development of policies for the peacemaking programs. Nielsen uses the lens of restorative justice for her analysis and concludes that peacemaking is a form of restorative justice while retaining its unique cultural roots. She compares European-based restorative justice programs and Navajo peacemaking on a number of issues, and discusses how peacemaking has solved challenges that still plague some restorative justice programs.

Nielsen's use of a term that is now popular in justice thinking around the world is provocative. Is peacemaking a form of "restorative justice"? One of the problems when attempting to find an analogue in English for a traditional Indian practice is that words are important. For example, examinations of traditional dispute resolution might conclude that since communities are small and "everyone" knows what is going on, there is a kind of "no fault" process. Personal injury lawyers who practice within the Navajo Nation pounce on that term, as they have used the translation of the traditional Navajo term for compensation, restitution, or reparation—nalyeeh—to advance the proposition that their clients must always be compensated—at the American trial lawyer's level of "adequate" compensation. That misconstrues the traditional Navajo concept. Although the term "mediation" is broad, and covers many kinds of dispute resolution activities, the notion of the "neutral" in mediation gives a wrong impression of how peacemaking works.

Nielsen uses an aware approach to Navajo peacemaking when she classifies it as a unique form of restorative justice. She recognizes that there is no one definition of the term and that it can encompass a broad range of informal problem-solving activities. Nielsen is an informed observer of traditional restorative or reparative processes, ranging from her experiences with a First Nations justice program in Alberta to her intimate observation of, and collaboration with, Navajo Nation justice, along with other colleagues at Northern Arizona University. She too concludes in her literature review, interviews, and observations that peacemaking "works." Nielsen's chapter has been heavily edited to leave out a repetitious description of the history of the Navajo Nation courts and peacemaking.

Chapter 9 by Philmer Bluehouse and James W. Zion was an invited piece by a special editor of *Mediation Quarterly* for a special issue to showcase "Native American Perspectives on Peacemaking." The article was a collaboration for which the two talked out what they would say. One of the items they discussed was whether or not peacemaking is a "ceremony." Bluehouse approached that question from his perspective as a student of Navajo traditionalism, a field researcher who interviewed male and female Navajo singers (traditional healing practitioners), and the director of the judicial branch peacemaking program. Bluehouse also has strong ties to an organization of traditional Navajo healers—medicine men and medicine women. Zion's contribution to the question of "ceremony" came from his background and education as a Roman Catholic and his understanding of its ceremonialism. The two agreed that if you define a "ceremony" as a transformative event, peacemaking is indeed a ceremony.

The other device the two used was the collection and relation of traditional stories to make their point that peacemaking is successful, from an anecdotal point of view. One of the teaching devices peacemakers use to attempt to transform fixed attitudes to prompt empathy and consensus is Horned Toad and Coyote stories—stories most often told to children during the winter to teach them bedrock Navajo values. This chapter, which concludes a collection of empirical studies of peacemaking, returns the reader to the cultural context of such research, and it is a good concluding chapter for the question, "Does it work?"

References

Grenier, Louise. 1998. *Working with Indigenous Knowledge: A Guide for Researchers.* Ottawa, ON: International Development Research Centre.

Mihesuah, Devon. 1996. *American Indians: Stereotypes and Realities.* Atlanta, Ga.: Clarity Press.

Nielsen, Marianne O. 2000. Non-Indigenous Scholars Doing Research in Indigenous Justice Organizations: Applied Issues and Strategies. Paper presented at the Western Social Sciences Association Annual Meeting, San Diego, California, April 26–30.

Nielsen, Marianne O., and Larry A. Gould. 1999. Non-Native Scholars Doing Research in Native American Communities: A Matter of Respect. Paper presented at the Academy of Criminal Justice Sciences Annual Meeting, Orlando, Florida, March 9–13.

6

Perceptions of Justice

The Effect of Procedural Justice in Navajo Peacemaking

Eric Kenneth Gross

Since 1982, the judicial branch of the Navajo Nation has revived the traditional peacemaking approach to deal with issues of interpersonal conflict on the reservation. Most family disputes and violence are currently addressed in either family court or peacemaking. The data presented in this article are drawn from an evaluation and assessment of peacemaking done in 1998. I sought to investigate the relative effectiveness of peacemaking in reducing the recurrence of interpersonal violence in comparison with its primary alternative venue: family court. If the data were to show that peacemaking was more effective in reducing the recurrence of violence, then it is necessary to provide some explanation for its relative effectiveness.

In this chapter, the issue of procedural, or process, openness is explored as an important factor explaining the relative efficacy of open process systems in reducing recidivism. Process openness is a function of how justice participants perceive their experience in the justice system. Our experience of life is, in large part, a function of how our life events are perceived. Life experiences that result in the perception of injustice lead to anger, frustration, and rage. Conversely, perceptions of justice lead to understanding and relative harmony. This chapter analyzes the perception of justice in Navajo peacemaking and family court.

One of the fundamental questions posed in this chapter is how people's perceptions of justice affect their feelings and attitudes about their justice experience. The conventional view expressed in the behavioral sciences and public policy is that people are primarily motivated by personal self-interest. The conventional theory is fundamentally utilitarian, wherein people are motivated to maximize personal advantage and control. However, the assumed validity of the self-interest model has been consistently shown to be inaccurate (Shultz, Schleifer, and Altman 1981; Tyler 1988; Tyler 1990; Lind and Earley 1992; Lind et al. 1993; Lind, Huo, and Tyler 1994; Tyler 1994; Cole 1999). And although only a relatively small group of social psychology researchers have comprehensively explored this issue, their research findings have consistently shown that perceptions of justice are not linked to self-interest *per se* but to perceptions of procedural fairness or systemic openness. The experience of "fair treatment" is actualized when process participants are enabled to tell their story to an important and respected third party. Moreover, they understand that their narrative is accorded influence and consideration in case deliberations. Even when dispute outcomes are adverse to the interests of the participant, satisfaction with the justice process is associated with such procedural opportunities (Huo, Smith, and Ryder 1996; Lind and Earley 1992; Lind, Huo, and Tyler 1994; Lind et al. 1993; Lind and Tyler 1988; Tyler 1994; Tyler 1988; Tyler et al. 1997; Tyler, Degoey, and Smith 1996).

If the perception of systemic injustice is understood as a source of sustained alienation from conventional social norms and is, therefore, associated with the proclivity to reoffend, then an examination of the effect of justice processes on offenders and secondarily on victims possesses considerable value (Braithwaite 1989; Cole 1999; Kennedy 1997; Mann 1993; Montada and Schneider 1989; Reiman 1998; Shaver et al. 1987; Tonry 1995). This raises the question of how such experiences influence people's attitudes and feelings. Process satisfaction and dissatisfaction is linked to whether a participant's experience has been accorded value and meaning; process satisfaction is not primarily linked to disputants achieving individual or group interests. Where injustice is systemic, it produces patterns of social, racial, and ethnic invalidation. Over time, the process becomes normative. Therefore, victimized groups (by race, ethnicity, age, location, and gender) over time develop the expectation of injustice and incorporate it in their lives. It is just something the system does to "us." This understanding creates a gap between the community and the criminal justice system. Sustained and perpetuated negative group identities are, in part, a function of an oppressive justice system. Such identities can be associated with tendencies to resolve life problems violently (Arrigo 1995; Huo, Smith, and Ryder 1996; Miller 1996; Tyler et al. 1997; Reiman 1998; Cole 1999; Ferrell 1999).

Specifically, what criteria do people use to determine whether justice has occurred? The social psychology literature indicates that people are seldom unsure about such criteria. Overwhelmingly, this literature shows that people experience injustice when the process deals with them mechanistically or when they are not permitted the opportunity to express their experience. The experience of justice is therefore profoundly associated with specific client needs. Ignoring these needs or merely giving them rhetorical attention negates the opportunity for the client to have an experience that would be perceived as fair.

How do people respond behaviorally when justice or injustice has occurred? The experience of consistent injustice, whether it is manifested as the unequal distribution of assets and rights in society (distributive norms) or of self or group invalidation through insufficient or irrelevant procedural avenues in the justice system, has been associated with the formation of rage and cynicism (Shaver et al. 1987; Montada and Schneider 1989). Absorption of the sociocultural projection of invalidation and moral condemnation from the dominant social classes will result (to an extent that varies on a range of sociopsychological variables) in sustaining structures conducive to the maintenance of high rates of crime and interpersonal violence (Sampson 1986; Sampson and Wilson 1998).

More specifically, what is meant by the expression "the perception of justice"? For the purposes of this chapter, this expression may be likened to the legal concept of the "totality of the circumstances," where the experience of justice, which is ultimately subjective (even if it is conditional on specific and identifiable social institutions), is a predictable outcome of specific systemic structures and processes. In the simplest terms, the perception of justice is something that is part of a sense of self. It is what we understand to be fair. One of the core ideas underlying this understanding is having the right to tell our own story. What is most meaningful and relevant to us is inevitably *our own story*. When the opportunity to tell our story is nonexistent or taken away from us, we experience a profound sense of injustice. Rage, frustration, and depression are predictable consequences of institutional invalidation.

The perception of justice is also a factor of the relationship between primary third-party decision makers and process participants (particularly the offender, or respondent). The relationship among key third-party decision makers (judges, prosecutors, mediators, and peacemakers) and core process participants is one that is critical to understanding settlement outcomes over time (Black 1976; Black 1993; Cooney 1998). In comparison with traditional Navajo justice processes, the Euro-American model is typically alienating to key case participants. This is a function of differences in social status and culture between process decision makers (third-party decision makers) and participants (offender and victim). Social and cultural variances act to separate offenders from court process, relegating them to positions of apparent inferiority and marginalization, a process that is replicated throughout the justice process. Most important, this dynamic supports the experience of unfair treatment and, therefore, is conducive to the formation of rage and systemic estrangement. The perception of institutionalized patterns of injustice is manifested on both the general societal level and on the specific procedural level (Champion 1989; Currie 1998; Reiman 1998; Cole 1999; Austin and Irwin 2000). Thus, marginalized groups experiencing exclusion exist in a relationship with the dominant class characterized by alienation and marked with rage.

Donald Black and Mark Cooney have proposed that the greater the distance in these variables (status and cultural distance), the greater is the probability that the process will be perceived as unfair and unjust and the greater is the resentment between the defendant and the justice system (Cooney 1998). From the point of view of the justice practitioners, the justice process is mechanical. Offenders are not seen as individuals but as cases with common and predictable characteristics belonging to well-established categories. From the perspective of adjudicated offenders, the experience is invalidating and revictimizing.

Opportunities for reducing rates of reoffending can be associated with the variables of social and cultural distance between judges, prosecutors, and naat'áanii (peacemakers) and other key third-party decision makers. When the distance between these variables and the offender is relatively large, there will be a greater probability of reoffending. Although this chapter does not substantively address this issue with respect to data analysis, it does examine the nature of this relationship with respect to the perception of "fair treatment" on the part of the process participants. Where the perception of fairness is high, it is possible that the potential for offender accountability and responsibility is also high.

It is possible to observe process openness in justice systems by measuring several key variables as found in these core questions:

Is there a variation in fairness between peacemaking and family court?

Is peacemaking perceived by process participants as more open compared with family court?

Does the role of judge or naat'áanii affect the participant's perception of process fairness?

Are differences in status and culture between key third-party decision makers and hearing participants important factors in case outcomes and subsequent rates of reoffending?

The current data set contributes some preliminary answers to these questions, which are reported below.

Method

The data in this study was collected in 1998 on the Navajo Nation. Individuals were selected who were involved in judicial cases regarding domestic violence and had hearings in either civil family court or peacemaking. Inclusion in the data set required that the hearing occurred at least ten months prior to the time of data collection. All participants identified themselves as Navajo Indians.

The dataset was divided into two discrete groups. The test group consisted of individuals (n = 63) who had taken their family violence cases to peacemaking, and the control group (n = 41), those individuals whose cases were adjudicated in family court, a civil venue. Each participant responded to a fairly complex survey administered by Navajo Nation court officials and the primary researcher in chapter houses located throughout the Chinle District of the Navajo Nation.

Findings

Variations between Peacemaking and Family Court

Family court, unlike peacemaking, is a hierarchical form of justice, where a judge presides over a hearing and renders a judgment. The case participants occupy a position in the authority hierarchy well below that of the judge and are required to abide by his or her decision. Therefore, if Black and Cooney (Black 1976; Black 1993; Cooney 1998) are correct, the research data should show that participants found family court to be less fair and satisfying than Navajo peacemaking. Even though rules and procedures in family court are derived from the Western canon of civil practice, in contrast to conventional adversarial criminal court practice, family court is relatively open and more supportive of personal testimony. If we were to conceive of authentic procedural justice as a forum where participants are empowered to tell their own story without needing to conform to a set of rules and timings regulated by outside authorities and where they are actively included in the form and substance of the hearing settlement, the family court could be described as almost a type of mediated justice. Family court is therefore closer in many ways to peacemaking than it is to conventional adversarial justice. This is an extremely important point, because the data presented below shows that it is perceived as significantly less fair and satisfying to participants than peacemaking is. This variation suggests that had the comparison been made with conventional adversarial justice, where inequities are much more extreme and the process almost entirely mechanical, the differences in process satisfaction between peacemaking and adversarial justice would be considerably more.

Variations in Perceived Fairness: Peacemaking and Family Court

If the experience of fairness is conditional on the openness of the justice process, then survey responses should show a significant difference between people whose cases were processed in family court and those handled in peacemaking. Figure 6.1 below shows that difference. A higher mean indicates "less fair." The difference in perceived fairness between the two venues is statistically significant where p < .001. It is possible to assert that case fairness is associated with process openness, where openness is primarily defined as having the opportunity to express one's story. A higher mean indicates less openness. Figure 6.2 shows that peacemaking participants expressed feeling a far greater opportunity to tell their story in comparison with family court participants.

Variations between Court Venues in the Rate of Reoffending

Was the case venue associated with differing rates of reoffending between the two venues? The hypothesis would require that where satisfaction with the justice process is greater, there should be correspondingly lower rates

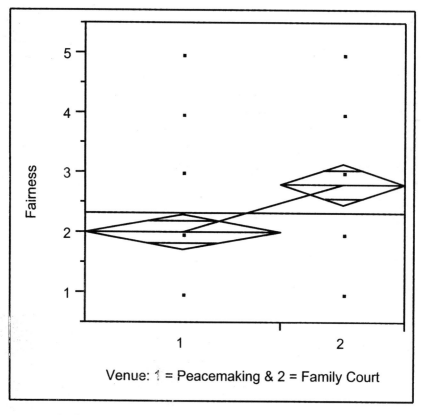

Figure 6.1 Process fairness by venue type: 1 = Peacemaking, 2 = Family Court

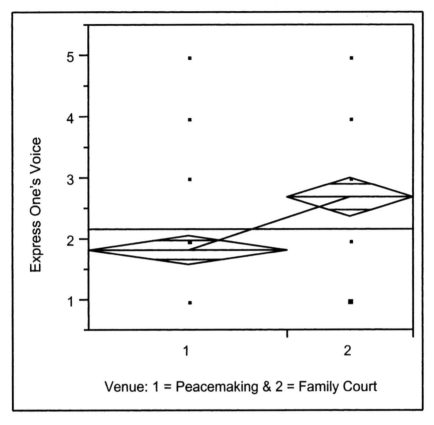

Figure 6.2 Having the right to express one's story: 1 = Peacemaking, 2 = Family Court

of reoffending. Respondents were asked if they had experienced a similar (related) problem with the "harm causer" since their peacemaking or family court proceeding. The data do show a difference, although it is only significant at a 90 percent level of certainty. Among the peacemaking cases, there was a reported reoffending rate of 23 percent, while among the family court participants, there was a 39 percent rate of reoffending, resulting in an approximately 60 percent higher rate of reoffending. These data provide preliminary support for the research hypothesis that open justice systems may result in lower relative rates of reoffending.

Finally, how did the two groups compare with respect to the question of whether the judge or naat'áanii was helpful in the justice process? Peacemaking respondents (many of whom had already had experience dealing with domestic violence issues in family court) stated that the naat'áanii was significantly more helpful than the judge in settling domestic disputes and bringing harmony to the disputants. The difference between the two groups was statistically significant where p < .001. (See figure 6.3.)

Extensive interview data further reinforce this finding. Peacemaking participants expressed considerably more satisfaction with the naat'áanii than family court participants expressed with the judge. This response suggests support for Black (1976; 1993) and Cooney's (1998) theories regarding the relationship between key third-party decision makers and satisfaction with the justice process, as well as resistance to justice outcomes. To reiterate, these theories posit that satisfaction and resistance to justice outcomes are mediated by differences in social status and culture between offenders and third-party decision makers. Moreover, interviews with peacemaking and family court participants consistently show a far higher satisfaction with the naat'áanii than with the family court judges. In virtually all studied cases, the naat'áanii was closer to the disputants with respect to social and cultural status than were the family court judges, although each of the latter are Na-

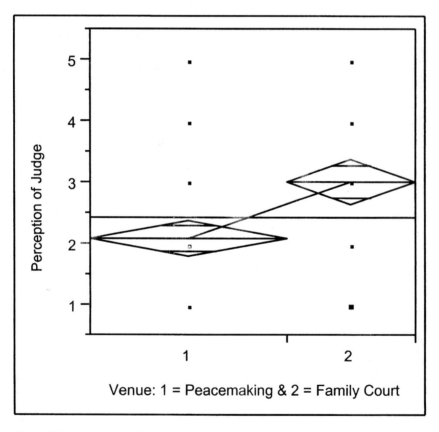

Figure 6.3. Perceptions of judge by venue type: 1 = Peacemaking, 2 = Family Court

vajos and are members of the community. They are fluent in the Navajo language and are widely known and respected throughout the Chinle District. Had the assessment comparison included a more conventional adversarial justice process, rather than the relatively friendly, mediational family court process, it can be presumed that the satisfaction difference would have been even greater between the two venues.

Conclusion

These data show that open systems are perceived significantly more positively than those that are only somewhat less open. It is not unreasonable to presume that were peacemaking compared with conventional adversarial justice in cases involving domestic violence, the results would be significantly more supportive of open justice systems. These data also show that peacemaking cases had a reoffending rate about 60 percent lower than cases processed in family court.

It would be important to replicate these results with further research, not only in Navajoland, but in other jurisdictions using similar open justice systems. Given that peacemaking participants consistently report more positive justice experiences and a greater experience of process fairness, and that peacemaking results in lower rates of reoffending, this justice paradigm could offer communities and justice agencies a powerful tool for dispute resolution and community justice.

References

Arrigo, B. A. 1995. The Peripheral Core of Law and Criminology: Social Theory and Conceptual Integration. *Justice Quarterly* 12 (3): 447–72.

Austin, J., and J. Irwin 2000. *It's About Time: America Imprisonment Binge.* Belmont, Calif.: Wadsworth.

Black, Donald. 1976. *The Behavior of Law.* New York: Academic Press.

———. 1993. *The Social Structure of Right and Wrong.* New York: Academic Press.

Braithwaite, John. 1989. *Crime, Shame and Reintegration.* London: Cambridge University Press.

Champion, D. J. 1989. Private Counsels and Public Defenders: A Look at Weak Cases, Prior Records, and Leniency in Plea Bargaining. *Journal of Criminal Justice* 17 (4): 253–63.

Cole, David. 1999. *No Equal Justice: Race and Class in the American Criminal Justice System.* New York: The New Press.

Cooney, M. 1998. *Warriors and Peacemakers: How Third Parties Shape Violence.* New York: New York University Press.

Currie, E. 1998. *Crime and Punishment in America.* New York: Henry Holt and Company.

Ferrell, J. 1999. Anarchist Criminology and Social Justice. In *Social Justice—Criminal Justice: The Maturation of Critical Theory in Law, Crime, and Deviance,* ed. B. A. Arrigo, 93–108. Belmont, Calif.: Wadsworth.

Huo, Yuen J., Heather J. Smith, and Tom R. Ryder. 1996. Superordinate Identification, Subgroup Identification, and Justice Concerns: Is Separatism the Problem; Is Assimilation the Answer? *Psychological Science* 7 (1): 40–45.

Kennedy, Randall. 1997. *Race, Crime, and the Law.* New York: Vintage Books.

Lind, E. A., and P. C. Earley. 1992. Procedural Justice and Culture. *International Justice of Psychology* 4: 227–42.

Lind, E. A., Yuen J. Huo, and Tom R. Tyler. 1994. . . . And Justice for All: Ethnicity, Gender and Preferences for Dispute Resolution Procedures. *Law and Human Behavior* 19: 269–90.

Lind, E. A., C. A. Kulik, M. A. Ambrose, and M. V. Park. 1993. Individual and Corporate Dispute Resolution: Using Procedural Fairness as a Decision Heuristic. *Administration Science Quarterly* 38: 224–51.

Lind, E. A., and Tom R. Tyler. 1988. *The Social Psychology of Procedural Justice.* New York: Plenum.

Mann, C. R. 1993. *Unequal Justice: A Question of Color.* Bloomington: Indiana University Press.

Miller, J. 1996. *Search and Destroy: African-American Males in the Criminal Justice System.* New York: Cambridge University Press.

Montada, L., and A. Schneider. 1989. Justice and Emotional Reactions to the Disadvantaged. *Social Justice Research* 3: 313–44.

Reiman, Jeffrey. 1998. . . . *And the Poor Get Prison: Economic Bias in American Criminal Justice.* Needham Heights, Mass.: Allyn and Bacon.

Sampson, R. J. 1986. Crime in Cities: Formal and Informal Social Control. In *Communities and Crime,* ed. J. Albert, J. Reiss, and M. Tonry, 271–311. Chicago: University of Chicago Press.

Sampson, R. J., and J. W. Wilson. 1998. Toward a Theory of Race, Crime and Urban Inequality. In *Community Justice: An Emerging Field,* ed. D. A. Karp, 97–118. Lanham, Md.: Rowman and Littlefield Publishers.

Shaver, P., J. Schwartz, D. Kirson, and C. O'Connor. 1987. Emotion Knowledge: Further Exploration of a Prototype Approach. *Journal of Personality and Social Psychology* 52: 1061–86.

Shultz, T. R., M. Schleifer, and I. Altman. 1981. Judgments of Causation: Responsibility and Punishment in Cases of Harm Doing. *Canadian Journal of Behavioural Science* 13: 238–53.

Tonry, Michael. 1995. *Malign Neglect: Race, Crime, and Punishment in America.* Belmont, Calif.: Wadsworth.

Tyler, Tom R. 1988. What is Procedural Justice?: Criteria Used by Citizens to Assess the Fairness of Legal Procedures. *Law & Society Review* 22 (1): 103–35.

———. 1990. The Social Psychology of Authority: Why Do People Obey an Order to Harm Others? *Law & Society Review* 24 (4): 1089–1102.

———. 1994. Psychological Models of the Justice Motive: Antecedents of Distributive and Procedural Justice. *Journal of Personality and Social Psychology* 67 (5): 850–63.

Tyler, Tom R., Robert J. Boeckmann, Heather J. Smith, and Yuen J. Huo. 1997. *Social Justice in a Diverse Society.* Boulder: Westview Press.

Tyler, Tom R., Peter Degoey, and Heather J. Smith. 1996. Understanding Why the Justice of Group Procedures Matters: A Test of the Psychological Dynamics of the Group-Value Model. *Journal of Personality and Social Psychology* 70 (5): 913–30.

7

Bił Háí'áázh ("I Am His Brother")

Can Peacemaking Work with Juveniles?

Jon'a F. Meyer

Not too long ago on the Navajo reservation, a teenage boy started the all-too-common downward spiral into a life of gangs and crime. His academic performance was dismal, with a D average and thirty-six absences in ninety days. After numerous court appearances for fighting and other gang activities, he was arrested for criminal impersonation and resisting an officer. Just when things were looking hopeless, the fifteen-year-old agreed to participate in a peacemaking program aimed at juvenile delinquents. Over the next year, he and his family participated in sessions that were guided by a traditional elder in which they discussed how his actions hurt him and those around him. Then, as a group, they refocused the teen on the Navajo ideal of hózhó (harmony) and formulated a plan of action so that he could correct his ways and live in hózhó. Between the sessions, program staff monitored him closely, making home and school visits to make sure he stayed on track. By the end of the program, the teen was getting A's and had discontinued his gang allegiances. Although the teen admits that he was skeptical of the program at first, he was particularly proud of his perfect attendance record and vowed to become a role model for his younger brothers to look up to.

The program in which the wayward teen participated wasn't a new approach invented by social workers to stem the growth of crime. It was the traditional form of justice employed by Navajos long before the arrival of whites and their ideas of justice to the Americas. Unlike the contemporary adversarial system, which focuses on punishing the guilty to prevent future crime, peacemaking instead tries to reduce deviance by reintegrating offenders into society and reestablishing harmony both within the individuals and between offenders and those around them. Navajos feel that harmony cannot exist when some people violate the rights of others; when this happens, everyone must be brought back into agreement through the use of ceremony and reparations. Peacemaking is one tool used to accomplish these goals (see other chapters in this volume for more information on peacemaking and how it works).

In 1993, the Navajo Nation initiated Yaa Da' Ya, a pilot program designed to work directly with juveniles and their families through peacemaking processes, where traditional teaching is strongly encouraged and implemented as a treatment plan. The program name, Yaa Da' Ya, neatly illustrates the goals of the approach; the name means "upward bound" in the Navajo language.[1] The program was based in Chinle, Arizona, a relatively sizable traditional community on the Navajo reservation. In 1990, Chinle, located at the center of the Navajo reservation, had a population of 25,418, of which nearly a fifth (17 percent, n = 4,442) were youths between the ages of ten and seventeen.

Brief History of the Program

The Yaa Da' Ya program was officially launched in April 1994, following a year of planning and process design. The program employed two front-line staff members: a family counselor and a family peacemaker liaison. The program served thirty-one juveniles during the first year of operation (1994), thirty-seven during 1995, fifteen during 1996, and twenty-seven during 1997, for a total of 110 youths. At the end of 1997, the program stopped admitting new clients due to the expiration of funding. The program was officially terminated on November 26, 1997, and the remaining cases were transferred to the previously existing adult peacemaking office for follow-up.

This evaluation uses information contained within the 108 completed case files (two of the 1994 cases could not be found). The greatest barrier I encountered was the lack of standardization among the files. Most files contained a one-page demographical information sheet to guide the intake process, but consistency beyond that was practically nonexistent, so much information was gleaned from reading summary reports of meetings and telephone calls, letters from various programs' personnel, records prepared for the family court's approval, and records from other agencies that were included in the juveniles' case folders. Because much of the information was handwritten (and not always legibly), some of the variables may have been miscoded in this research. Despite these limitations, however, the files presented a rich set of data, as discussed below.

Due to the sometimes high incidence of missing data, two forms of percentages are included in this report. The first percentage represents the "true" percentage, that is, the percentage of all 108 clients who fell into a particular category. The second percentage is the "valid" percentage, that is, the percentage of clients for whom the variable could be recorded who fell into a particular category. Both figures are presented so that readers may better draw their own conclusions about the findings. In cases where the true and valid percentages are the same, the second percentage is not reported.

If anything, the cases show that Navajo youth experience the same problems and issues as mainstream off-reservation youth, although possibly to a greater degree (e.g., grief over loss of supportive grandparents may be more of an issue for some youths who participated in Yaa Da' Ya due to the significant value assigned to grandparents in Navajo culture).

The Yaa Da' Ya Program Approach: A Case Study

Before presenting the findings, it is necessary to explain how Yaa Da' Ya handled its cases. This section presents a case study to demonstrate the program's approach and how it operated. During the third week of April 1994, a concerned mother came into the Yaa Da' Ya office to request services for her fifteen-year-old gang-involved son, who was in custody while awaiting trial on assault and other charges. He had repeated seventh grade three times and had been expelled from school after intimidating a teacher and participating in a number of violent episodes at school. He had been caught fighting at the residential program to which he was sent after being adjudicated a child in need of supervision (CHINS), so he was made a ward of the court and sent to the Navajo Nation's juvenile detention facility. Like the boy discussed in the beginning of this chapter, this young man seemed to be off to a very bad start. It was after these events that his mother requested Yaa Da' Ya's services.

During the first week of May, the juvenile was temporarily released for a month to help gather information for his upcoming criminal trial for interfering with judicial proceedings. By the end of May, Yaa Da' Ya had scheduled the youth's first peacemaking session. Eight people participated in the three-hour session, during which the parties talked about how much they cared for the youth and how much they wanted him to succeed. Traditional lectures were presented by the peacemaker about the youth's role in his family (both as a child and as an older sibling) and in society and how his alcohol and substance abuse were preventing him from achieving his goals. During the session, the juvenile recognized that he needed to change and agreed to participate in "rehabilitation treatment and traditional ceremonies to redirect his life in a positive manner."[2] He agreed to obtain residential counseling from Behavioral Health Services (BHS) in the areas of gang violence, alternatives to violence, and substance and alcohol abuse. He agreed to take advantage of the traditional healing ceremonies offered through BHS, including a sweat lodge ceremony. The family agreed to provide three traditional Navajo healing ceremonies for the boy. The youth and his mother agreed to attend biweekly individualized counseling sessions with Yaa Da' Ya staff, and he agreed to participate in group counseling offered through Yaa Da' Ya (e.g., youth awareness tours of a local prison, lectures by contemporary leaders on gender roles, and motivational talks). A review peacemaking session was set for six weeks after the first session to ensure that the boy was still on track with the many commitments he had made during his first session.

Two weeks later (the first week of June), the boy's charges of interfering with judicial proceedings were dismissed, and the family court judge signed into a court order the peacemaking agreement that the boy and his family had created. By that point, Yaa Da' Ya had arranged for the boy to enter Twin Trails Treatment Center (TTTC), a residential program that treats alcohol- and substance-abusing youths from the Navajo Nation. While waiting for space to open at TTTC, the boy attended counseling sessions and came in several times "just to talk" with program staff. He seemed open to counseling and was happy he was getting into residential treatment.

By the middle of June, the juvenile was at TTTC, so the Yaa Da' Ya staff traveled there to conduct his biweekly counseling sessions, at which they discussed his gang involvement and other issues. Due to his residential treatment, the review peacemaking session had to be rescheduled for the end of August. During this time, Yaa Da' Ya staff worked at getting the youth reenrolled in school. At his review peacemaking session, it was determined that he had met all but one of the conditions of his agreement. A second agreement was drawn up after the boy agreed to continue counseling and to seek the three ceremonies recommended at the first peacemaking session.

By the third week of September, the boy was enrolled at an alternative school and was doing fine. Within a month, however, he was ditching school and had been caught writing notes to other students in his class. He complained that he had not been scheduled for aftercare through TTTC although he wanted it. During November, the juvenile missed his first aftercare appointment at TTTC, saying that he had no transportation to get to his appointments. While this was going on, the boy's mother rescheduled his final review peacemaking session twice.

By the time January arrived, the youth had been terminated from school due to excessive absences, and his probation officer was wondering why he had not yet completed his community service hours from a prior criminal case. Even the Yaa Da' Ya staff was unhappy with his progress and threatened to send his case back to family court if the final review peacemaking session did not take place as scheduled.

At last, the final session was able to take place. The youth still had not had the three recommended ceremonies done due to the expense involved, but TTTC offered to contribute funds toward getting them performed. The boy had withdrawn from his gang but was afraid of being harmed due to doing so. He decided to pursue a GED through the alternative school and finally began working on his community service sentence. The Yaa Da' Ya staff actively monitored his case until April 1995, then kept periodic updates in his file. No additional negative incidents appeared in his file.

This case summary briefly illustrates how the Yaa Da' Ya program progressed. Although the boy had legal problems, it was his mother who sought out Yaa Da' Ya's assistance rather than the case being transferred into the program. Immediately, the two program staff members went to work on behalf of the youth, writing a formal referral to TTTC and coordinating his entry into that program. The juvenile attended a peacemaking session and two follow-up sessions, at which treatment plans were drawn up with the youth's input and with assistance from those who care about him (i.e., relatives and caseworkers). The program staff met with the boy and kept in regular touch with his school, treatment providers, and probation officer.

The case is a fairly typical one in that there was some resistance to full participation by both the juvenile and his parent, but this resistance was overcome. The financial difficulties inherent in some parts of the treatment plan are also highlighted, but it is encouraging to note that funds were available from other support services to help defray the sometimes onerous costs. This case also typifies the difficulties in classifying the outcomes in this evaluation; this youth was finally classified by the evaluator as "no serious problems, but not a good outcome." It was commendable that he left his gang and went back to school but unfortunate that he was expelled again due to excessive absences and behavioral problems and that he had begun to present treatment problems as well. Importantly, however, he was not involved in any fights after leaving his gang. This was no easy case, but, despite his relapsing, the youth and his family obviously benefited from his involvement with Yaa Da' Ya.

The case also illustrates how the program addressed its four goals: (1) provide peacemaking sessions to adjudicated and at-risk youth, using traditional teachings, healing ways, and ceremonies as treatment options; (2) develop a network of opportunities for clients; (3) coordinate aftercare and relapse-prevention activities and monitor clients and service providers to ensure that the youths comply with the agreements designed during their peacemaking sessions; and (4) develop a monitoring and feedback system to allow for continual evaluation of and change as necessary to the peacemaking element of the program. The staff worked quite diligently for all of their clients in order to meet the first three goals. Although not obvious from this particular case summary, the program was able to adapt and better itself for dealing with future clients (e.g., learning to better match peacemaker style with individual client needs, refining the program's monitoring efforts, and improving its ability to work with other service agencies to assist clients with meeting the terms of the agreements made during peacemaking).

Demographics

Yaa Da' Ya served a variety of Navajo juveniles aged six to eighteen and one twenty-one-year-old, whom the program staff identified through working with the family who took her in as a daughter. The greatest percentage of clients were aged fifteen to seventeen; this category comprised a full 53 percent (n = 57, valid = 55 percent) of the clients. The mean age of the participants was fifteen years of age (std. dev. = 2.32). Nearly two-thirds (63 percent, n = 68, valid = 64 percent) were male.

The family makeup of the program participants varied immensely. Most of the clients were from families with two to five children (56 percent, n = 61, valid = 73 percent), although 6 percent (n = 6, valid = 7 percent) were only children, and 16 percent (n = 17, valid = 20 percent) had five to nine siblings. The clients' mothers were more likely than their fathers to share a home with them (81 percent versus 43 percent). Not surprisingly, the mothers were also more likely to maintain contact with their children (93 percent vs. 63 percent), but the typical father maintained some contact with his child.

The vast majority (78 percent, n = 84, valid = 87 percent) of participants were enrolled in school at the time that Yaa Da' Ya's services were sought out, but the typical student was struggling academically. Many were failing academically (25 percent, n = 27, valid = 56 percent), and fewer than half (45 percent, n = 48, valid = 52 percent) were in high school although most were high-school aged. In fact, a full third (34 percent, n = 37, valid = 41 percent) had been held back for at least one year, and an additional 28 percent (n = 30, valid = 33 percent) may have repeated a grade.[3] In addition, suspensions were quite common among the participants; an average of five days were spent by each participant on internal or external suspension (range = 0–24 days for the thirty cases for which suspension data were available).

One reason for the students' poor academic performance was their unsatisfactory attendance records. The thirty-five students for whom attendance data were available missed an average of four full days and twenty-two partial days of school. Because each student's records covered different lengths of time (e.g., all of a term versus only a portion of that term), the absence rates were standardized by combining both types of absences and dividing by the total number of days covered by the school records. The results show that the typical student was absent for 59 percent of the school days covered by his or her records, and only two students missed fewer than one-fifth of their school days. Although GPA, suspension, and attendance records were available for only a small subset of the program participants, there is no reason to suspect that their records differ substantially from those whose records were incomplete (e.g., only half of the clients for whom GPA was available had been identified at intake as having academic problems).

Alcohol and substance abuse were rather common in the juveniles' lives despite legal statutes prohibiting possession or consumption of any alcohol on the reservation by either adults or youths. More than one-third (36 percent, n = 39) of the files mentioned prior alcohol use by the clients, and nearly a third (32 percent, n = 34) mentioned use of drugs, mostly marijuana and inhalants (e.g., sniffing gasoline). Relatively few of the participants had experience with more serious drugs such as cocaine.

In addition to the youths' own abuse of alcohol and drugs, abuse of alcohol by their parents was not uncommon; 21 percent (n = 23) of the juveniles had at least one parent whose alcohol abuse was noted in the files. Similarly, 14 percent (n = 15) of the youths had parents whose relationships with one another were noted to be abusive. Possibly related to the above factors, 10 percent (n = 11) of the participants had attempted suicide or reported suicidal ideations.

The juveniles' prior criminal records varied greatly. Nearly one-fourth (24 percent, n = 26) had been arrested for or admitted to committing violent crimes, including battery, aggravated battery, armed robbery, and other acts of violence. Property offenses appeared just as often as violent crimes (25 percent, n = 27). Prior arrests for alcohol-related crimes were less common (16 percent, n = 17) and were typically for public intoxication. Drug offenses were relatively uncommon (5 percent, n = 5) and tended to be for possessing marijuana. Some of the youths had other prior offenses: driving-related charges (typically driving without a valid license, 7 percent, n = 8), being beyond the control of one's parents (7 percent, n = 7), criminal impersonation (4 percent, n = 4), and nine other assorted arrests. When taken together, two-thirds (69 percent, n = 75) had been arrested for or admitted to at least one prior offense. In addition, nearly a tenth (9 percent, n = 10) of the program participants were reported to be gang members.

Program Variables

Although the program was originally designed to serve only juveniles transferred from the courts, only half (51 percent, n = 55) of the program's cases met this criterion. An additional two cases were referred due to parental crimes (e.g., a mother charged with endangering her two daughters after hosting a party where alcohol was served), and four cases were filed by social workers hoping to improve the living or social situations of youths in their caseload. More than two-fifths (44 percent, n = 47) of the cases, however, were direct requests by a parent or other interested party to initiate Yaa Da' Ya involvement in a juvenile's life. The high percentage of direct requests may be due to the manner in which the program was publicized. Program representatives attended chapter meetings to explain Yaa Da' Ya to community members, leading some to seek intervention for nonadjudicated youths.

Parents were the most common requesters of record. Even in cases transferred from the court, a person in the juvenile's life served as the point of contact for Yaa Da' Ya, and for 70 percent (n = 76, valid = 72 percent) of cases, this was one or both parents. Other relatives or step-relatives were the requesters in seven cases, and nonrelatives served as requesters in nineteen cases (including two victims who requested services for seven juveniles who had harmed them, four cases initiated by social workers, and a case brought by a school employee). Of interest, the juveniles themselves sought the program's help in combating drug or alcohol addiction or other problems in four cases.[4]

The reasons the juveniles were brought in or referred to Yaa Da' Ya fell into five major categories: (1) more than half (57 percent, n = 62, valid = 60 percent) of the participants were noted as being beyond the control of their parents; (2) nearly half (44 percent, n = 48, valid = 47 percent) were having problems in school that attracted their guardians' attention, including ditching, fighting, expulsion, or other problems; (3) more than one-fourth had been runaways (29 percent, n = 31, valid = 30 percent); (4) a small but substantial number (7 percent, n = 8, valid = 8 percent) had experienced family disharmony (e.g., a divorcing couple felt intervention might help their children deal with separation issues); and (5) one-fourth listed only the transfer from court as motivation for seeking Yaa Da' Ya's services (22 percent, n = 24, valid = 23 percent).[5]

The Yaa Da' Ya program was designed to cater to both traditional and contemporary participants and allowed clients to choose peacemakers who best fit their own religious beliefs. The requests showed that a variety of individuals sought the program's services (traditional Navajo = 33 percent, n = 36; Native American Church = 25 percent, n = 27; Christian = 19 percent, n = 21; Mormon = 5 percent, n = 5).

The Yaa Da' Ya intervention plan called for three peacemaking sessions (two regular sessions followed by an exit session). Possibly due to the lower seriousness of the charges faced by the youths than was originally anticipated by the program designers, the reality was that only one or two sessions was typical. Only three clients completed all three sessions. The highest number (43 percent, n = 46) of participants completed just one session, with follow-up tracked through staff members' supplemental reports, based on site visits and telephone calls with the clients, their families, their schools, and the other programs in which they participated.

One reason for the limited number of peacemaking sessions was the cost incurred by the parents. In order to compensate the peacemakers for their time, each session cost the parents thirty dollars. A number of the parents, especially single mothers, depended on government assistance programs, and this additional fee was unwelcome. Nearly one-fifth (18 percent, n = 19) of the files contained some mention of the parents complaining about the fee. Yaa Da' Ya staff conducted free case staffings in lieu of peacemaking for a few clients, and some clients were unable to participate in the peacemaking portion of the program due to their parents' inability (or unwillingness) to incur those costs. These clients were still monitored by the program staff and were able to participate in all other aspects of the program.

Parental cooperation stood in the way of many clients' progress. Only one-third (32 percent, n = 35, valid = 38 percent) of the parents cooperated with the Yaa Da' Ya program. The others refused to attend peacemaking sessions, participate in the parenting counseling to which they were recommended, bring their children to the program office for required meetings, or sign paperwork allowing their children to participate. Parental refusal to cooperate appeared to stem from their own programming needs, which were unaddressed due to denial that they had problems of their own. Alcoholic parents, for example, tended to be unwilling to seek help for themselves when asked to as part of the overall Yaa Da' Ya intervention.

One of the goals of Yaa Da' Ya was to use traditional ceremonies to bring the young clients back into harmony when the peacemakers felt this approach was warranted. To this end, more than one-fifth (22 percent, n = 24) of the clients' families were directed to seek traditional ceremonies on behalf of the juveniles. Of interest, only four families had the ceremonies done (an additional four families for whom a ceremony had not been recommended also had one done). It is likely that expense played some role in this lack of follow-up treatment; some families noted that the ceremonies cost several hundred dollars for materials and compensation for the practitioner. Those who had ceremonies completed typically had them funded at least in part by other offices (e.g., BHS provided some funds for this purpose) or had family members who could conduct them.

Outcome Variables

There were four outcome variables obtained from the program records. The first two were measures of recidivism: future crime and future substance use. Remarkably few of the program participants were arrested (10 percent, n = 11) or were detected abusing drugs or alcohol (9 percent, n = 10) after their involvement with Yaa Da' Ya, although the program staff followed some cases for three full years and typically followed others for at least one year.

The third outcome measure, detailed in table 7.1, sought to summarize the youths' levels of success in and following the program. Cases that had good general outcomes, regardless of level of participation in Yaa Da' Ya, were coded as such and formed the second largest category of outcomes (25 percent, n = 27, valid = 26 percent). It is important to note that cases classified as having good outcomes were not limited to clients who met the goals designed during their peacemaking sessions or for whom the treatment appeared to "work." This variable was a more general measure so that cases could be classified as having good outcomes even if the treatment did not appear to work, as long as the client's life appeared to have taken a positive direction (e.g., one juvenile failed to reenroll in school but did obtain and maintain full-time employment to support himself, his mother, and his younger brother and was reported by his relatives to have learned to "differentiate right from wrong"). Successful clients were those whose lives appeared to have changed for the better, either through improvements

Table 7.1 Overall description of case outcome

Value Label	Frequency	Percent	Valid Percent
Not a good outcome	44.0	40.7	41.5
Good outcome	27.0	25.0	25.5
No serious problems, but not good outcome	27.0	25.0	25.5
No treatment, but staff worked for client	8.0	7.4	7.5
Could not be classified	2.0	1.9	Missing
Total*	108.0	100.0	100.0

The total includes eight clients (percent = 7.4, valid percent = 7.5) for whom the Yaa Da' Ya staff provided services although the clients did not take part in a session.

noted by school personnel, positive attitude changes noted by parents, or other constructive behavioral modifications made by the juveniles. Simply reenrolling in school or ceasing to run away from home was not enough to be considered a successful case; the juvenile had to appear to make sincere changes. This variable was created to allow for meaningful statistical comparisons among groups.

A second category, which accounted for another fourth (25 percent, n = 27, valid = 26 percent) of the cases, included clients who had no further serious problems documented in their files but for whom the outcomes could not necessarily be classified as good. Clients in this category stopped participating in at least some of the negative behaviors that brought them to the attention of Yaa Da' Ya but still had problems in their lives (e.g., most of the clients in this category discontinued their criminal activity or reenrolled in school but continued to break school rules or to be difficult for their parents). While the nature of their deviance was reduced, these were not truly successful cases.

The final category, which accounted for the largest percentage (41 percent, n = 44, valid = 42 percent) of the cases, included clients for whom the outcome was decidedly uncomplimentary. These youths returned to their bad habits or never discontinued them, or added new criminal activities to their repertoire. In an additional 7 percent (n = 8, valid = 8 percent) of the cases, there was no treatment provided by Yaa Da' Ya, but the program staff worked on behalf of the juveniles, for example, by coordinating reenrollment in school or making referrals to social services. See table 7.1 for the general breakdown of this third outcome measure.

The fourth and final outcome measure was whether or not the client reenrolled in school with Yaa Da' Ya's assistance. Because the vast majority of the youths were already in school, it is encouraging to note that Yaa Da' Ya helped nearly one-fifth (19 percent, n = 21, valid = 20 percent) of the youths reenroll in school (this number includes ten of the thirteen clients who were not enrolled at intake, and eleven clients who withdrew or were expelled after coming to the program). In fact, the ability to get their clients back into school appeared to be one of Yaa Da' Ya's strong points. In this capacity, the Yaa Da' Ya staff persuaded the clients to reenroll (for many youths, the motivation to reenroll emerged during peacemaking), contacted schools, and coordinated reentry of the youths. This was not always an easy task because each school had requirements (e.g., learning contracts and promises to attend regularly) before accepting even alternative students. In further support of Yaa Da' Ya's abilities to perform this task is the fact that most of those whom the program helped reenroll had been out of school for two or more years.

Bivariate Analysis

In the next section, the general outcome (i.e., the third outcome measure) is broken out by demographic and program variables to determine which factors were associated with positive outcomes. This analysis is not intended to determine which youths should be included or excluded from participating in programs such as Yaa Da' Ya, but it may help people understand for which youths Yaa Da' Ya seemed to have the most beneficial effects. This type of analysis may also highlight concerns that future programs should consider during their design and implementation stages.

Bivariate Analysis of Demographic and Program Variables

As shown in table 7.2, it does not appear that positive general outcome was statistically related to the majority of client demographics. In fact, only three demographic variables were associated with an increased likelihood of a positive outcome. This can be interpreted as meaning that positive outcomes were equally likely for all but the three breakout groups of individuals. Clients who had committed prior property offenses appeared more likely than those without similar records to succeed in Yaa Da' Ya ($V = .24$, $p < .05$), as were those who had committed any offense ($V = .25$, $p < .05$). These findings may reflect the fact that these juveniles were more likely to be court ordered into the program ($V = -.43$, $p < .0001$), giving them and their parents more incentive to cooperate. Those with arrests for violent offenses (versus property offenses), on the other hand, despite being court ordered into the program, may have been more hardened delinquents for whom a positive outcome was more difficult to predict.

Of interest, youths with a history of alcohol abuse were substantially more likely than those who lacked such a history to succeed in Yaa Da' Ya ($V = .27$, $p < .05$). This may reflect the program staff's ability to get such youths into the residential or outpatient alcohol treatment programs that they needed and staff members' ability to serve as guides throughout and following the treatment process. Once clients' addictions were addressed in treatment, they were better prepared to succeed. In fact, one of the primary goals of the initial peacemaking sessions was to persuade youths that they had problems, then to convince them of the importance of committing themselves to completing a treatment program. In this context, peacemaking served a valuable function, providing at-risk youths with the motivation in addition to the skills to succeed.

In addition to the three demographic factors, two program variables were related to general outcome. First, the more peacemaking sessions

Table 7.2 Whether demographic and/or program-related factors were related to program outcome (using Cramer's V)

Factors	Significant relationship found for	No significant relationship found for
Demographic	• prior property offense ($V = .24$, $p < .05$); youths with such records succeeded more • any prior offense ($V = .25$, $p < .05$); youths with such records succeeded more • history of alcohol abuse ($V = .27$, $p < .01$); youths with such records succeeded more	• client's age, number of siblings, or gender (although females were nearly twice as likely as males to have good outcomes [37% v. 19%] and males were more likely to fall into the "somewhat good" category [21% v. 40%, $V = .23$, $p = .06$]) • whether the client's mother (or father) shared a home with the youth, client's mother (or father) had contact with the youth, client's parents abused alcohol (or had a history of domestic violence) • client's grade level in school, GPA, or enrollment in school at intake • prior violent offense, alcohol-related arrest, client history of substance abuse, or prior substance abuse–related arrest (although the fact that there were very few clients in this category may have clouded any findings)
Program	• number of peacemaking sessions completed; youths who completed more sessions were more successful ($V = .35$, $p < .001$) • parental cooperation with Yaa Da'Ya; youths whose parents cooperated were more successful ($V = .69$, $p < .0001$)	• whether the case was a direct request or an official transfer from court or social services, or identity of the requester of record (although cases initiated by crime victims tended to have more positive outcomes) • the client said to be experiencing school problems, family disharmony, or as being beyond the control of his or her parents • Yaa Da' Ya's success in getting the youth back into school • program fees, although they were noted as an issue

completed, the more likely a youth was to succeed in the program and to have a positive outcome (V = .35, p < .001). Whereas 63 percent (n = 27) of juveniles who failed to attend any peacemaking sessions had negative general outcomes, only one-fourth (26 percent, n = 17) of the youths who attended at least one session had negative outcomes.[6] In fact, the likelihood of a positive general outcome increased with each additional session (5 percent of clients who completed no sessions had positive general outcomes, compared to 33 percent of those who completed one session, 57 percent of those who completed two sessions, and two of the three [66 percent] who completed three sessions). Although it is possible that those who attended more sessions had more supportive families than those who failed to attend any peacemaking sessions, it is clear that the peacemaking portion of the program had beneficial results for the youths who took advantage of it.[7] It was during those sessions that the youths (and their families) were focused on the benefits of healing themselves and their families and achieving reintegration into society.

Parental cooperation with Yaa Da' Ya was also strongly related to positive general outcomes for the clients (V = .69, p < .0001). Nearly all (91 percent, n = 31) of the clients whose parents cooperated with the Yaa Da' Ya program intervention derived some positive outcomes from the program (good outcome = 68 percent, n = 23; somewhat good outcome = 24 percent, n = 8). This stands in stark contrast to the 32 percent (n = 18) of the youths with uncooperative parents who had some form of positive outcome. In fact, 68 percent (n = 23) of the youths with cooperative parents had good outcomes, compared to only 7 percent (n = 4) of those with uncooperative parents. (See table 7.2.)

The examination of the two recidivism outcome measures and the client's likelihoods of abusing alcohol or drugs was complicated by the small number of clients who were noted to have committed crimes after the program, so they are not reported here. Even so, it was instructive to note that prior alcohol or drug use was associated with future criminality. Clients who had abused alcohol (phi = .26, p < .01) or drugs (phi = .23, p <.05) were more likely than nonabusing clients to commit crimes after entering the program. In addition, those who had abused alcohol (phi = .29, p < .01) or drugs (phi = .26, p < .01) before participating in Yaa Da' Ya were more likely to be detected using alcohol or drugs after intervention. These findings are not surprising and do not invalidate those reported above because they focus exclusively on future arrests while the general outcome was a more holistic measure that included future criminality as only one of several factors.[8] In addition, some of the arrests occurred early during their participation in the program, well before the youths had a chance to benefit from the program.

Because the original intent of the program was to serve only court-referred youth, analyses were conducted on only those cases. As expected, the results for the subsample were very similar to those noted above, but many could not be reliably interpreted due to the reduced sample size (i.e., the subsample contained only sixty-one cases), so they are not reported here. Two particularly strong results deserve special mention, however. As found for the sample as a whole, the more peacemaking sessions completed by each client, the more likely she or he was to have a positive outcome ($V = .42$, $p < .001$), and clients whose parents cooperated with the program were significantly more likely to have a positive general outcome ($V = .70$, $p < .0001$).

Summary

It is encouraging to note that the Yaa Da' Ya program appears to "work" for a variety of juveniles. Success appeared unrelated to whether a case had been transferred from court or social services or was a direct request. The program appeared to work equally well across age and grade levels and regardless of whether the clients were enrolled in school at the time of intake. How well the clients performed in school appeared to be irrelevant in their success in the program, as was having a record of alcohol-related, drug-related, or violent offense arrests. Family dynamics (e.g., family size or amount of parental contact with client) also played no statistically significant role in the youths' success in the program. The program, then, appears to serve a wide cross-section of youths; this was not a program that functioned for only a small subsample of clients.

Parental cooperation appeared to play a large role in the clients' successful reintegration into society. Nearly all juveniles whose parents cooperated with Yaa Da' Ya enjoyed at least some success following the program, compared to fewer than one-third of those whose parents were less cooperative. Based on a review of the case files, parental uninterest in the program appeared to be based on denial of their own problems (e.g., alcoholism), concern about the monetary costs of the program, anger at the system for not punishing their wayward children "enough," or general indifference regarding their children's progress. A number of the parents lacked parenting skills and resented the program staff's attempts to get them into classes aimed at improving how they interacted with their children. Other parents couldn't be bothered with attending family-oriented sessions or ensuring that their children made it to counseling appointments. Future programs must address this important reality—that parents may impede rather than encourage their children's success. Future programs may consider including more support for parents in an attempt to enhance their likelihood of cooperation. Even intermediate steps such as providing transportation to sessions for clients who could not otherwise attend appointments could be helpful. The Yaa Da' Ya staff tried to schedule counseling appointments at school for those youths who were enrolled, which appeared to increase the likelihood of those clients to receive needed counseling. Steps such as this improve parents' levels of cooperation because the program requires less time investment on their behalf, while not compromising any of the program goals.

The peacemaking portion of the Yaa Da' Ya intervention appears to have been a worthwhile innovation. The more sessions the juveniles completed, the more likely was their general outcome to be positive. The least success-ful cases were those of youths who failed to attend any peacemaking ses-sions, while the most successful cases were those of youths who attended two or more sessions. It is important to recognize that the peacemaking sessions were not simply additional counseling sessions. Instead, they were a community forum in which family and friends and other interested parties talked about a youth's problems and as a group decided how best to help the youth prevent future deviance. The presence of so many parties ensured that the youths heard about the effects of their delinquency on those they cared about. Following this important stage, the youths played a central role in the plans that arose from the peacemaking sessions.

In conclusion, it can be said that the Yaa Da' Ya program was beneficial to those who participated fully. Those who attended the peacemaking ses-sions and whose parents cooperated with the program were significantly more likely to better their lives by discontinuing their criminal activities, eschewing their bad acquaintances, dealing with their dependence on alco-hol or drugs, enhancing their scholastic records, and improving their gen-eral attitudes toward life and their families. Those juveniles who did not take advantage of Yaa Da' Ya's program offerings, however, did not fare so well. In the majority of cases, they were likely to continue or escalate the actions that brought them to the program and to fail to derive many benefits from the program. It is obvious from this evaluation that youths who do not participate wholly in programs that seek to help them cannot benefit fully from those programs.

It is also clear that peacemaking-based programs can work with juve-niles, giving them a rationale and chance to change for the better by using traditional approaches to reduce deviance and increase harmony in society. The ability of peacemaking to cause positive change is not limited to adults, for whom some of the typical peacemaking lectures seem to make more sense (e.g., lectures on traditional gender roles or marriage). The lectures employed by the peacemakers in this program were tailored to the younger audience, typically involving statements about the value of continuing one's education even after dropping out of school, assertions that others (especially loved ones and friends) are truly interested in the youth's success and that the youth must be the first to recognize a need for change and take a central role in making any changes in his or her attitude and life, suggestions to get involved in sports or afterschool activities, mentions of the need to get along with others, and other age-appropriate advice. Even the common exhortation used with adult disputants to set a good example for children to follow was adapted for this younger audience, effectively transformed into admonishments to set an example for one's younger siblings and to recognize one's importance as a role model for younger children. In short, the same dynamics that make peacemaking effective with adults were successfully employed with a juvenile audience. Peacemaking is not limited to adults and their disputes, and the process can be expanded into other areas where healing is needed or where disputes exist.

Notes

I acknowledge the support of the Ford Foundation and the Rutgers University Research Council in completing this article. I also thank James W. Zion and Philmer Bluehouse for their comments on earlier drafts. The title translation comes from Robert Young and William Morgan, *Colloquial Navaho: A Dictionary,* New York: Hippocrene Books, 1994, page 3.

1. In addition, the first word of the program name is an acronym from "young adjudicated adult." As originally envisioned, Yaa Da' Ya would take juvenile delinquents who faced lengthy jail terms and try to redirect their lives in a positive manner by helping them develop lifelong plans. In the end, only about half of the program clients were court referred.

2. Quotation from the juvenile's case file.

3. The method of calculating academic delay was simple, but not without its drawbacks. The participants' grade levels were subtracted from their ages to gain a baseline measure, then each student was assumed to have begun school at age six. Because the clients who fell into the one-year delay category could easily have begun school later due to their exact dates of birth, it is not certain that those students had repeated a grade. One program participant was a year ahead of same-aged peers.

4. The requesters in the remaining seven cases were never established due to lack of cooperation from the parents in court transfers, so the requesters were considered to be the family court itself.

5. In addition, one participant was referred by social services due only to the poor living conditions experienced by the youth, and another's file listed only worry about the juvenile's substance abuse. The percentages do not add up to 100 because some clients fell into multiple categories.

6. The juveniles were divided into the three groups presented in table 7.1 and discussed in the accompanying text: good general outcome, bad or negative outcome, and those who can be described as having only a somewhat good outcome (e.g., those who made progress but not enough to be classified as successful cases).

7. Of the ninety-two clients for whom both parental cooperation and number of peacemaking sessions could be ascertained, twenty-four youths with "uncooperative" parents attended one or more peacemaking sessions, and four clients with "cooperative" parents failed to attend any sessions. As would be expected, however, the two variables were related ($V = .50$, $p < .0001$).

8. Four juveniles were classified as having good outcomes despite being arrested after their acceptance into the program: (1) After his arrest for swinging at a security officer, one client completed his 341 community service hours for the offense for which he was transferred into Yaa Da' Ya, then settled down to work and start a family; (2) after being jailed for disorderly conduct and substance abuse, another client completed a three-month residential treatment program following the arrests, reentered school, and "matured a lot" while participating in Yaa Da' Ya; (3) another client was arrested for carrying a deadly weapon but otherwise was doing excellent—even his school was "surprised by [his] progress"; and (4) a chronic runaway was arrested and detained for eight hours but had stopped running away from home, had started obeying her parents, had repaired her relationship with her mother, had avoided joining a gang despite pressure to do so, had gone to daily tutoring to improve her academic performance, and had completed a traditional ceremony to help her deal with the death of her brother.

8

Navajo Nation Courts and Peacemaking

Restorative Justice Issues

Marianne O. Nielsen

Peacemaking as carried out by Navajo peacemakers is a form of restorative justice, but the basic principles of peacemaking predate Euro-based restorative justice models and programs by centuries. Because the current peacemaking program is the result of different cultural processes, peacemaking may have already surmounted many of the issues that are of concern about restorative justice programs operating in the dominant society. Some of these solutions may be of use to non–Native American programs, but some will not because of their rootedness in Navajo *(Dine')* specific cultural practices and values. This chapter contains a short comparison of peacemaking principles and the restorative justice model and a discussion of ten issues that have been raised about restorative justice programs and how these may or may not apply to peacemaking.

The Restorative Justice Paradigm and Peacemaking

The primary goal of restorative justice programs is to bring justice back into the community using a process that respects "the feelings and humanity of both the victim and the offender" (Van Ness and Strong 1997, 25). This means the empowerment of victims, the community, and offenders (McCold 1996, 97). The current criminal justice system operates based on a model that focuses on upholding the authority of the state, deterring offenders, and punishing wrongdoing. Repairing the harm done to the victim and the community has become nearly irrelevant (Van Ness and Strong 1997, 10).

The restorative model is based on a number of principles that vary greatly from the retributive, deterrent, protective principles of the adversarial system. These principles include that the victims need to regain control of their lives, overcome a feeling of powerlessness, and receive vindication; the community needs to restore its order and its members' confidence of safety and reassert its common values; and offenders need to have "contributing" injuries (such as alcohol or child sexual abuse) and injuries resulting from the crime healed (Van Ness 1996, 23–24). In addition, victims and offenders need personal involvement in the process so that the offenders know whom they owe and the victim can be reempowered, which, for example, reduces fear of crime (Hudson and Galaway 1996).

The restorative justice model can be summarized in three propositions: Crime is primarily a conflict between individuals (not between an individual and the state) resulting in injuries to victims, communities, and offenders; the aim of the criminal justice process should be to reconcile parties while repairing the injuries caused; and the process should facilitate active participation by victims, offenders, and their communities instead of being dominated by the government (Van Ness 1996, 23). The goal of restorative justice is that "the community seeks to restore peace between victims and offenders, and to reintegrate them fully into itself; the goals for victims can be expressed as healing and for offenders as rehabilitation" (Van Ness 1996, 28). In general, the establishing of blame for past behavior is less important than problem solving for the future (Kennedy and Sacco 1998, 206). McCold (1996, 94) expresses the restorative model in terms taken from Jewish culture, which sound remarkably similar to the principles of Navajo peacemaking: "The community's injury is to *shalom,* right relationship, among members of the community. The damage is against peace, and requires a local effort to restore harmony."

Victim-offender reconciliation programs, mediation, and perhaps arbitration are the most common types of restorative justice programs in nonindigenous societies. In these programs trained mediators work to empower participants, promote dialogue between victims and offenders, and encourage mutual problem solving (Van Ness 1996, 24).

Peacemaking is not the kind of alternative dispute resolution found in Euro-based systems; it differs markedly from the examples above. Seidschlaw (1997), in discussing indigenous peacemaking in North America, points out a number of differences between peacemaking and mediation. Mediation is a one-time service with a cost associated with it; peacemaking is primarily a way of life that fulfills one's sense of responsibility to the community. Peacemaking functions best in the context of community culture and values; in mediation this context is not an important part of the process. Spirituality, specifically Native American beliefs, is an integral part of peacemaking. Prayers are used to set the stage for peacemaking by mentioning the issues and the need to show respect to all participants, including the spiritual. Prayers remind the participants that they are part of the spiritual world and that they must use their "sacred mind and sacred language" to solve the problem facing them (Philmer Bluehouse, pers. comm., July 24, 1998). Mediation, on the other hand, exists within an environment that brings individuality and material achievement into the process and probably works best if it ignores cultural values.

Similarly, Navajo Nation peacemaking is a unique form of restorative justice because of its singular dynamics rooted in Navajo relationships and ways of doing things (Zion 1995). As Zion and Yazzie (1997, 55–56) state, it is not alternative dispute resolution, it is original dispute resolution. It also differs from dominant society restorative justice programs: The peacemaker is not a neutral mediator but may be a blood or clan relative; mediation excludes feelings where peacemaking promotes their expression; consensus is sought in peacemaking rather than an arbitrary decision by the mediator; peacemaking relies on prayer as a means of involving the spiritual, but this is irrelevant to mediation; the naat'áanii has a teaching and problem-solving role not held by a mediator; support group members (family, clan, community) are included as participants in peacemaking rather than excluded; and in peacemaking, the Navajo and other spiritual narratives are used as guides to problem solving, unlike the absence of spiritual guidelines found in most mediation programs (see Zion 1995). In addition, the naat'áanii is not a trained professional in mediation but a respected community member with special expertise in Navajo spirituality. The peacemakers have already been trained in accordance with Navajo traditions as naat'áanii before they join the Peacemaker Division. They then receive sixteen hours of training from the peacemaker director in peacemaking techniques, administrative duties (paperwork), the relationship between the technical support unit of the judicial branch and the peacemakers, the peacemakers' responsibilities to the technical support unit, and the importance of the Navajo (or Christian) creation and journey narratives as the source of law, ethical standards, and guidance on contemporary issues, such as domestic violence (Philmer Bluehouse, pers. comm., July 24, 1998). With these marked differences between the Navajo and nonindigenous models of restorative justice, it is likely that the issues currently of concern about restorative justice programs may have a different relevance to peacemaking.

Issues in Restorative Justice and Their Relevance to Peacemaking

Although there are many issues that arise in any discussion of restorative justice, only ten are discussed here: the relationship between the retributive and the restorative justice systems, victim perceptions of justice, offender perceptions of justice, due process, community perceptions of justice, antagonism from criminal justice personnel, lack of program resources, program effectiveness in reducing incarceration and recidivism, mediator skills, and expanding clientele to include organizations, repeat offenders, and violent offenders.

Hudson and Galaway (1996, 11) raise the issue of *the relationship between the two models of justice*. They ask if the restorative justice system should be separate from or part of the criminal justice system. There are arguments on both sides, which are thoroughly presented in Galaway and Hudson (1996), and discussing them here would be too time consuming. The most important point for the purposes of this chapter is that the question is being asked at all. In the Navajo criminal justice system, the question has already been answered: Peacemaking is an essential part of the criminal justice system. It should not replace the Euro-based components of the system, because these are still needed for specific types of offenders, and as an alternative to peacemaking. It has been suggested that the fear of court sanctions makes peacemaking a more attractive option (James W. Zion, pers. comm., June 29, 1998). On the other hand, the goal of the Navajo judicial branch is to move more and more disputes into the hands of the peacemakers, even serious offenses, as will be discussed shortly. Peacemaking is seen as a more effective mechanism for decreasing the social ills that underlie criminality, thereby reducing Navajo involvement in criminal behavior (Yazzie 1996).

One of the most important aspects of *victim perceptions of justice* is whether or not the victims feel that they are voluntarily participating in restorative justice programs. Umbreit (1994) found that a small percentage of victims in his sample felt that they had been coerced into participating and thereby felt revictimized. Wright (1996, 229) suggests that the victim's knowledge that the offender may otherwise be prosecuted or go to prison leads to feelings of pressure. Griffiths and Hamilton (1996, 197) point out that indigenous women and female adolescents are particularly vulnerable to pressure. Power structures within indigenous communities may also compromise the fair operation of restorative justice programs for certain community members (Griffiths and Hamilton 1996, 188).

Ashworth (1993) suggests that restorative justice programs do not provide clear criteria for consistent settlements to the victim or to the community. It might be difficult for victims to get what they consider a just reparation since some offenders may not have the resources to make full reparation. Along the same line, he argues that there are few criteria for measuring harm done to the community and what would be fair reparations to it. Research by Umbreit (1994) found confirmation of one of these issues and introduced another. First, he discovered that some victims felt that the punishment given the offender was inadequate. Second, some victims were concerned that mediation lacked the authority to enforce completion of mediation agreements.

Peacemaking cannot happen without the participation of the victim, the wrongdoer, and their respective families or clans. There have been cases when a reluctant victim was compelled by the court to take part in the process, when the judge felt it was in the victim's best interests (Philmer Blue-house, pers. comm., July 24, 1998). According to Zion:

> A judge may or may not exercise the discretion to refer a case based on many factors. For example, a judge would not send a case into peacemaking where the victim of a violent offense is reasonably afraid of a perpetrator or coercion by relatives. A court could, however, require "shuttle diplomacy" peacemaking, which is traditional, whereby the peacemaker conducts extended negotiations with a victim without facing a perpetrator or with a victim and perpetrator's relatives. (1998, 4)

As an added protection, the process ensures that the victim has a strong support group present. As well, the victim will have a chance to express his or her feelings in a controlled environment. Since a consensus is needed before the procedure is over, the victim should be able to get whatever reparation he or she thinks is equitable and should come out of the process with issues resolved.

As well, the offender can be compelled by a court order to participate in peacemaking. Reasons for this can include being needed to assist in the healing of others and for self-healing. Offenders have also been pressured by their families to participate (Philmer Bluehouse, pers. comm., July 24, 1998). This is discussed further in the section on due process.

Offender perceptions of justice are a third issue. Offenders may feel that pleading guilty (if necessary) and diversion from the system into mediation will offer them a better chance, even though they might have had a valid defense against the charges (Wright 1996, 229). Wright (1996) and Ashworth (1993) both point out that some victims may be more vindictive than others and make greater demands. Similarly, victims may discriminate on economic grounds, leading to inequity (Harland 1996, 511). Umbreit (1994, 105) reports that a small number of offenders felt that the punishment they received was too severe or out of proportion to the offense. At the opposite end of the spectrum, some victims of a serious offense may be satisfied with a symbolic form of reparation such as an apology. This is an issue of proportionality, the achievement of which is one of the aims of the criminal justice system. Hudson and Galaway (1996, 13) point out that this question is really the result of confusing the retributive and the restorative models, since in the restorative model, "fairness is not uniformity but satisfaction."

This response applies equally well to peacemaking. The objective of peacemaking is not punishment or blaming; it is to restore the relationships among all the participants. What it takes to do so must be agreed upon by all parties present and must be enforced by all parties present. If the wrongdoers or aggrieved cannot live with the arrangement, they have two recourses:

They can ask to reconvene the peacemaking, or they can take the problem to the Navajo courts.

Due process has been raised as a related issue. Ashworth (1993) suggests that there is a conflict between the victim's right to participate and the procedural rights of the offender in some kinds of restorative justice. He suggests that the victim might have undue influence, especially on the court process. This is particularly a concern in serious crimes.

Due process is inherent to peacemaking. As Zion states:

> Peacemaking does not violate due process of law because no decision can be imposed on an unwilling party. Procedural due process arises when an individual is to be deprived of liberty or property or be denied a substantive legal right. Given consent, there is no deprivation of a right. The peacemaker rules clearly require that an individual's procedural rights are protected. Peacemaking does not deny the right to a trial by jury. If an individual does not consent to peacemaking or a decision, that person can return to court for a jury trial. Peacemaking does not deny access to the courts, because an individual can refuse to make an agreement and come back before the court. (1998, 3)

In a more fundamental way, according to Navajo justice thinking, when an individual acts out, thereby demonstrating an imbalance in body, mind, and spirit, he or she is asking for community help and invoking community responsibility and obligations (k'é) to them (Philmer Bluehouse, pers. comm., July 24, 1998). An individual, therefore, is willing to take part in the process by definition.

Community perceptions of justice is an issue in that there is currently a political climate of "get tough" on offenders. Restorative justice programs may be seen as "soft" by those with this kind of agenda (Harland 1996, 510). It has also been suggested that offering some kinds of offenders diversion is incompatible with the goal of offering restitution and assistance to victims (Umbreit 1995). Research by McElrea (1994) indicates that, on the whole, victims are not as vindictive as imagined and that most of them want to help "straighten out" the offender, especially if the offender is young. Research done in the late 1980s and early 1990s found public support for reparation, restitution, and community service programs as long as the victim agrees to participate in the procedure. Even so, these programs were not seen as suitable for violent or repeat offenders (Lee 1996, 340).

Griffiths and Hamilton (1996, 188) suggest that not all indigenous communities may want to deal with serious offenders. Some communities practiced banishment for serious offenses, repeat offenders, or in cases where the individual refused to abide by community-imposed sanctions. These communities may think of the Euro-based criminal justice system as the modern equivalent of removing the offender from the community.

Support for peacemaking seems fairly widespread throughout the Navajo Nation, based on the estimated one thousand cases handled by peacemakers in 1997, despite some logistical problems that may have held down numbers (James W. Zion, pers. comm., June 29, 1998). The option of proceeding with serious offenses through the adversarial courts is always available, which means that victims in peacemaking are there because they want to be there.

Nevertheless, there has been and still is a small degree of resistance to peacemaking among some political leaders and community members (see Nielsen 1996). Most of this relates to a discrediting of Navajo values by acculturated Navajo Nation members and concerns of political leaders about peacemakers having too much autonomy.

Antagonism from criminal justice personnel, according to Marshall (1995), arises mainly from the attempts of these personnel to use the new programs to fill their own organizational needs. They sometimes impose restrictions that interfere with the operation of the restorative program. Because the criminal justice system is more offender oriented than victim oriented, the restrictions most often affect the interests of the victims.

This is a very relevant issue for peacemaking. Nielsen (1996) and Gould (1997) both found resistance by Navajo Nation criminal justice personnel to peacemaking (see also Bluehouse 1996). There were concerns expressed by a few Navajo Nation judges, lawyers, and court clerks about how peacemaking fitted into the Navajo court system, and by some Navajo police officers about Navajo peacemakers having little knowledge of Western law (Gould 1997). These concerns seem to be related to confusion by criminal justice personnel about the difference between Navajo restorative justice and Western-based retributive goals and procedures, and to the acculturation of criminal justice personnel into Euro-based values about justice and its mechanisms.

Lack of resources such as funding, expertise, and political will is also an issue for restorative justice. McElrea (1994) expresses the fear that restorative justice programs may be adopted as a means of reducing the costs of courts and prisons without recognizing that communities need financial resources to properly operate these new programs (see also Harland 1996, 512). A related issue is the lack of human resources in the community. Griffiths and Hamilton (1996) raise the issue of the "healthiness" of community members, leaders, and others who play key roles in restorative programs in Canadian Aboriginal communities. Because of the tragic impacts of colonialism, many indigenous communities have social problems, such as widespread alcoholism, family violence, and child abuse. Community members who act as mediators will have to deal with their own personal issues before they can help others. A final resource needed by these programs is political will (Harland 1996, 515), which the current climate suggests is in short supply.

This is also an important issue for peacemaking. Although peacemakers are paid a fee by participants, this is more a token of commitment than a living wage. Zion (pers. comm., June 29, 1998) suggests that only a handful of the over 250 peacemakers rely on peacemaking as a regular source of income. Funding is also scarce for the technical support unit of the program, where program statistics are recorded, training is developed and offered, and educational materials are gathered and prepared. Discussions are currently under way about possible changes in structure that could alleviate some of this funding stress. On a more positive note, there is a great deal of political will and few problems with finding stable, capable community members to act as peacemakers. Support for peacemaking seems general throughout the Nation. In terms of the peacemakers themselves, the community must first choose the peacemakers, and then the participants must choose the peacemaker who will assist them; therefore, incompetent peacemakers are quickly weeded out, thanks to word of mouth.

The effectiveness of restorative programs in reducing incarceration and recidivism is another issue. Umbreit (1995) notes that although restorative program staff often tout mediation as an alternative to prison, there is little evidence that these programs decrease incarceration. Some research has found that mediation has contributed to reducing the length of sentences and changing the locale of the sentence served from prison to jail. There is also some question whether or not these programs reduce recidivism. Umbreit (1994, 117), for example, found a "marginal but non-significant impact of the mediation process" among juveniles. He suggests that the mediation process may be overshadowed by the contrasting influences of a dysfunctional family and criminal friends. However, in the Euro-based society, as Harland states, "the perception that it is not the business of the criminal justice system to try to right the underlying social and cultural wrongs that maintain and encourage the existence of a stable and visible class of criminals is both deeply ingrained and a convenient excuse for its abject failure to reduce crime" (1996, 511). Restorative justice programs may try to respond to the underlying causes of the crime and the needs of the parties involved, but they still suffer some restraints because of the widespread nature of the above attitude, and because true "healing" of all parties is not an objective.

This is not the case with peacemaking. One of the primary purposes of peacemaking is precisely to identify the underlying problems that are leading to the disharmony and to develop a plan to combat them. A specific example of how this operates is provided by the Navajo Courts' Minority Male Program. People charged with driving while intoxicated (DWI) were diverted into peacemaking, where the problems leading to the intoxication were sought, found, and dealt with. Although no statistics are given, Yazzie and Zion (1996, 170) report that recidivism rates dropped. The objective of peacemaking is not punishment, and unless the participants agree that incarceration will in some way benefit the wrongdoer, incarceration is not a likely outcome. If consensus is reached that the wrongdoer should serve time, a referral will be made back to the courts for sentencing.

Mediator attitude and competence were a concern to small numbers of both victims and offenders (Umbreit 1994, 98–99, 105–6). When mediators were unable to control the proceedings, the victim or the offender felt revictimized or victimized. Hudson and Galaway (1996, 3) warn that giving the community responsibility for justice procedures will likely mean that the processes of restorative justice will have to be "deprofessionalized," that is, placed in the hands of nonprofessional community members, because "[b]y their very nature, professions remove power from others and concentrate it in their own alleged area of expertise."

Again, this is not an issue for peacemakers. Peacemaking in and of itself is a form of community obligation; it is a return to traditional structures that placed leadership in the community. The peacemakers must have expertise and knowledge in Navajo and other creation and journey narratives, which is acquired through living and having learned "Navajo thinking" through traditional oral history. The training they receive from the technical support unit is not to make them more "professional," but to acquaint them with organization requirements. In addition, peacemakers who cannot control sessions will quickly lose their clientele.

Expanding clientele to include repeat and violent offenders can be an issue in restorative justice not only because of public resistance to "going easy" on these offenders but because these kinds of cases require more time to prepare and work through (Marshall 1995). While questions of the suitability of serious cases such as rape and aggravated assault have been raised, there is also evidence that as long as the victim is willing to participate, victim-offender mediation may be successful (McElrea 1994). Very little research has been done on expanding restorative justice programs to include organizations. The issue raised previously about resources to support programs is also a concern here. It should be pointed out that there is also an opposite concern about "widening the net" of social control to include offenders who, for example, might have had their charges dismissed (Hudson and Galaway 1996, 12). This issue boils down to a question of which offenses should be dealt with by restorative justice and which by the retributive system.

For peacemakers, there is a relatively simple answer: Since it is not a matter of punishment but reconciliation and reparation, any offense is eligible, as long as the people affected are willing to actively participate. Peacemaking has been used once so far in a wrongful death–products liability civil case against a corporation. Cases of death and rape have been resolved. Widening the net is also not an issue since any dispute, no matter how trivial or serious, is eligible if the participants agree to conduct peacemaking. Furthermore, there are no systemic repercussions such as a criminal record or a police file resulting from peacemaking, so there is no reason for keeping a participant out of peacemaking.

This brief review of ten issues suggests that some of the major issues currently facing restorative justice programs in the nonindigenous society are not relevant for peacemaking. There are only three issues—lack of resources, community perceptions of justice, and antagonism from criminal justice personnel—that peacemaking seems to share with restorative justice programs.

Conclusion

Native American nations in the United States are justifiably afraid that the dominant society will continue to impose social institutions on them that are not in their best interests. Although legal pluralism is an undeniable fact in the United States, mainstream American society is not known for its tolerance or respect for difference. One of the underlying issues that must be acknowledged is the possible threat to peacemaking that could come from a perceived lack of legitimacy. This is already an issue with Navajo Nation members who have been so acculturated into dominant society values that they question traditional Navajo justice procedures. Add members of the dominant society's state and federal criminal justice systems who see Navajo justice procedures as inferior to those of the dominant society, and pressure to drop or modify peacemaking becomes a very real, imminent danger. As Zion states so well, it would be "our old problem of trying to pound a round peg (Indian justice) into a triangle of power, force, and authority" (James W. Zion, pers. comm., June 29, 1998). An insidious strategy would be for these groups to push for peacemaking to be standardized to fit nonindigenous restorative justice programs such as alternative dispute resolution or mediation, which these individuals might see as more familiar, more legitimate, less threatening to the status quo, and untainted by "Indianness." However, as Austin (1993, 47) states:

Indian systems do not need instructions on empowerment, balancing disparities in bargaining positions, principles of ethics in mediation, or the kinds of disputes that mediation systems can or cannot handle. They do not need, and must not have, outsiders peering in to nod affirmance or indicate disapproval. Indian systems need support to do what they know how to do best—use fundamental principles of equality and responsibility to talk out disputes for harmony.

If Native American restorative justice systems such as peacemaking are left to develop on their own, they may present valuable lessons to the Euro-based retributive and restorative systems. The shift in thinking toward restorative justice in the Euro-based system is based on the ineffectiveness of the current system in battling crime, the tendency of incarceration to worsen offender involvement in crime rather than deter or rehabilitate offenders, and the dissatisfaction of victims with the current system (Van Ness and Strong 1997, 6). As Marshall states, "[restorative justice] is a practice that contains the seeds for solving a new problem—the inadequacy of the criminal justice system itself, as it lurches from crisis to crisis, based on a primitive philosophy of naked revenge" (Marshall 1995, 230). As was seen in the previous discussion of issues, Navajo peacemaking has developed solutions to many of the problems that plague nonindigenous restorative programs. Of course, some of these may not be usable by nonindigenous society because of their rootedness in Navajo culture. Some researchers, such as Goldberg (1997), even go so far as suggesting that Native American justice procedures are so deeply based in Native American spirituality that they cannot be replicated in the non-Native world at all. Other scholars disagree, believing that nonindigenous systems are so aware of their own ineffectiveness that they will be open to new ideas (James W. Zion, pers. comm., June 29, 1998).

One of the significant characteristics of current restorative justice thinking is its willingness to look outside the practitioners' society for ideas and possibilities (Van Ness and Strong 1997, 117). This bodes well for the relationship between peacemaking and other restorative justice programs, both indigenous and nonindigenous. Peacemaking strategies that seem to have a strong potential for usefulness to non-Navajo justice programs include the use of victim and offender support groups and the use of consensus to deal with both victim and offender concerns. As well, peacemaking and other restorative programs have common issues for which they are searching for solutions, such as the lack of funding resources and the development of community and criminal justice support.

Sharing strategies and ideas can only make them all stronger.

Note

This chapter is an edited version of Marianne O. Nielsen, "Navajo Nation Courts, Peacemaking, and Restorative Justice Issues," *Journal of Legal Pluralism,* 44: 105–26, 1999. Reprinted with permission of the journal and the author.

References

Ashworth, Andrew. 1993. Some Doubts about Restorative Justice. *Criminal Law Forum* 4: 277–99.

Austin, Raymond D. 1993. Freedom, Responsibility and Duty: ADR and the Navajo Peacemaker Court. *The Judges' Journal* 32 (2): 8–11, 47, 48.

Bluehouse, Philmer. 1996. The Ceremony of Making Peace: Excerpt from *People of the Seventh Fire,* edited by Dagmar Thorpe. *Native Americas* 13 (3): 54–57.

Galaway, Burt, and Joe Hudson, eds. 1996. *Restorative Justice: International Perspectives.* Monsey, N.Y.: Criminal Justice Press.

Goldberg, Carole E. 1997. Overextended Borrowing: Tribal Peacemaking Applied in Non-Indian Disputes. *Washington Law Review* 71: 1003–19.

Gould, Larry A. 1997. The Dilemma of the Navajo Police Officer: Traditional versus European-Based Means of Social Control. Paper presented at the Commission on Folk Law and Legal Pluralism Congress, Moscow, Russia, August 18–22.

Griffiths, Curt T., and Ron Hamilton. 1996. Sanctioning and Healing: Restorative Justice in Canadian Aboriginal Communities. In *Restorative Justice,* ed. Burt Galaway and Joe Hudson, 175–91. Monsey, N.Y.: Criminal Justice Press.

Harland, Alan. 1996. Towards a Restorative Justice Future. In *Restorative Justice,* ed. Burt Galaway and Joe Hudson, 505–16. Monsey, N.Y.: Criminal Justice Press.

Hudson, Joe, and Burt Galaway. 1996. Introduction. In *Restorative Justice,* ed. Burt Galaway and Joe Hudson, 1–14. Monsey, N.Y.: Criminal Justice Press.

Kennedy, Leslie W., and Vincent F. Sacco. 1998. *Crime Victims in Context.* Los Angeles: Roxbury.

Lee, Angela. 1996. Public Attitudes Towards Restorative Justice. In *Restorative Justice,* ed. Burt Galaway and Joe Hudson, 337–47. Monsey, N.Y.: Criminal Justice Press.

Marshall, Tony F. 1995. Restorative Justice on Trial in Britain. *Mediation Quarterly* 12: 217–31.

McCold, Paul. 1996. Restorative Justice and the Role of Community. In *Restorative Justice,* ed. Burt Galaway and Joe Hudson, 85–101. Monsey, N.Y.: Criminal Justice Press.

———. 1997. *Restorative Justice: an Annotated Bibliography.* Monsey, N.Y.: Criminal Justice Press.

McElrea, F. W. M. 1994. Restorative Justice—The New Zealand Youth Court: A Model for Development in Other Countries? *Journal of Judicial Administration* 4: 33–54.

Nielsen, Marianne O. 1996. A Comparison of Developmental Ideologies: Navajo Peacemaker Courts and Canadian Native Justice Committees. In *Restorative Justice,* ed. Burt Galaway and Joe Hudson, 207–23. Monsey, N.Y.: Criminal Justice Press.

Seidschlaw, Kurt D. 1997. Peacemaking and Mediation. Paper presented at the Western Social Sciences Association Annual Meeting, Albuquerque, New Mexico, April 23–26.

Umbreit, Mark S. 1994. *Victim Meets Offender: The Impact of Restorative Justice and Mediation.* Monsey, N.Y.: Criminal Justice Press.

_____. 1995. Restorative Justice Through Mediation: The Impact of Offenders Facing Their Victims in Oakland. *Journal of Law and Social Work* 5: 1–13.

Van Ness, Daniel W. 1996. Restorative Justice and International Human Rights. In *Restorative Justice,* ed. Burt Galaway and Joe Hudson, 17–35. Monsey, N.Y.: Criminal Justice Press.

Van Ness, Daniel W., and Karen Heetderks Strong. 1997. *Restoring Justice.* Cincinnati, Ohio: Anderson.

Wright, Martin. 1996. Can Mediation be an Alternative to Criminal Justice? In *Restorative Justice,* ed. Burt Galaway and Joe Hudson, 227–39. Monsey, N.Y.: Criminal Justice Press.

Yazzie, Robert. 1996. *Hozho Nahasdlii*—We Are Now in Good Relations: Navajo Restorative Justice. *St. Thomas Law Review* 9: 117–24.

Yazzie, Robert, and James W. Zion. 1996. Navajo Restorative Justice: The Law of Equality and Justice. In *Restorative Justice,* ed. Burt Galaway and Joe Hudson, 157–73. Monsey, N.Y.: Criminal Justice Press.

Zion, James W. 1995. Living Indian Justice: Navajo Peacemaking Today. Paper presented at the Alternative Dispute Resolution Conference, Vancouver, British Columbia, October 15 (approx.).

_____. 1998. Opinion of the Solicitor, Judicial Branch of the Navajo Nation, No. 98-02: Bill of Rights Objections to Peacemaking, June 4, 1998. Unpublished.

Zion, James W., and Robert Yazzie. 1997. Indigenous Law in North America in the Wake of Conquest. *Boston College International and Comparative Law Review* 20: 55–84.

9 Hózhǫǫ́jí Naat'áanii

The Navajo Justice and Harmony Ceremony

Philmer Bluehouse and James W. Zion

The Navajos in today's Arizona, New Mexico, and Utah had their own justice methods for centuries. Despite that, the government of the United States imposed adjudication methods on Navajos in 1892. After almost a century of adjudication, in 1981, the courts of the Navajo Nation began a process of consciously returning to traditional ways. Although Navajo judges had used principles of traditional law prior to that time, it was only recently that the Navajo Nation judiciary began an open and intentional program of reviving it.

As it is with other American justice planners, the judges and lawyers of the Navajo Nation are attempting to bring individuals into the dispute resolution process so that they can resolve their own problems. That was one reason the Navajo courts returned to traditional mediation and arbitration. However, there is a difference: Traditional Navajo "mediation" is not mediation as others understand it, and Navajo "arbitration" is different as well.

Navajos are very aware of their justice traditions and, as associate justice Raymond D. Austin of the Navajo Nation Supreme Court puts it, Navajos are "going back to the future" by reviving traditional justice methods (Austin 1991). To go forward into the next millennium (and the next half-millennium of contact with non-Navajos), there has been a return to old justice ways. That includes initiatives to use Navajo common law in opinions and policy documents, the return of justice responsibilities to communities through the Navajo Peacemaker Court, and research on Navajo values to use as principles of law.

The Navajo courts are a leader among the 170 or more American tribal courts: They preserve Navajo cultural values to an unusual extent, and Navajos are actively using their contemporary traditional law (that is, ancient law in modern settings). That persistence, which is the product of the Navajo language, religion, and traditions, motivates conscious judicial initiatives. The courts of the Navajo Nation apply Navajo common law as the law of preference. This approach reflects the customs, usages, and traditions of the Navajo people, formed by Navajo values in action.

In 1982, the Navajo Nation Judicial Conference created the Navajo Peacemaker Court (Zion 1983). This unique method of court-annexed "mediation" and "arbitration" uses Navajo values and institutions in local communities. Today, it struggles to overcome the effects of adjudication and laws imposed by the United States government. The alien Navajo Court of Indian Offenses (1892–1959) and the Bureau of Indian Affairs (BIA) *Law and Order Code* (written in 1934; adopted by the Navajo Nation in 1959) made Navajos judge others, using power and force for control. That arrangement is repugnant to Navajo morals. The BIA court and code illustrate the failure of legal structures and methods imposed on Indians by non-Indian outsiders. Given the contemporary enthusiasm for alternative dispute resolution, Navajo judges must also guard against new imposed methods. Navajo justice has different goals and methods, which are more successful than imposed or imported models. This chapter describes the foundations of traditional Navajo justice and traditional dispute resolution methods and makes comparisons with non-Indian mediation and arbitration.

The traditional Navajo legal system—a horizontal one—is based on clan relationships. All Navajos identify clan membership through their mother. They are members of their mother's clan and are "born for" their father's. Thus, each Navajo has relationships and relatives in extended families. Differences or disputes can be adjusted between individuals using learned values and with the help of family or clan members on the basis of the strength of relationships.

The two dynamic forces of traditional Navajo law are k'é and *k'ei*. K'é translates into English as compassion, cooperation, friendliness, unselfishness, peacefulness, and all the other positive values that create an intense, diffuse, and enduring solidarity (Witherspoon 1975, 37). Navajo ceremonies, stories, and traditions, and for that matter the language itself, teach and reinforce those values and the utility of solidarity. K'é is an essential part of the clan system and is the dynamic that makes it work as a horizontal system of law and dispute resolution. K'ei is a special kind of k'é: it refers to the clan system of descent relationships and groups of relatives a person is connected to, tied by the virtues of k'é (37). Thus, Navajos know their clan relatives and interact with them, prompted by strong values that create Navajo solidarity. Those values are virtues that become an ingrained emotional cement to bond the individual to the clan and the clan to the individual. Navajo children learn the importance of their clan relationships, and they express them in daily life by introducing themselves by clan, parentage, and grandparentage. The k'é values are expressed in traditional lore, stories, and ceremonies, which are a common part of Navajo life, and Navajos cite them in ordinary conversations as a kind of case law. In Navajo culture, words often have more powerful connotative force than in English. It is difficult to describe the powerful impact of the terms discussed here.

The Navajo language has great connotative force. Words are strong, taken literally, and they often have a great deal of meaning by connotation. The way a Navajo speaks tells the listener a great deal about his or her state of Navajo knowledge or ability to relate to traditional values. If the individual appears to be aloof, that may mean that he or she does not know the values being related to the listener. If the individual is abruptly direct, given the great weight of words, that most likely means that the person knows the values. This cues the peacemaker and allows him or her to set the stage for the person's response to peacemaking. In addition, the way a person speaks will let the peacemaker know the nature of the problem and the individual's response. The peacemaker wonders, "Is it *hashkéji* (moving toward disharmony) or *hózhǫ́ǫ́jí* (moving toward harmony)?" Language is a powerful tool and an essential component of peacemaking.

Most Americans have heard of the Indian concept of "elders." An "elder" is not simply a person who is old and thus wise. An elder is a distinguished person who earns that status. As is true of most Indian groups, Navajos identify their elders by recognizing their spirituality, good works, and personal achievements. For Navajos, that person is the naat'áanii.

The word "naat'aanii" has been inaccurately translated as "headman" or "principal leader." This unfortunate translation is the product of American Indian policy. Non-Indians need to have some powerful leader to deal or treat with to conclude peace or take land. Most tribes did not have strong leaders with absolute or hierarchical power, as was typical of European vertical systems of authority. Most tribal leaders were persuasive and not coercive. The Navajo "peace chiefs" were civil leaders, and the word naat'áanii refers to a person who speaks strongly, wisely, and well. They are leaders who are known for their ability to guide others and plan for community solidarity and survival. Their authority comes from the force of k'é in k'ei relationships. Beyond relationships in the family and clan, Navajos acknowledge their naat'áanii as community leaders because of demonstrated leadership abilities.

In Navajo society, there are war leaders, or war planners (*hashkééjí naat'ááh*), and peacemakers, or peace planners (*hózhǫ́ǫ́jí naat'ááh*). Both have demonstrated leadership abilities, depending on whether war or peace is necessary. In the way of warfare, leadership is a tool of last resort. Peace planning has been a predominant force in Navajo life, as is reflected in the emergence narrative, where peace planning was done with the intent of promoting peace. War is avoided at all costs. This dictates always seeking peace and harmony. Peacemaking guidelines were established in the emergence narrative. As one elder peacemaker said, "I have waited for the day I would hear again of the peacemakers as was provided for in the Emergence No Sleep Ceremony. I'm glad we are getting away from war ways, which our children have learned much of—they are so used to war ways, they have become our own enemy. We must speak of peace and harmony to be back in hózhó." The modern term for a peacemaker is *hózhǫ́ǫ́jí naat'áanii*—peace and harmony way leader, the key person in the Navajo Peacemaker Courts and its operation.

The Navajo horizontal (peace planning) system of justice uses Navajo norms, values, moral principles, and emotions as law. K'é and k'ei are only two of these precepts. There are many others, which are expressed in Navajo creation and journey scripture, songs, ceremonies, and prayers. Navajos also have sayings that are in fact legal maxims. The denial of k'é and k'ei is expressed in the maxim "He acts as if he had no relatives." A person who acts that way betrays solidarity and kinship; he or she is not behaving as a Navajo and may behave in a "crazy" way (see Kaplan and Johnson 1964, 216–17).

Hózhǫ́ǫ́jí Naat'áanii

The Navajo term hózhǫ́ǫ́jí naat'áanii denotes the process of peacemaking. Navajo common law is a process that uses principles that are internalized by songs, prayers, origin scripture, and journey narratives. It builds on k'é solidarity in a procedure to summon assistance from the Holy People and humans to diagnose how people are distant from k'é or their k'ei relations (to identify the disharmony that creates disputes), teach how Navajo values apply to the problem, and restore the continuing relationships of the parties in their community. It is in fact a justice ceremony.

In the Navajo worldview, disharmony exists when things are not as they should be. This condition is called "anahoti'," the opposite of harmony. Hózhó is a fundamental Navajo legal term, and it is related to the forces of solidarity (k'é) and clan membership (k'ei). It is difficult to translate hózhó into English because of differences in perceptions. Hózhó measures the state of being in complete harmony and peace. It provides the framework of Navajo thought and justice. It takes into account both the hashkééjí naat'ááh (war planning or war philosophy) and the hózhǫ́ǫ́jí naat'ááh (peace planning or peace philosophy). Hózhó is the balance obtained from the two plans. Peacemaking applications are simple, because hózhó measures the root cause of one's conduct and prompts the participants to seek solutions to regain that hózhó. It means that reality and the universe are unified, and there is unity in existence itself. Reality is not segmented or compartmentalized in the Navajo worldview. There is no separation of religious and secular life. Everything has its place in reality and in a relationship to the whole that is something like the clan relationship. All animate and inanimate beings, and all supernatural beings (or forces), have their proper places and relations with each other. Thus, hózhó is a state of affairs or being where everything is in its proper place, functioning in a harmonious relationship with everything else (Witherspoon 1975, 8). It is also a state that sometimes translates as "beauty," as in the phrase non-Navajos often hear, "walk in beauty." The term hózhóójí refers to the Beautyway, one of the fundamental Navajo ceremonies. As with the Beautyway, the goal of hózhóójí naat'áanii is to restore disputants to harmony. Hózhóójí naat'áanii is itself a ceremony. Navajo prayers are based on the concept that the processes of prayer and ceremony create hózhó, or harmony. Many Navajo prayers (including those said by Christians) end with a repetition of the phrase hózhó nahasdlii four times. This repetition expresses a feeling of the restoration of hózhó, meaning something like "the world is hózhó again" (Farella 1984, 165, 167). At the conclusion of the prayer, which ends a ceremony, individuals are again in their proper place, functioning harmoniously and in beauty with everything else. Hózhó nahasdlii is the end goal of hózhóójí naat'áanii, which, as a peacemaking ceremony, uses a similar orientation as the Beautyway ceremony.

The process is closely related to Navajo concepts of illness and healing. When people are ill, they are out of harmony and must be restored to harmony to be well. Some describe Navajo healing as holistic, where supernatural power can be directed to remove or overcome evil and to restore order (Kaplan and Johnson 1964, 221). Navajo healing ceremonies are effective and use two major processes: suggestive words and symbols to purify the patient, and a reaffirmation of solidarity with the community and deities by making the patient the center of goodwill and reintegration with the group (Kaplan and Johnson 1964, 228). The process of helping a patient return to harmony involves invoking supernatural powers for assistance, driving out evil forces, and using the force of solidarity (k'é) to help the patient achieve a return to continuing relationship with the group.

The peacemaker's role in the justice ceremony is to guide the parties to hózhó. The peacemaker's authority is persuasive, not coercive. Coercion (forcing someone else to do one's will) is alien to Navajo thought about human relationships. It is contrary to Navajo morals and can be an evil in itself. (This overstates some very subtle Navajo thought; one can use *coercion* in the sense that one can "force" the assistance of the supernatural through prayer. Just as authoritarianism is an abuse of authority, an abuse of supernatural coercive power is witchcraft, one of the most feared evils.) A naat'áanii uses authoritative (not authoritarian) persuasion to lead and guide others. Navajos have a great deal of respect for tradition, so relevant information from Navajo narratives helps provide authority.

For example, if there is a land dispute, this story may be told by the peacemaker to guide the parties:

Before humans assumed their present form, the Holy People had their own problems to address. During that time, Lightning and Horned Toad had a dispute. Horned Toad was walking on some land when suddenly Lightning confronted Horned Toad and asserted that he, Lightning, owned the land and Horned Toad must leave immediately. Horned Toad replied, "My brother, I don't understand why you should have possession of this land, and I certainly don't lay claim to it." He continued along. Again, Lightning asserted his claim, and he threw a bolt of lightning as a warning. Horned Toad said, "I am very humble, and I can't hurt you as you can hurt others with your bolt of lightning. Could we talk about this tomorrow? I'll be waiting to talk with you on top of the refuse left there by Brother Water." Lightning agreed.

The following day, Horned Toad arrived, wearing his armor. Lightning announced his arrival and asserted his power by throwing more lightning bolts at Horned Toad.

Horned Toad sat atop a pile of driftwood, which was left behind after a storm. From atop that pile, he discussed the matter with Lightning. Horned Toad said, "You are very powerful; you can certainly strike me down with a bolt of lightning." "I certainly can," said Lightning. "That's not what we are here about," said Horned Toad. "We are here to discuss the land ownership issue, and we must talk." "There is nothing to discuss; the land is mine!" Lightning got angry and threw another bolt of lightning, which hit the Horned Toad. "Brother, you did not hurt me," he said. The bolt bounced off Horned Toad's armor. "Brother," he said, "this armor was given to me by the same source as your bolts of lightning. Why is it we are arguing over the land, which was also loaned to us?"

This story takes land complainants back to the true "owner," and it is a forceful traditional precedent to take the parties to common ground. In the process, a naat'áanii will teach Navajo values to guide people in the right way. Many values use the strong moral and emotional connotations of k'é, particularly in the context of k'ei obligations.

Comparisons with Other Forms of Mediation and Arbitration

General American mediation uses the model of a neutral third person who empowers disputants and guides them to a resolution of their problems. In Navajo mediation, the naat'áanii is not quite neutral, and his or her guidance is more value laden than that of the mediator in the American model. As a clan and kinship relative of the parties or as an elder, a naat'áanii has a point of view. The traditional Navajo mediator was related to the parties and had persuasive authority precisely due to that relationship in a k'ei way. The *Navajo Nation Code of Judicial Conduct* (1991) addresses ethical standards for peacemakers and states that they may be related to the parties by blood or clan, barring objection.

Peacemakers have strong personal values, which are the product of their language and rearing in the Navajo way. Those values are also the teachings of Navajo common law. A peacemaker, as a naat'áanii, is selected because of personal knowledge of Navajo values and morals and the demonstrated practice of them. Peacemakers teach values through prayer and a "lecture" to tell disputants what is right and wrong. Navajo peacemakers, unlike their American mediator counterparts, have an affirmative and interventionist role to teach parties how they have fallen out of harmony by distance from Navajo values.

A peacemaker is a guide and a planner. As a guide, a peacemaker helps the parties identify how they have come to the state of disharmony. Non-Indian dispute resolution tends to focus on the act that caused the dispute. Navajo peacemaking is more concerned with the causes of the trouble. A peacemaker tries to find the sources of disharmony and conflict. Persuasion and guidance help the parties make practical plans to resolve problems. Lectures—which are not simply speeches that urge people to do good and avoid evil—help them explore concrete means of repairing disharmony.

A peacemaker intervenes but is not coercive. Navajos have definite opinions about good and evil and about how parties can be at variance with hózhó and the good way. The intervention has the end of making the parties come to feelings of being at one with all, of being beautiful in the resolution of the dispute at hand, and of having restored a good relationship with others. The peacemaker summons supernatural help through prayer and uses ceremonial knowledge as a guide to promote goodwill, self-examination, and reintegration in continuing relationships. Navajo peacemaking, like Navajo healing, actively involves the disputants in the process. This is not a doctor treating a passive patient; the patient is actively involved in the cure.

Peacemaking is not quite "mediation" in the sense of a completely neutral intermediary who leaves the process wholly in the hands of the parties. It is almost, but not quite, "arbitration." Peacemakers generally do not make decisions for others, because coercion is wrong (but under the rules of the peacemaker court, a peacemaker can make decisions for others if the parties agree to use that method). The peacemaker's authority is persuasive, but it has an element of arbitration. An individual selected for personal qualities and respect can use guidance, instruction, and persuasion to help others, and if the parties respect what the peacemaker does, they will most likely follow the guidance they receive. It is much like the process of complying with the healing instructions of a medicine man or woman. Perhaps we can best say that a naat'áanii's word is law.

These attempts to translate Navajo legal terms into English show that it is dangerous to use English terms to describe what Navajos actually do. For that reason, non-Navajos should take great care when applying an English term to describe Navajo processes. The English words "mediation" and "arbitration" do not accurately reflect how Navajos feel about their justice ceremony. Navajo legal terminology shows that Navajo culture approaches justice processes with different values and procedures than those of mainstream American society. Just as the non-Native society is now having problems with adjudication in courts, Navajos also suffer because of this approach. Navajos are still coping with a century of coerced law—law that makes individual acts criminal and subject to punishment, rather than emphasizing restoration to harmony with others and the community. Given the differences between Navajo and general American alternative dispute resolution processes, no outsider should come in to impose any other way of handling social problems.

Conclusion

Navajos have a valuable system of law that is different from the American adjudication system. It is a horizontal system of justice that relies on the essential equality of Navajos and on their solidarity in kinship relations. It differs from modern alternative dispute resolution, which attempts to avoid state coercion or authoritarianism (when coercion is excessive) by perhaps going too far in the direction of neutrality. Navajo peacemaking is an example of restorative justice.

The Navajo Peacemaker Court and its hózhǫ́ǫ́jí naat'áanii are a model for non-Navajo initiatives. The dynamics of community solidarity, reinforcement of relationships, and wise guidance by community leaders who have the people's respect can be developed in other systems. Following the creation of the Navajo Peacemaker Court, in 1982 officials and leaders from

Australia, New Zealand, Canada, and South Africa studied it as a possible model. In 1991, the Manitoba Public Inquiry into the Administration of Justice and Aboriginal People recommended the use of Native peacemakers in that Canadian province (1991, 654). A group of South African visitors to the Navajo Nation recognized the similarity of peacemaking to their native processes, and some of them said that Navajo peacemaking would work there. In 1992, the Canadian Royal Commission on Aboriginal Peoples examined the operations of the peacemaker court for possible use in Canada.

As Navajos go back to the future, others can join them.

Note

This chapter is an edited version of Philmer Bluehouse and James W. Zion, "*Hozhooji Naat'aanii*: The Navajo Justice and Harmony Ceremony," *Mediation Quarterly* 10 (4): 327–37. Reprinted with permission of *Mediation Quarterly*.

References

Austin, Raymond. 1991. Navajo Common Law Principles and Alternative Dispute Resolution. Unpublished manuscript.

Farella, John R. 1984. *The Main Stalk: A Synthesis of Navajo Philosophy*. Tucson: University of Arizona Press.

Kaplan, Bert, and Dale Johnson. 1964. The Social Meaning of Navaho Psychopathology and Psychotherapy. In *Magic, Faith and Healing: Studies in Primitive Psychiatry Today,* ed. Ari Kiev, 203–29. New York: Free Press of Glencoe.

[Manitoba] Public Inquiry into the Administration of Justice, Aboriginal Justice Inquiry of Manitoba and Aboriginal People. 1991. *Report of the Aboriginal Justice Inquiry of Manitoba, Vol. 1: The Justice System and Aboriginal People*. Altona, Manitoba: Friesen.

Witherspoon, Gary. 1975. *Navajo Kinship and Marriage*. Chicago: University of Chicago Press.

Zion, James W. 1983. The Navajo Peacemaker Court: Deference to the Old and Accommodation to the New. *American Indian Law Review* 11: 89–109.

PART

4

CONCLUSIONS

Commentary on Part 4

James W. Zion and Marianne O. Nielsen

Thus far, the chapters of the book were written by individuals who developed Navajo peacemaking, established its policies, promoted it, advocated it, or came in to study it as supporters. This part on "Conclusions" opens with a speech given by United States Supreme Court Justice Sandra Day O'Connor to an annual gathering of Indian law specialists convened by the Supreme Court of Oklahoma, the Indian Sovereignty Symposium. Aside from the questions "Does it work?" and "How does it work?" one of the problems with the revival of traditional Indian justice methods is acceptance by the general legal culture. O'Connor's endorsement of Navajo peacemaking as a legitimate and acceptable justice method to a prominent national Indian law conference was important. However, today, about ten years after that statement of approval, justices of the United States Supreme Court are again questioning the legitimacy of traditional Indian justice. Among the questions posed in opinions of the court are "Can Indians from another Indian tribe understand the customary law of the tribe whose justice is being applied to them as a matter of fairness?" "Is Indian justice acceptable to general American culture?" (at end, is it "barbaric"? showing lingering American ignorance of traditional Indian law). "How can we accept traditional Indian law when there is no federal judicial review to assure compliance with American concepts of civil rights?"

Thus far the critics of traditional Indian law have ignored four important provisions of the Indian Tribal Justice Act of 1993 in asking their questions and making assumptions that, at end, there is something not quite right with it. Chief Justice Tso, accompanied by J. W. Zion as a lawyer, participated in intensive lobbying on the act, and they got four relevant provisions in it: One of the findings of the act is that "traditional tribal justice practices are essential to the maintenance of the culture and identity of Indian tribes and to the goals of this chapter." There is a subsection in the provisions for tribal justice support and tribal justice systems that states that one of the functions of tribal justice support must be to "Provide funds to Indian tribes and tribal organizations for the continuation and enhancement of traditional tribal judicial practices." Another provision for funding is that "Nothing in this chapter shall be deemed or construed to authorize the Office [of Tribal Justice Support] to impose justice standards on Indian tribes." Fourth, among the six congressional disclaimers in the act is that it cannot be read to "alter in any way any tribal traditional dispute resolution forum."

American Indian law has usually been established by case law—federal "Indian common law." Given that one of the major canons of American Indian law is that Congress has the ultimate authority to make Indian law, the four provisions in the Indian Tribal Justice Act are important. First, the act establishes the bedrock legitimacy of traditional tribal justice practices, such as Navajo peacemaking, and that goes beyond Justice O'Connor's personal endorsement as a legislative command. Second, traditional practices, justice systems, and methods of dispute resolution are established as core Indian country justice functions for base funding (which has not been allocated in annual federal budgets to date). Third, one of the major problems with contemporary Indian nation justice systems is that they are largely imposed systems, beginning with the courts of Indian offenses in 1883, which was set up to destroy customary Indian justice practices, and the provision that no new standards may be imposed to reverse that policy. Fourth, Congress disclaimed that it has any power to alter traditional dispute resolution fora in any way.

There is a dispute at present between Justice O'Connor's endorsement of Navajo peacemaking and doubts about the legitimacy of customary Indian law voiced by other justices. That would be dangerous if Indian law continued to be developed by case decisions. However, Congress has spoken to traditional initiatives such as Navajo peacemaking, and that should determine the outcome of the argument.

The second chapter in this part, by Robert Yazzie and James W. Zion, is a compilation of two documents: The first is an invited chapter for an international collection published by an Australian scholar, outlining a possible policy using Navajo thinking; the second is the actual draft policy.

In the first part of the chapter, Yazzie and Zion take another look at peacemaking and use the invited chapter to do a policy background piece for justice planning to address violence. They use a traditional Navajo story as their centerpiece and launching-off point (the Hero Twins fighting the "monsters") and Navajo linguistics to examine Navajo perceptions and culture. When the Five-Fingered People (Navajos) emerged onto the surface of the earth from a world below, excesses in that world created monsters that ravaged the land and the people. The Hero Twins, Monster-Slayer and Born-for-Water, were born to the deity Changing Woman, and after the Twins got weapons from their father, the Sun (also the father of some of the monsters), the two set out to slay or weaken the monsters. The Navajo word for "monster" has a deeper meaning, and *naayéé* can include things that get in the way of people leading a successful life. Yazzie and Zion propose that paradigm for justice planning to deal with, or prevent, the violence that results when the monsters within people take control.

The second part, the draft policy statement, is based upon the policy background piece, and it has been left in its original format for easy citation by scholars. This statement provided a plan for increasing the number of criminal cases handled by peacemaking and extended the idea of the "family as probation officer." It also stressed using peacemaking in criminal cases.

Although the policy was not formally adopted for institutional and political reasons, the study that preceded it and elements of the policy were integrated into legislation. It was in the minds of Chief Justice Yazzie and Zion when they made recommendations for amendments to the *Navajo Nation Criminal Code*. Some of its ideas were adopted in code revisions in 2000, where many offenses were decriminalized by providing no jail time or fine for a crime and substituting peacemaking to fix nalyeeh, or restitution or reparation to victims of crimes. Treatment considerations in the plan became the law. Treatment providers told chief probation officer Vincent Craig that they needed court supervision of defendants in need of treatment for a minimum of eighteen months, so probation for any one offense was extended to two years, and there is a five-year probation period for multiple offenses. The thinking was that if peacemaking became a mainstay of criminal procedure, it should extend the length of supervision to match treatment programs.

We believe that chapter 11 is unique. First, it is an example of how indigenous thinking can be used to develop justice policy. Second, while the policy is framed in Western language and style, it integrates what Yazzie calls "Navajo thinking" in an actual justice plan. This chapter is another demonstration of the "voice" issue. Navajo society is integrationist in that it takes ideas from other cultures (voluntarily or in dealing with what to do about imposed concepts or systems), but the contemporary attitude (reflected in this book) is that Navajos want to identify and flesh out Navajo ideas for contemporary use.

Third, elements and approaches of the plan were used for law reform and a federally funded drug court. The substance was put in United States Department of Justice drug court applications that were incorporated into grant documents as deliverables. Among the major provisions of the drug court plan were an eligibility requirement that a drug- or alcohol-dependent defendant must accept responsibility for his or her actions as a minimum (a guilty plea was not required); defendants and their families were to be part of the development of an individualized treatment plan for the defendant in peacemaking; treatment professionals could be involved in peacemaking to give defendants and their family members information on what treatment meant and how they could contribute to a plan; and cases should return to peacemaking when there was noncompliance. The traditional probation officer concept of involving families as enforcers of treatment plans was not intended to widen the net for defendants for sanctions or punishment but to implement a treatment approach based on the idea that entire families should be involved in rehabilitation for substance abuse.

Indian drug courts, often called "wellness courts" in Indian country, are far different from the standard American model. They involve families, give respectful treatment to families, and, in the instance of Navajo Nation drug courts, use peacemaking to solve problems as they arise in treatment. The policy was also used to influence the development of United States Department of Justice programs for funding drug courts in Indian country.

The final chapter, by James W. Zion, is a forward-looking and somewhat personal piece that relates his observations about and hopes for peacemaking in the future. Using the metaphor of the many facets or sides of a crystal, he attempts to peer into the future based upon the experience of the past. It took almost ten years for peacemaking to take life after its creation, and at the conclusion of twenty years, we now have a good picture of its theory and sufficient experience with it to see that it is a successful method of indigenous justice. Navajo society is changing; just as custom grows to fit the circumstances of a given time, Navajo society evolves as well. It has been called an integrative society that takes the best from borrowed ideas and rejects that which does not work for Navajos. The dream is that upcoming generations of Navajos will, as it is with this generation, take pride in having a Navajo identity.

One of the most important conclusions about peacemaking is that it is not simply a justice method or technique. Peacemaking mirrors ceremonial thought, and it is driven by Navajo philosophies of peaceful interaction and group well-being. It stresses relationships and interdependence. It is in fact a philosophy of life.

This last section demonstrates three things: recognition of peacemaking by a prominent justice of the United States Supreme Court, how "Navajo thinking" (and likely indigenous thought in general) can be elaborated into a policy study, and how such thinking and an Indian voice can be put in policies that can be used in Western-based legal systems. It concludes with the dream of returning the ability for people to solve problems to the people who have them. The point is that justice systems should not "do for," but instead they should "do with." Dreams can become reality, just as in 1981 the dream of the Navajo Nation chairman, judiciary committee, and members of the council became reality.

10 Lessons from the Third Sovereign: Indian Tribal Courts

Sandra Day O'Connor

Today, in the United States, we have three types of sovereign entities—the federal government, the states, and the Indian tribes. Each of the three sovereigns has its own judicial system, and each plays an important role in the administration of justice in this country. The part played by the tribal courts is expanding. As of 1992, there were about 170 tribal courts, with jurisdiction encompassing a total of perhaps one million Americans.

Most of the tribal courts that exist today date from the Indian Reorganization Act of 1934. Before the act, tribal judicial systems were based around the courts of Indian offenses, which were set up in the 1880s by the federal Office of Indian Affairs. Passage of the Indian Reorganization Act allowed the tribes to organize their governments, by drafting their own constitutions, adopting their own laws through tribal councils, and setting up their own court systems. By that time, however, enormous disruptions in customary Native American life had been wrought by factors such as forced migration, settlement on the reservations, the allotment system, and the imposition of unfamiliar Anglo-American institutions. Consequently, in 1934, most tribes had only a dim memory of traditional dispute resolution systems and were not in a position to recreate historical forms of justice.

Swift replacement of the current systems by traditional dispute-settling institutions was not possible. Therefore, while a few tribes, such as the New Mexico Pueblos, have "traditional courts" based on Indian custom, most modern reservation judicial systems do not trace their roots to traditional Indian fora for dispute resolution. Rather, because the tribes were familiar with the regulations and procedures of the Bureau of Indian Affairs, that model provided the framework for most of the tribal courts. Nevertheless, many tribes today attempt to incorporate traditional tribal values, symbols, and customs into their courtrooms and decisions. Some tribal courts, in proceedings that otherwise differ little from what would be seen in state or federal court, have incorporated traditional features of Indian dispute resolution to try to infuse the proceedings with values of consensus and community. For example, the placement of litigants and court personnel in a circle aspires to minimize the appearance of hierarchy and highlight the participation and needs of the entire group in place of any one individual.

The tribal courts, while relatively young, are developing in leaps and bounds. For example, many tribes are working to revise their tribal constitutions and to codify their civil, regulatory, and criminal laws to provide greater guidance and predictability in tribal justice. At the same time, tribes have expanded the use of traditional law. Many tribal codes now combine unique tribal law with adapted state and federal law principles. The number of law-trained Native Americans has increased. Both state and federal courts continue to recognize the tribal courts as important fora for resolution of reservation-based claims involving both Indians and non-Indians.

Tribal courts today face significant challenges. They must work to satisfy the sometimes-competing demands of those inside and outside the tribal communities. But while the challenges are great, the effective operation of tribal courts is essential to promote the sovereignty and self-governance of the Indian tribes. As the Court on which I serve has recognized, "Tribal courts play a vital role in tribal self-government, and the Federal Government has consistently encouraged their development" (*Iowa Mut. Ins. Co. v. LaPlante,* 480 U.S. 9 [1987]).

To fulfill their role as an essential branch of tribal government, the tribal courts must provide a forum that commands the respect of both the tribal community and of non-tribal courts, governments, and litigants. To do so, these courts need to be perceived as both fair and principled. And at the same time the courts seek to satisfy these conditions, they strive to embody tribal values — values that, at times, suggest the use of different methods than those used in the Anglo-American, adversarial, common law tradition.

While tribal courts now include within their jurisdiction a broad range of issues, they naturally take a particular interest in the issues that are most pressing to the population they serve. Issues related to the family, and to the control of natural resources such as land, water, oil, fish, and timber, are of particular interest to the tribal courts, both because important tribal traditions are implicated and because these issues have a vital and recurring impact on the welfare of the community.

In addressing the matters that come before them, the decision-making process by tribal courts need not, and does not always, replicate the process undertaken in state and federal courts. Tribal courts often act more quickly, and more informally, than do their counterparts. The factors considered to reach a decision, the procedures used, and the punishment or resolution arrived at may differ in reflection of tribal values. Tribal court judges frequently are tribal members who seek to infuse cultural values into the process.

While tribal customs and beliefs vary, of course, from tribe to tribe, some general patterns emerge. In place of the Anglo-American system's emphasis on punishment and deterrence, with a win-lose approach that often drives parties to adopt extreme adversarial positions, some tribal judicial systems seek to achieve a restorative justice, with emphasis on restitution rather than retribution and on keeping harmonious relations among the members of the community. Furthering these traditional Native American values in contemporary circumstances has permitted tribal courts to conceive of alternatives to conventional adversarial processes.

The development of different methods of solving disputes in tribal legal systems provides the tribal courts with a way both to incorporate traditional values and to hold up an example to the nation about the possibilities of alternative dispute resolution. New methods have much to offer to the tribal communities and much to teach the other court systems operating in the United States. For about the last fifteen years, in recognition of the plain fact that the adversarial process is often not the best means to a fair outcome, both the state and federal systems have turned with increasing interest to the possibilities offered by mediation, arbitration, and other forms of alternative dispute resolution. In many situations, alternative methods offer a quicker, more personal, and more efficient way of arriving at an answer for the parties' difficulties.

The special strengths of the tribal courts—their proximity to the people served, the closeness of the relations among the parties and the court, their often greater flexibility and informality—give tribal courts special opportunities to develop alternative methods of dispute resolution. For example, vital issues touching on domestic relations, child custody, probate, tort, and criminal prosecutions may be solved more satisfactorily using a nonadversarial method. A cooperative process is particularly useful where family issues, particularly related to children, are involved, because the process helps the parties work together to arrive at a fair and workable solution. An adversarial process, in contrast, may worsen the strains between members of the family and create new conflicts to fuel the old. Too, family problems lend themselves to methods of resolution shaped by the particular character of individual tribal courts, because family issues—involving child custody, juvenile crimes, marriage, and inheritance—are ones where tradition provides critical guidance for social behavior.

Many tribal courts have already developed methods that meet the needs of their communities and use the underlying traditions and values to the extent possible. A good example is the Navajo Peacemaker Court, which was formed in 1982 by the Judicial Conference of the Navajo Nation to provide a forum for traditional mediation. The Navajo Peacemaker Court is now an active, modern legal institution, which incorporates traditional Navajo concepts into a judicial process for dispute resolution. The process is directed by a mediator, who acts to guide and encourage parties to resolve their dispute. The process relies on parties' participation and commitment to reaching a solution, rather than on the imposition of a judgment by an impersonal decision maker. The Navajo Peacemaker Court successfully blends beneficial aspects of both Anglo-American and Indian traditions.

The Northwest Intertribal Court System, a consortium of fifteen tribes in the Pacific Northwest, was set up in 1979 to provide court services and personnel to the individual tribal courts of member tribes. Several of the member tribes have supplemented their formal tribal court system with peacemaker programs — programs that are based on traditional values of consensus and respectful attention to individuals.

The Indian communities' interest in the development of alternatives for dispute resolution has led to the development of the Indian Dispute Resolution Services, a group formed about six years ago to provide training in conflict resolution. That organization is helping Indian communities to settle unresolved disputes around the country and to provide fair and timely outcomes for parties.

Mediation can be effective not only within a tribal community, but also between the tribe and other groups. The Native American Heritage Commission and the Community Relations Service of the United States Department of Justice have collaborated on several mediation cases involving the repatriation of Indian remains. Some mediation took place between tribes and developers who had discovered remains at construction sites; others took place between tribes and universities that wanted the remains for academic research. Mediation worked to settle successfully the many conflicts that arose over the proper treatment and assignment of such ancestral remains and funerary objects.

The development of methods of alternative dispute resolution may help tribal courts to expand the exercise of their authority over more civil cases. Historically, the great majority of cases heard in tribal courts involve criminal matters, with relatively few civil disputes decided. This might reflect the time and expense required for civil cases, the courts' reluctance to handle civil cases because of a lack of familiarity or advanced legal training, or perhaps because tribal courts serve a less litigious community. Development of alternative methods of dispute resolution allows the tribal courts to take advantage of their strengths in order to provide efficient and fair resolution of such conflicts.

It is to be hoped that the tribal courts will continue to explore additional possibilities for alternative methods of dispute resolution. These methods need not be limited in scope to disputes within a tribe but could be used also to resolve conflicts between one tribe and another, and between a tribe and the state and federal government, political units, private investors, or contractors. At its best, such a method would provide a cooperative, relaxed forum for the conclusion of disputes, with use of a process that would include all interested parties to ensure their involvement and their consent, and, at the same time, offer important practical advantages by accomplishing its tasks more agreeably, more quickly, and less expensively than the adversarial mode. By expanding such techniques, the tribal courts may set out the paradigm for other courts to follow.

While tribal courts seek to incorporate the best elements of their own customs into the courts' procedures and decisions, the tribal courts have also sought to include useful aspects of the Anglo-American tradition. For example, more and more tribal judicial systems have established mechanisms to ensure the effective appealability of decisions to higher courts. Too, some tribes have sought to provide tribal judiciaries with the authority to conduct review of regulations and ordinances promulgated by the tribal council. And one of the most important initiatives is the move to ensure judicial independence for tribal judges. Tribal courts are often subject to the complete control of the tribal councils, whose powers often include the ability to select and remove judges. Therefore, the courts may be perceived as a subordinate arm of the councils rather than as a separate and equal branch of government. The existence of such control is not conducive to neutral adjudication on the merits and can threaten the integrity of the tribal judiciary. Some tribes, like the Cheyenne River Sioux Tribe in South Dakota, have amended their constitutions to provide for formal separation of powers.

A vital improvement made by tribal judicial systems is the growing number of law-trained, well-prepared people participating in the system, both as lawyers and as judges. Many tribal judges have taken steps to craft ethical guidelines and to institute tribal bar requirements for the lawyers who practice before them, and have participated themselves in further training for the task of judging. Both lawyers and judges must be knowledgeable and principled if the tribal judicial systems are to engender confidence in the fairness and integrity of their courts. Whether in tribal court, state court, or federal court, the exercise of a court's jurisdiction is a serious matter, and all persons—Indian and non-Indian—who come before a court are entitled to just and reasoned proceedings.

The judicial systems of the three sovereigns—the Indian tribes, the federal government, and the states—have much to teach one another. While each system will develop along different lines, each can take the best from the others. Just as "a single courageous State may, if its citizens choose, serve as a laboratory" (*New State Ice. Co. v. Liebmann,* 285 U.S. 310, 311 [1931] Brandels, J., dissenting) for the development of laws, the experiments and examples provided by the various Indian tribes and their courts may offer models for the entire nation to follow. To give but one example, the Navajo Peacemaker Court has been studied by officials not only within this country, but also from Australia, New Zealand, Canada, and South Africa, for possible use. The Indian tribal courts' development of further methods of dispute resolution will provide a model from which the federal and state courts can benefit as they seek to encompass alternatives to the Anglo-American adversarial model. And, while tribal courts currently seek to expand the role of traditional law in their judicial systems, they may well choose to incorporate some of the features of the Anglo-American system, such as access to an effective appeal and the independence of the judiciary.

The role of tribal courts continues to expand, and these courts have an increasingly important role to play in the administration of the laws of our nation. The three sovereigns can learn from each other, and the strengths and weaknesses of the different systems provide models for courts to consider. Whether tribal court, state court, or federal court, we must all strive to make the dispensation of justice in this country as fair, efficient, and principled as we can.

Note

This chapter is an edited version of "Lessons from the Third Sovereign: Indian Tribal Courts," a speech presented at the Indian Sovereignty Symposium IX, Tulsa, Oklahoma, June 4, 1996. Reprinted with permission of the author.

11 "Navajo Thinking": Peacemaking Planning and Policy

Robert Yazzie and James W. Zion

Once again, crime and violence are national priorities. The cries in response to reported violence are "Tougher laws!" "Increased penalties!" and "More police!" (Gibbs and Carney 1993). Violence is not a new issue, and "[i]n some 100 years of national sovereignty, Americans have been preoccupied repeatedly with trying to understand and control one form of violence or another" (National Research Council 1993).[1]

Violence is a Navajo Nation issue as well. In October 1993, the Navajo Nation Council, galvanized by reports of gang vandalism and family violence, resolved to make gang violence and family disruption a legislative priority. Should the council's upcoming debates focus on more laws, more penalties, more police, and more gaols? Too often, policy makers and legislators limit their debates to legal procedures, what to do with individual offenders, and talk of "rights"; that is, "micro justice" (Nader 1980), where planners ask what to do with people rather than address causes and systemic problems. Policy makers become so preoccupied with what to do with individual offenders that they fail to address larger problems. They sometimes forget to look at causes, trends, and the big picture.

Navajo Macro-Justice

This policy study seeks to view law, justice, and social problems in a new way to respond to violence and social disruption. It attempts to use "macro justice" to address the nature and causes of violence in the Navajo Nation. Courts must anticipate new conditions and emerging events and adjust their operations to meet them.

Navajo macro justice requires a careful reexamination of institutions, relationships, and approaches. Most tribal courts use the state model of adjudication and adversarial litigation. Are those procedures legitimate in the context of a given culture? Who are the actors in Indian justice systems and what is their role?

Adjudication and adversarial process may not be the best approach to deal with monsters. The Navajo Nation may wish to abandon or modify imported procedures following a century of experimentation with them. Are there ways to put the power to solve problems back in the hands of the people who are the victims of violence? Are there alternatives to the imposed procedures that destroyed traditional justice and created this situation? They can surely be developed through a careful reexamination of Navajo institutions, expectations, and relationships.

We must also reexamine the relationship between the Navajo Nation and the United States government. Congress fails to follow through when it creates new programs or responsibilities. One example is the Indian Civil Rights Act of 1964 (Pub. L. 90-284, title II, April 11, 1968, 82 Stat. 77 [25 U.S.C. §§ 1301-1303]). In addition to discounting the objections of many Indian nations, including the Navajo Nation, Congress, for more than twenty years, failed to provide adequate funding for Indian nations to implement the act (United States Commission on Civil Rights 1991, 72). In 1990, Congress passed the Indian Child Protection and Family Violence Protection Act (Pub. L. 101-630, title IV, November 28, 1990 [25 U.S.C. §§ 3201-3211, 1992 supp.]). It authorized $30,000,000 per year for fiscal years 1991 to 1995 for Indian nation child protection and family violence programs (25 U.S.C. § 3210 [i], [a].).

Although the act became law on November 28, 1990, the BIA did not begin to develop the regulations required by it until June 1, 1993. Although the BIA asked for $1.5 million for family resource centers and $5 million for family violence prevention programs that year, to date programs under the act have not been funded because the BIA has not asked for monies to implement the protection and prevention programs ("BIA says . . ." 1993; Singer 1993, 8–10.) Tribal self-determination programs and funds for tribal courts are "no longer a high priority" for the bureau ("BIA says . . ." 1993).

Although its inaction in the face of widespread violence against women and children is inexcusable, Congress also abdicated its trust responsibility to assure justice in Indian country. The continuing reality is that until Congress honors the basic human rights of Indians and their governments, people will be hurt and will die. The relationship between Indian nations and the United States needs a thorough overhaul. Official neglect is a monster.

The Names of the Monsters

We will name the monsters, describe their ways, and discuss weapons to use on them in the context of Navajo thought and society. We see the monsters in the workload of the trial courts of the Navajo Nation. In fiscal year 1993 (April 1, 1992, to March 31, 1993), the Navajo Nation courts received 47,979 new cases and brought forward 42,739 from the previous fiscal year (Navajo Nation Judicial Branch, n. d.). An examination of the workload of the trial courts shows that 51 percent of the docket of the district courts are criminal cases; 45.7 percent are traffic matters; and 1.8 percent, civil actions. In addition, 26,631 new criminal charges were filed in fiscal year 1992, and with the 19,958 cases brought forward, the total caseload was 46,589 cases.

The major categories of criminal charges involved alcohol and personal violence: They were (1) offenses against the public order (a caseload of 17,159 charges—36.8 percent of them criminal); (2) DWI (3,194—13.5 percent); (3) offenses against persons (6,243—13.4 percent); (4) intoxicating liquor possession or sales (5,848—12.5 percent); and (5) offenses against the family (2,659—5.7 percent). Property crime was comparatively low; criminal damage to property (2,027—4.2 percent), theft (687—2.7 percent), trespass and burglary (489—1 percent), forgery (315—less than 1 percent), and robbery 3 make up slightly over 8 percent of the criminal docket. The five major categories of crime were approximately 82 percent of that docket. Other violent crimes against persons were low: weapons and explosives charges (470—1 percent), sexual offenses (e.g., sexual assaults; 214—less than 1 percent) and robbery 1 were comparatively few.[2] There were few drug or controlled-substances cases (184—less than 1 percent).

The largest category of offenses, those against public order, show a need to address two problems: public intoxication and disorderly conduct. The judicial branch proposes to address public intoxication by decriminalizing it as an offense. The major purpose of the existing law is to prevent deaths from exposure to the cold by taking disabled people into custody.[3] Disorderly conduct is a more serious issue than it may otherwise appear. It is a catchall for less serious conduct, but it should be taken seriously. A study of Navajo drinking patterns shows that it takes place out of doors or at public gatherings, including "stomp dances," Enemyway ceremonies, and other gatherings (Topper 1980). Another study of violence says that "Intoxicated Navajo fight almost exclusively with family members" (National Research Council 1993). Disorderly conduct is an important offense because officers frequently make arrests for alcohol-related fighting. It is associated with high numbers of DWI charges and offenses against persons; it is most likely associated with offenses against the family and sexual assaults. If the conclusion is correct, that most Navajo Nation crime is related to alcohol and assaults involving relatives, then disorderly conduct charges should be more closely scrutinized.[4] The same holds true for assaults.

Sexual misconduct is a more difficult problem. We do not know the extent to which offenses against the public order, offenses against the family, and sexual offense are interrelated. Violence against women often involves the use of sexuality for punishment or control, and sexual assaults at public gatherings are reported to be common. As it is with other offenses, defendants attempt to excuse their conduct by saying, "I was drunk."

How people behave under the influence of alcohol is determined by cultural practices and beliefs. Cultural patterns of Indian drinking have been identified (National Research Council 1993). However, if we tolerate drunkenness as a form of "time out," this aggravates the problem (MacAndrew and Edgerton 1969, 83–99).[5] There is an identified psychopathology known as "crazy violence" or "crazy drunken violence," which Navajos use to explain deviant and bizarre behavior (Kaplan and Johnson 1964). Violence should never be excused by explanations for behavior that takes responsibility out of the hands of the individual. If alcohol-related crime is taken seriously, with drunkenness seen as an aggravating and not a mitigating factor, that should have an impact on defendants. Although the Navajo Nation gaols are overcrowded, the court's policy toward alcohol-related crime should be that special attention will be given to it. Some nongaoling options include use of the Navajo Peacemaker Court to address denial, mandatory restitution to victims, involvement of offender and victim families, and intensive probation coupled with required treatment.

How do these patterns apply to youth crime? In fiscal year 1993, 724 delinquency cases were filed in the Navajo Nation family court, and 248 were brought over, for a total caseload of 972 matters. The major categories of delinquency were public intoxication (a caseload of 157—14.6 percent), assault or battery (140—13 percent), "other" offenses (a broad range; 183—12.8 percent), property damage (104—9.7 percent), and disorderly conduct (98—9.1 percent). DWI, unlike adult crime, was only 4.3 percent of the delinquency docket (47 cases). Possession of liquor petitions (66) were only 6.1 percent of the caseload. There is some violent crime involving juveniles, as is shown by resisting arrest (36—3.3 percent), weapons (32—1.9 percent), and threatening (30—1.7 percent) charges. Juveniles appear to be more involved in property crime, as is shown by theft (88—8.2 percent), burglary (44—4.1 percent), and trespassing (33—3.0 percent) petitions. There were few charges for inhalation of toxic substances (16—1.4 percent) and possession of marijuana (11.1 percent). Again, the low number of filings may reflect a law enforcement problem, the use of prosecutorial discretion, or other factors, and it does not necessarily mean that those problems are not present in larger numbers.

Although youth crime follows a wider pattern, the same problem of alcohol-related crime and personal violence found in adult crime is present. There are few treatment, detention, or foster care facilities for youthful offenders. Court programs should address educating young people about their roles and behavior, because those avenues are limited. Children look to their parents and relatives for example. In some instances, parents and relatives provide liquor to the young, encouraging drunken behavior. In others, relatives have become too dependent upon the criminal justice system to deal with their children. Delinquency procedures should include use of the Navajo Peacemaker Court to require children to confront their conduct, with relatives present to see what is happening to their children. Given the fact that at least 35 percent of juvenile charges involve property damage or injury to others, the Navajo Nation should consider increasing parental liability for restitution. There is a concept of a "traditional probation officer," where parents and clan members assume responsibility for paying for the injuries caused by relatives and watch an offender closely.[6] Parental and custodian liability for youthful offenders could be used to revive the effective role. The peacemaker court can be used to counsel children and relatives in a specific case, and peacemaker courts should be instituted in school systems as a means of teaching children their traditional Navajo responsibilities.

Children's status offenses are few. Of the 378 cases filed and 135 brought forward (for a caseload of 513 "child in need of supervision" [CHINS] cases), 266 (51.8 percent) were for traffic violations, 159 (30.9 percent) were children "beyond control," 87 (16.9 percent) were truants, and there was one "other" petition. CHINS cases are unique to our justice system, because it processes children for offenses that would not be a crime if committed by an adult. While they are comparatively minor, they point to possible misconduct when a child is an adult. Children who are truant or "beyond control" need special care, because they may be victims of adult neglect. The focus of such cases should be the family situation as a whole.

The injury done to children is reflected in the figures for dependent and neglected children. In fiscal year 1993, 428 petitions were filed and 346 were brought forward for a caseload of 774. The largest category of cases was physical abuse or neglect (427—55.1 percent).[7] The number of guardianship cases (119—15.3 percent) shows the extent to which private remedies to deal with child abuse are used and needed. Guardianship is essentially a procedure where a family member can petition the court to deal with poor parenting, neglect, or abuse by appointing another person—usually a relative—to care for the child. Many tribal social service programs and courts prefer to avoid the stigma of legally removing a child from parents by instead placing the children with other relatives. Guardianship is important to grandparents and other relatives, who wish confirmation of a familial arrangement for child placement. Those relatives need a guardianship decree to receive benefits, place children in schools, provide for medical treatment, qualify for housing, and so forth. Actions to remove children legally from parents or placements were 25 percent of the dependent-neglect docket.

That includes termination of parental rights (53—6.8 percent), custody (34—4.3 percent), and Indian Child Welfare Act referrals (34—4.3 percent; Fahey 1975, 10, 12). The family court had twenty-one sexual abuse cases (2.7 percent) and eight "other" cases.

Here too, placement and treatment facilities are limited. Placement outside the child's home or family is a last resort, due not only to Navajo family values, but also due to the lack of any other placement option. One of the best approaches to child welfare in this area is requiring families to deal with their own children and to assume responsibilities toward them. The Navajo Peacemaker Court is proving to be a successful approach for dependent-neglect cases, because it unites family members to discuss their children's problems and assists with the placement process. Child sexual abuse (which is most likely present in many of the 1,158 "offenses against the family" criminal cases) is particularly difficult to address. Some abusers attempt to justify sexual conduct with a child or with a stepchild on the grounds that it was "traditional" to have relations with a girl who had just reached puberty, or "traditional" to have sexual relations with a wife's young sister or child from a previous relationship. Incest was one of the most horrible of crimes under Navajo common law. Peacemaking can be used to address abuser denial. In cases where proof of sexual contact is lacking, a child's family can be alerted to the possibility of abuse and develop safeguards to prevent it in the future.

The family court domestic relations caseload shows other cases that affect children. The largest category of cases (673—35.2 percent) was divorce, followed by name changes (271—14.1 percent). Other categories of cases that affect children included orders to show cause (to enforce court orders; 218—11.4 percent), "other" family matters (217—11.3 percent), paternity (134—7 percent), child support (70—3.6 percent), and modification of prior decrees (55—2.8 percent). The other work of the family court included probates (159—8.3 percent), quiet title actions (44—2.3 percent), and validations of marriage (27—1.4 percent).[8] There were forty-one peacemaker actions in family court, which covered a wide variety of family disputes.

The domestic relations cases, as with guardianships, are important because they give individuals a private remedy for injuries done to them in a family setting. A divorce action can be an important means of private protection to prevent family violence or child abuse. A domestic relations action is an individual procedure to address abuses that social welfare officials or police may not detect or do not have the resources to address. Although the Navajo Nation does not wish to encourage divorce as a matter of public policy, it is important for petitioners—particularly women—to have a means to get relief. At present, DNA-People's Legal Services cannot handle divorces, except for situations involving domestic violence, due to high demand. The Navajo Nation law of separation (for which there is no statutory provision) is unclear. Many women who want a divorce, or at least support, cannot get into court, due to their poverty and lack of access to a lawyer.[9]

When members of the public cannot get a simple and inexpensive day in court, two things happen: women and children remain in abusive or neglectful environments, and the potential for violence increases. There should be private civil remedies to allow woman and child victims to escape a bad situation at their own choice and to lower the victimization. Adequate civil remedies also prevent violence by providing peaceful alternatives to settling disputes through personal family violence. Although we do not yet have figures to show the extent to which recent domestic violence proceeding laws are working, family judges are reporting a sharp increase in filings. This shows the extent to which the Navajo Nation public wants private remedies to deal with victimization. Also, the large numbers of private actions, in comparison with filings by the Navajo Nation on behalf of children, shows that offering private remedies is a viable option to increasing social service functions.

The district court's civil actions are also relevant to the topic of violence. They are a means for the public to resolve disputes peacefully and provide compensation for injuries. Although civil cases were only 1.8 percent of the district court's work, they are important. Contract actions were 62.9 percent (caseload of 953) of the docket. The usual pattern of these cases is that they are brought by lending institutions to collect loans, repossess property sold on credit, or resolve other contractual disputes. Unemployment and a lack of income opportunities are tied to crime and violence, and offering civil remedies to businesses is tied to the Navajo Nation's business climate and the opportunities it offers. To the extent poor individuals need access to courts in civil actions to curb consumer abuses, small-claims procedures are necessary.

The second highest category of civil cases was torts and personal injuries (with a caseload of 133 matters—8.8 percent of the civil docket). A tort action is a private remedy for an injury. In the past, Navajos filed criminal charges to deal with personal injuries, but the overburdened criminal justice system did not deal adequately with this problem. To some extent, the burden of injuries to others should be shifted to the civil docket, except for matters that require punishment or criminal sanctions. Civil remedies are a means to prevent abuses caused by government officials; there were fifty-nine civil rights actions (3.9 percent of the civil docket) and fifty-four prisoner relief petitions (3.6 percent). District courts possess the power to order specific relief to prohibit conduct or to require an action, and there were forty-four such cases (2.9 percent). There are many kinds of civil actions, and the categories of "other" (122 — 8 percent) and "miscellaneous" (92 — 6.1 percent) were a significant portion of district court workload.

These are the monsters. As the figures show, the biggest problems are alcohol, violence within family units, and harm to children. The Navajo Nation repeatedly demands significant increases in the federal contribution to justice in Indian country, but this is unlikely to come in these days of federal budget cutbacks. The Navajo Nation inherited a "policing" model of justice from the United States, but this is breaking down. Only the most violent of crimes are prosecuted in the courts of the Navajo Nation, due to gaol overcrowding and a decree that sharply limits the numbers of prisoners the gaols can hold.

Western adjudication is a police model. It assumes that social order is maintained by using force and authority. That is the policy that underlies the formation of Indian police and courts in the nineteenth century (Barsh and Youngblood 1976) and the Navajo Nation system. Modern federal initiatives such as promoting tribal courts and recommending model codes only reinforce a model that is designed to promote federal governmental authority and assimilation. Recent legislation and proposals to increase the federal presence in Indian country are another aspect of the police model. Given the fact that most of the social problems of Indian country arise in the family, do we need to "federalize" family conduct and subject family members to federal action?

Adjudication is another aspect of the police model. Although it offers private remedies, people must seek the services of attorneys to invoke them. Licensed attorneys, whom people hire to advocate their positions, are authority figures who attain their privileged position through a tightly regulated system of education and discipline. Most Navajos cannot afford a private attorney to seek remedies for violence or neglect of familial duties.

The Ways and Habits of the Monsters

Although in theoretical and practical terms, we may not have enough information about the causation of violence, we have various avenues by which to identify problems and to take coordinated action to address them.[10] The courts of the Navajo Nation must consider their role in this process. It is obvious that, given a lack of gaols and treatment facilities, the courts will have to increase their probation activities when dealing with adult criminal and juvenile offenses. To do so, we need better understanding of the nature of problems that come before the courts.

There are many theories about alcoholism, but courts are most concerned with the dynamics of escapism within the use of alcohol. One of the biggest problems is denial. It is a difficult phenomenon. It manifests itself in criminal cases, where defendants plead guilty at rates in excess of 90 percent. There are many reasons for this, despite the fact that Navajo Nation judges carefully counsel defendants on their rights. One is that alcohol-dependent defendants simply submit themselves to punishment, then return to their prior behavior. That is a form of denial—denial of the individual's responsibility to care for him- or herself. Another form of denial is the refusal to accept personal responsibility for the consequences of individual conduct by dealing with it. That is, DWI defendants deny they have a drinking problem; abusers deny domestic violence or blame the victim for it; sex abusers deny the act and are adept in hiding it; parents deny responsibility for their children; children deny their responsibilities to their parents (particularly in elder abuse situations).

The usual approach to the common problem of denial is to use professionals to communicate with people who deny. The effectiveness of this approach relies upon the degree of respect people have for authority figures. It may be minimal, as with the person who is forced to speak to a probation officer, social worker, or mental health professional. The circumstances may inhibit communications: Judges see thousands of defendants each year; probation officers are overburdened; social workers cannot keep up with their caseloads; police do not want to be counselors; school teachers prefer to teach. We cannot expect to receive or raise the resources to fully use a professional counseling approach to deal with denial.

One weapon, or policy initiative, for the Navajo Nation to use in addressing social problems is traditional leadership authority to address denial. The Navajo Peacemaker Court builds on the tradition of the naat'áanii—the Navajo civil leader. Peacemakers reinforce the tradition that the people who have a dispute should be the ones who decide how to resolve it. The incentive for resolution is the presence of the participants' family members. A peacemaker gets at denial through the lecture, which is a practical review of the problem in light of Navajo values. Family members are also effective agents to eliminate or reduce denial.

A recent peacemaker court case illustrates the point: Parents brought their children into peacemaker court to prevent them from committing incest. The case involved two first cousins who were committing incest in violation of both Navajo and Anglo values. The families were able to touch at least one of the couple to dispel his denial that there was anything wrong going on. The Navajo Peacemaker Court is proving to be an effective tool to reach DWI defendants. Although many argue the effectiveness of mandatory minimum gaol sentences in DWI cases, we may also argue that punishment is more effective when a drunken driver must face his spouse, children, family, and even victims in an intimate setting to discuss his conduct.

The peacemaker court seeks to return justice to the community as well as to the parties to dispute a problem. Too often, communities rely upon their police and courts to solve problems and become dependent upon official action. When a lack of personnel or resources produces official inaction, the public loses respect for its government. Dependence upon governmental authority produces another form of victimization, and communities hide behind locked doors to avoid directly becoming victims of violence. An active participating community can have a great impact on community problems. For example, if it is correct that drunken behavior can be curbed through the exercise of public opinion, then Navajo chapters have the means to deal with their violent or dangerous drinkers through direct action. A chapter can appoint and actively support peacemakers, and chapters have the ability to call community peacemaking meetings to return to the old Navajo procedure of discussing deviant conduct as a group.

Although the peacemaker court was originally designed to solve most legal problems, it has been an underused avenue until recent days. Most of the domestic relations matters just discussed can be addressed through peacemaking. It is an appropriate place for guardianships, name changes, probates, and even divorces. The problem lies with cases where the parties cannot afford the services of a peacemaker or the public experts provided by the Navajo Nation government. The Navajo Nation must make an investment in the process.

A root cause of social disruption is the destruction of traditional family and clan arrangements. Traditional social controls in the form of the Navajo language, religion, and social structure were destroyed by boarding schools, a transition to a wage economy, consumerism, and modern media (e.g., radio, television, films, and the personal video player). Are traditional social controls still effective? They can be if communities choose to put them back in place. There are roles for families, clans, and chapters to address violence, mistreatment of children, and alcohol-related misconduct.

Weapons

This approach recognizes shortcomings in modern adjudication, the police model, and institutions that take power away from individuals and groups of people. One of the major initiatives that the Navajo Nation must begin is to move justice back to the chapters and involve families in the justice process. The Navajo Nation is large, too vast to cover with police, given limited resources. This shortcoming in policing and treatment resources mandates a change in policy. In addition, individual and community empowerment—and opportunity to speak and deal with one's own problems—is more in harmony with Navajo thinking.

There may be instances when litigants, who do not want consensual justice methods, refuse to cooperate with peacemaking or prefer action by a judge. What can the courts do to address those problems and forge other weapons to use against the monsters?

There is an ancient European tradition of access to the courts that can be revived by the Navajo method of adjudication. It comes from an ancient European belief that poor people should receive special treatment, that they should have a right to speak freely to have their grievances resolved.[11] The legal right of access comes from canon law, which had "the concept of a dual system procedure, one solemn and formal, the other simple and equitable. The simple procedure was available to certain types of civil cases, including those involving poor or oppressed persons and those for which an ordinary legal remedy was unavailable. It dispensed with legal counsel as well as with written pleadings and written interrogatories" (Berman 1983, 250–51). English common law recognized a similar right, expressed in the doctrine of *in forma pauperis*. Under English common law, litigants who swore they had less than a stated minimum income had fees waived and received appointed counsel in civil cases. Under American law, fees are waived under limited circumstances, and there is no right to appointed counsel in a civil case.[12] There is a due process right of access to the courts for relief. Governments cannot "unreasonably" restrict access, and denial can be a violation of due process of the law (see Antieau 1969).[13] The American legal doctrine is more restrictive than canon law or English common law, but there is a right of access to the courts to demand relief. Modern court performance standards recognize the right and require court planners to consider access to justice as a priority.[14]

Other European precedents address easy access to courts by people who cannot afford lawyers. In the later Middle Ages, Europeans sought to develop procedures for judicial accommodation to ease the impact of law upon people who were at a special disadvantage in demanding justice. Three principles emerged: First, there was an obligation to provide special protection for widows, orphans, the aged, crippled or seriously ill persons, the poor, "and in general, the wretched of the earth." Second, to ease the impact on those groups, their cases were to be handled by a summary hearing and rapid decision to avoid "long-drawn-out and expensive forms of ordinary suits and proceedings" (Borah 1983, 11). Third, all lawyers were obligated to serve the poor and needy at reduced fees or no fees at all, or the state would provide an official to offer free legal representation (Borah

1983, 11–12). Those ideas went to the Americas with the conquest of the New World.

The Spanish struggled for many centuries to frame their relations with Indian nations.[15] There were three schools of Spanish thought about Indian law and government: first, that Indians have their own societies and that they are entitled to their own institutions and laws; second, that there is but one society (namely Spanish) and that Indians should be fully integrated into it; third, that there are two republics—Indian and Spanish. Spanish law for the Americas acknowledged the first point of view by decrees that ordered Spanish bureaucrats to observe the "usages and customs of the Indians" (Haring 1975, 101).[16] The Indian groups of Mexico quickly learned Spanish institutions and legal procedures, and the governors of New Spain studied how to accommodate Indian complaints and stem frustration (Borah 1983). On April 9, 1591, a royal order created the Juzgado General de Indios (General Court of Indians) for Mexico. It, and an accompanying letter, provided for a summary court to "hear suits by Indians against Indians, Indians against Spaniards, and Spaniards against Indians." It also created an office for attorneys, to be paid from fines or levies on Indian communities, who would represent Indians without fee.

The concept of the General Court of Indians was simple: It provided speedy, simple, and inexpensive legal remedies for Indians and Indian groups. All a litigant needed to do was to seek out one of the staff attorneys, relate the complaint to him, and he would do the rest. After hearing a complaint, the court attorney would prepare all the necessary papers and process them through a summary legal procedure. Although there is disagreement among historians regarding the motives or the effectiveness of the court, its principles can be used to modify Navajo Nation court procedures. A similar tradition in England was that of the justice of the peace. Those individuals held positions of respect, and the office was sought for the honor it gave. English justices of the peace stopped riots, informed the central government of any problems in their jurisdiction, heard the complaints of the poor, and regulated ale houses. They also used summary procedure, questioning people about the nature of the offense against them (Notestein 1962).

The courts of the Navajo Nation should achieve the same goals: Provide speedy and simple remedies for those who cannot afford a lawyer or the expense of normal legal proceedings. This would represent a shift from adversarial proceedings conducted by lawyers to a system that would receive the public and process their cases without cost. It would require court staff members and modern equipment to prepare court papers and orders. Court staff members could brief the judge on the nature of the case and do everything necessary to provide for summary hearings.

Judges would have to modify their present usages somewhat. Rather than rely upon lawyers to question witnesses to bring out all the facts of a case, the judge would have to ask the questions. This is "inquisitorial procedure," which goes back to canon law and is still used by some European courts. The canon law doctrine was that a judge must be convinced of the judgment to be rendered by questioning parties and put himself in the position of the person before the court to ascertain what he does not know or what he wishes to hide (Notestein 1962). Judges can receive case briefings from members of the court staff to become familiar with each case, then allow the parties to tell their stories. If anything is unclear, a judge can ask appropriate questions to get all the information needed for a decision.

Slay the Monsters!

The foregoing analysis uses Navajo legal thinking and modern strategic planning. In Navajo legal thinking, it is important to identify the source of problems to deal with them. Navajos do not believe in punishment for its own sake. They believe it is better to identify reasons for misconduct and deal with them. The analysis uses court statistics to identify the biggest problems in terms of offenses and also the public demand for judicial services. That is strategic planning.

In the criminal area, the Navajo Nation courts must focus on the rights of victims. This is not only a modern trend in American criminal law, but a fundamental tenet of Navajo common law. It is nalyeeh, or a demand to be made whole for an injury. Nalyeeh is also a process for reconciliation of victim and offender, whereby people in ongoing family, clan, and community relationships "talk out" their problems for resolution. The Navajo common law principle dictates a policy that the Navajo Nation courts must develop summary procedures to allow victims to demand restitution (or reparation). Where an offense involves a family member, the Navajo Peacemaker Court is the best forum to use consensual problem solving to restore or build proper relationships.

Many social problems are better addressed using civil rather than criminal remedies. In our analysis, we discovered that Navajos are using the guardianship action as a private child welfare remedy. Navajo Nation social service agencies, which are a variant on the police model and assume that professional intervention works best, are overburdened with cases and focus primarily on sexual abuse. They ignore child neglect cases, so grandmothers and aunts exercise their traditional duties toward children by seeking appointment as guardians. Navajos have long recognized that prompt intervention is necessary to keep children out of the cycle of violence, and family members have a duty to intervene when children are placed at risk. The Navajo Nation courts previously promulgated summary domestic or family violence remedies to address family disruption, and summary procedures for child support enforcement will be implemented in the near future.

We call the plan "Slay the Monsters!" We will get at the monsters of alcohol-related violence and dysfunctionalism in families and communities through summary remedies. As it was with the General Court of Indians, individual Indians will be able to go to a Navajo Nation courthouse for immediate relief. In modern times, the court advocate (or commissioner) will use a computer rather than a quill pen to record the individual's grievance. Using standard computer forms, the commissioner will process the paperwork for restitution in a criminal case, reference to the Navajo Peacemaker Court, or summary proceedings. A commissioner will meet with the parties to discuss the documentary evidence they must present to the court and coordinate the appearance of witnesses. The commissioner will then schedule a hearing before the court and present a prepared file to a judge. The hearings will be relaxed, and the judge will question the parties. In 1991, the Navajo judges adopted the *Navajo Nation Code of Judicial Conduct*. This encourages judges to use Navajo ethics regarding consensual agreements through discussion to conduct informal hearings.

This is not simply an academic essay. It is a plan for action. A draft of this essay was presented to LaNeta Plummer of Southern Arizona Legal Aid. Plummer contacted the Navajo Nation courts to ask how funding from the national Legal Services Corporation could best serve Navajo justice needs. The text of this essay became a proposal for those funds, and the Slay the Monsters program became reality on July 1, 1994. Using the federal funds provided, the Navajo courts will hire a planner to write plain-language computer forms and a manual that outlines summary procedures. The priority areas are child support enforcement, victim compensation in criminal cases, peacemaking, family violence intervention, guardianships, simple divorces, and other kinds of domestic relations cases. Following development of the forms and manual, the courts will hire two commissioners for each court and have them available at computers to serve the public. The funds are limited to the Window Rock and Chinle districts in the Arizona portion of the Navajo Nation, but the forms and manual will be available to the other five judicial districts, and this plan will be used to seek funding from other sources.

In 1982, the Navajo Nation courts chose to "go back to the future" in the Navajo Peacemaker Court. The judges revived traditional Navajo justice in a modern setting. This plan also goes back for something else new. It uses traditional Navajo justice thinking and medieval concepts about summary justice to provide prompt and efficient remedies.

The non-Indian police model does not serve Navajos well. It does not meet their expectations. Navajos look to their judges as leaders whom people can seek out at will. As it was during the time of creation, Navajo leaders will seek out the monsters and slay or weaken them in procedures that attempt to get at the source of problems. The Navajo Peacemaker Court will be used to a greater extent, coordinated with summary adjudication methods. The primary drive behind this policy is to generate simple justice methods that allow victims of crime and social disruption to have their problems solved in ways they understand. Police and courts took away this power. It is time to return the ability to frame the future to the hands of the people.

[Editors' Note: The Navajo Nation judicial branch uses general and theoretical policy studies of justice issues and conference presentations as foundations for specific policies. "Slay the Monsters," the original title of the essay that forms the first part of this chapter, was an invited contribution to a book on popular justice that developed an approach to future justice policies. The proposed policy statement follows.]

The Policy

Preamble

Hózhǫ́ǫ́jí, which can be translated into English as harmony with oneself and one's environment, is a traditional cornerstone of Navajo existence. Modern principles of criminal probation, when combined with Navajo peacemaking, embody the dual concepts of learning and redemption for a spiritually based reintegration into the community. That reintegration involves offenders, victims, their relations, and their communities. It should be the objective of both probation and peacemaking to use education and rehabilitation to address offenders and their conduct. This policy is designed to consolidate the functions of the Probation Services Division and the Peacemaker Division of the judicial branch of the Navajo Nation to offer healing and community justice. This policy will use the hózhǫ́ǫ́jí (peace way) principles and the procedures of peacemaking and *hashkéji* (harsh, or war, way) methods of probation for a balanced approach to dealing with offending and the harm caused to victims of crime.

1. Findings

a. *The nature of crime in the Navajo Nation.* Court statistics show that the Navajo Nation courts are dealing with increased levels of violent crime, including assaults and batteries, DWI (which often causes serious injuries), crimes against the family, and crimes against the public order, involving family violence and fights at public events. Gang violence recently emerged as a serious public safety issue, and the courts are beginning to see gang-related violent crimes. Family violence is a major and serious social problem.

b. *Alcohol-related crime.* Studies of Navajo criminal activity state that violent crime exists primarily within the family, and it is most often alcohol related. Drug-related crime is also a problem within the Navajo Nation. There should be a specific program that addresses alcohol- and drug-related crime, with progressive measures to treat alcohol and drug dependence.

c. *Lack of jail space.* At present, there is jail space for only 237 (164 male and 73 female) inmates throughout the Navajo Nation, including space for both pretrial detention and post-conviction incarceration.[17]

d. *Community sentencing.* The only alternative available to jailing is an enhanced use of community sentencing strategies.

e. *Victim's rights and offender competence.* Modern sentencing practice instructs that courts should do more to ensure victim rights and work to empower offenders by giving them competence to address personal shortcomings and develop skills to abandon offending.

f. *Cycle of violence.* Studies show that children who are abused or neglected are equally likely to enter the cycle of violence as teens and then go on to offend as adults. Sentencing and court policies should address the earliest effective intervention possible to address children as victims of crime and as later offenders. The same principles hold true for sexual offenses, when victims can become sexual predators.

g. *Community justice.* Given the geographic expanse of the Navajo Nation and limited law enforcement and justice resources, modern justice trends, and the principles of Navajo common law, the courts should work to empower communities by giving them the capacity to become directly involved with justice programs.

h. *Individual and family responsibility.* Sentencing policies and criminal justice procedure should be designed to promote individual and family responsibility rather than police or social work models, in which outsiders assume responsibility to control individual behavior.

i. *Principles of Navajo common law.* Navajo common law anticipated many of the foregoing findings, which are the product of contemporary justice research, long ago. Navajo common law process, which involved families, was designed to correct the offender's action and not the offender; ensure victim compensation (in nalyeeh); promote individual responsibilities of the family, clan, and community; and promote community stability.

The policy incorporates both modern justice principles and Navajo common law.

2. Authority

This policy is promulgated by the chief justice of the Navajo Nation as an interpretive policy pursuant to 7 NCC § 371 (1995) and the collegial authority of the Judicial Conference of the Navajo Nation.

3. Purposes

The policy is designed to merge the functions of the Probation Services and Peacemaking divisions of the courts of the Navajo Nation to better address adult and juvenile offenses by a system of diversion into peacemaking, with support and supervision services in probation. The policy is designed to improve the community sentencing and diversion capabilities of the courts of the Navajo Nation and involve communities in justice process. This policy also incorporates principles of Navajo common law for a more comprehensive methodology to deal with crime and violence.

4. Relation to Other Statutes, Rules, or Policies

This policy uses the uniform sentencing policy of the courts of the Navajo Nation (Navajo Nation Judicial Conference Resolution No. JB-AU-03-94, August 13, 1994), the rules and policies of the Peacemaker Division, and the standard operating procedures of the Probation Services Division.

5. Organization

a. *No change in structure.* The Peacemaker and Probation Services divisions remain as separate administrative divisions of the judicial branch of the Navajo Nation. This policy addresses a merger of the functions of the two divisions.

b. *Coordination.* The directors of the Peacemaker and Probation Services divisions (chief probation officer) shall coordinate the activities of each division in accordance with these policies, and peacemaker liaisons, probation officers, and other court personnel will use this policy in accordance with its spirit and purposes.

c. *Other personnel.* Subject to the availability of funds, there will be a program director and judicial district healing and community justice coordinators to implement this policy. The program director shall be under the supervision of the chief justice of the Navajo Nation, and the healing and community justice coordinators shall be under the supervision of the court administrator of the assigned judicial district.

6. Scope of Program

This policy will apply to adult criminal cases in district court and to delinquency cases in the family court division. In other actions involving children or family violence, this policy may be used when appropriate.

7. Points of Diversion

a. *Diversion principles.* This policy is premised on the concept that the courts can effectively address offending and social disruption by the diversion of cases into peacemaking, with the support of the probation function. It also uses the concept of making contracts or agreements with offenders, developed in peacemaking, and supervised in probation, with the family as a "traditional probation officer."

b. *The diversion points.* The specific times of diversion include (1) prior to the filing of a charge (deferred prosecution); (2) at the time of arraignment or initial appearance, without plea or upon a plea of guilty, not guilty, or no contest; (3) prior to the imposition of a sentence; or (4) following the imposition of a sentence.

c. *No admission to guilt required.* A defendant may choose to withhold a plea pending diversion or to plead not guilty or no contest.[18] However, an eligible defendant must accept responsibility for the act that underlies the charge and its effects. Such an acceptance of responsibility shall not constitute an admission against interest. Eligible defendants shall have the right to be protected from self-incrimination and shall have use immunity for any fact or matter related in peacemaking.

8. The Decision to Divert a Case into This Program

a. *Deferred prosecution.* A case may be diverted into this program with the approval of the presiding judge of the judicial district with jurisdiction, subject to the availability of resources for the given case and eligibility under this policy.

b. *Arraignment or initial appearance.* The presiding judge may make a diversion into this program at the time of arraignment or initial appearance, subject to eligibility as stated in this policy.

c. *Pre-sentence diversion.* The presiding judge may make a diversion for the purposes of recommending a sentence following diversion for a reasonable period of time.

d. *Post-sentence diversion.* The presiding judge may make a diversion into this program on probation, suspended imposition of sentence, suspended execution of sentence, or to assist the defendant to comply with the court's conditions of sentence.

9. Conditions of Eligibility

a. *Participation not a right.* Participation in this program is a privilege and not a right. This program is designed for defendants or juveniles who are found to be a good risk for rehabilitation. To avoid straining the program, the court has the discretion to use this program in a limited number of cases.

b. *Waiver of speedy trial rights.* An eligible defendant must waive the right to a speedy trial for the duration of the diversion program.

c. *Alcohol- and drug-related offense.* The offense for which the eligible defendant is charged must be related to the use of alcohol or drugs, or the defendant must be alcohol or drug dependent.

d. *Restitution and nalyeeh.* The defendant must make the commitment to make restitution to any individual or entity injured by the underlying act for which the defendant is charged, and the defendant must produce family members or sureties to ensure that agreed compensation is actually paid.

e. *Family involvement.* The defendant must assure the court that members of his or her family will commit themselves to the program's process, including peacemaking, probation, cooperation with treatment or service providers, and all other aspects of the program. The defendant must show the presence of a family or other support group.

f. *Cooperation.* A defendant must show a willingness to fully cooperate with all aspects of the diversion and comply with all conditions made by the court, peacemaking, probation officer, treatment program, or other relevant agency. The cooperation must be substantial and done in good faith.

g. *Nature of the offense.* Diversion may be made without regard to the nature of the offense; however, the nature and frequency of prior offenses may be considered to assess the likelihood of success in diversion. Diversion may be made irrespective of the views of a victim as long as victim compensation is adequately addressed.

h. *Payment of fees.* The defendant and the defendant's family must pay all fees for peacemaking, treatment, or other services.

i. *Other conditions.* The court or the program may establish other conditions of eligibility, which may arise from time to time or which may be suited to the individual case.

j. *Police report.* When possible, the defendant's police report or other information should be obtained to assess the nature of the offense.

k. *Notification of prosecutor.* When possible, the assigned prosecutor should be consulted on the eligibility and suitability of the defendant or the case for the program.

l. *Terminology.* A defendant who successfully enters this program will be called a "participant."

10. The Diversion Decision

Upon the recommendation of the program that an individual is a successful participant, the court may enter a diversion order with such terms and conditions as are suitable to the case, including standard conditions of probation applied to the diversion, acceptance of the waiver of the right to a speedy trial, and the time period for the diversion. Diversions may be extended from time to time when a treatment or rehabilitation program recommends that such an extension is necessary to complete a treatment program. The time and conditions of diversion should be designed to take maximum advantage of available treatment and support services.

11. Peacemaking Process

Upon diversion, the participant will be immediately referred to the Peacemaker Division for assignment to a peacemaker.

a. *Peacemaking.* The peacemaking session must involve the participant, the participant's family or support group members, any injured and that injured's family or support group, and any other person whose presence is necessary or useful for the process. The peacemaking session may include treatment professionals or service program personnel.

b. *Agreement.* Upon the completion of an agreement by consensus in peacemaking, the agreement will be reduced to writing and signed by the participant and any person who will take responsibility for the participant's actions (e.g., the payment of restitution, fees, participation in a program, undertaking certain actions, or refraining from certain conduct).

c. *Family commitment.* A key to the success of peacemaking agreements is the willing participation of a participant's family members or support group to assist the participant and ensure that he or she complies with the conditions of the agreement reached in peacemaking. Such individuals must commit themselves to cooperate fully with the peacemaker, the probation officer, and treatment or service program personnel. That includes, when necessary, reporting any breach of the agreement or any new offense to the appropriate personnel.

d. *Injured persons.* Any individual who is injured by an act of the participant may not be compelled to participate in peacemaking if that person does not so desire. However, any injured person may send a representative to peacemaking to speak for him or her. There may be long-term communications with the injured person as part of the peacemaking process (i.e., "shuttle diplomacy").

e. *Court endorsement of the agreement.* The court may reserve the discretion to approve any or all agreements that result from peacemaking or to defer to the program for approval. The peacemaker may consult with the court, a probation officer, or a treatment or service program professional, or obtain other assistance in making the agreement final.

12. Probation Officer Responsibilities

a. *Receipt and review of peacemaking agreement or court order.* The probation officer must be provided a copy of the peacemaking agreement or court order for review. The probation officer may make suggestions for additional conditions, and standard conditions of probation will apply to the participants.

b. *Counseling.* The probation officer will then review the agreement with the participant to ensure that he or she understands the terms of the agreement and knows what terms and conditions must be followed. The counseling session can include the participant's family or support group.

c. *Monitoring.* The probation officer will monitor compliance with the peacemaking agreement.

d. *Case conferences.* The probation officer may hold case conferences with the peacemaker, treatment or service program personnel, the presiding judge, and others to discuss the progress of the diversion and the success of the participant.

e. *New offense or violation of conditions.* The probation officer may, upon consultation with the peacemaker or program personnel, report any new offense or material violation of terms and conditions to the court for a new prosecution or termination of the participant from the program. The probation officer must reasonably determine that the diversion is an unredeemable failure or that it is in the interests of public safety or substantial justice to terminate the participant from the program. Upon termination, the participant may be prosecuted for the original offense, prosecuted for a new offense, sentenced, or committed to the execution of any prior sentence. The participant's noncooperation or noncompliance may be taken into consideration in sentencing.

f. *Role of community justice coordinator.* When there is funding for the position, a district community justice coordinator will perform the functions of this position or be responsible for the oversight of the diversion process.

13. Court Oversight

In the discretion of the court, the presiding judge may require periodic reports from the peacemaker or probation officer on the progress of a participant and compliance with the court's orders or terms and conditions of the program, and the court may conduct periodic case review meetings with the participant, support staff, or others. The court may also conduct periodic reviews on the record.

14. Sharing of Information

Information shall be freely shared among the court, peacemakers, probation officers, treatment and service programs, and other relevant agencies, provided, however, no information developed during the course of the program be used as evidence against a participant in any future court proceeding or prosecution other than the fact of noncompliance with the terms and conditions of this program. No information shall be provided to any police officer, prosecutor, or state or federal law enforcement officer without the specific leave of the presiding judge. Any person who violates this section should be immediately excluded from the Navajo Nation for contempt of court if that person is not a Navajo, or charged with contempt of court if that person is a Navajo.

15. Administrative Subpoenas

Any peacemaker, probation officer, or community justice coordinator may apply to the clerk of court and receive a subpoena to compel the attendance of persons to peacemaking or a session with a probation officer or to compel the production of documents or things.

Notes

This chapter is an edited version of Robert Yazzie and James W. Zion's "'Slay the Monsters': Peacemaker Court and Violence Control Plans for the Navajo Nation," in *Popular Justice and Community Regeneration,* edited by Kayleen Hazlehurst, 67–87 (Westport, Conn: Praeger, 1995), reprinted by permission of Praeger and the authors; and Navajo Nation Judicial Branch, *Healing and Community Justice Policy* (Window Rock: Judicial Branch, n. d.), reprinted with permission of the author.

1. This study of the scientific aspects of violence reports and builds upon several twentieth-century studies, including the National Advisory Commission on Civil Disorders (1967), the National Commission on the Causes and Prevention of Violence (1968), the Commission on Obscenity and Pornography (1968), and the Scientific Advisory Committee on Television and Social Behavior (1969).

2. Public order offenses include public intoxication and disorderly conduct; offenses against persons include assault, aggravated assault (with a weapon), battery, and aggravated battery; and offenses against the family are most commonly incest and child sexual abuse. These violent crime figures do not show the extent of violence and criminal conduct in the Navajo Nation. They do not address issues such as policing in large rural areas or prosecutorial discretion in light of overcrowded jails. They do show the problems presented to the courts.

3. This is a serious issue, aside from the case statistics. Studies of death in New Mexico show that excessive cold, exposure, or neglect was the second leading cause of death from unintentional injury in New Mexico and the third leading cause for Indian women. Death from exposure and excessive cold "occurs almost exclusively among American Indians" (Sewell et al. 1993, 127–28). One study states that American Indians are 22 percent more likely to die from exposure, with risk factors of alcohol and remote geographic locations. See Sewell et al. (1993).

4. The literature consistently shows this characterization of Navajo crime. See Ferguson (1968); Lubben (1975); Levy, Kunitz, and Everett (1969); Jensen, Stauss, and Harris (1977); and May (1982).

5. MacAndrew and Edgerton (1969) apply the theory of tolerance to drunken behavior to the stereotype "Indians can't hold their liquor" and conclude that Indian drinking patterns are associated with stereotypical perceptions (pages 136–64).

6. The greatest category of child neglect may be "dumping" children on grandparents or leaving them alone while on drinking bouts. Physical abuse and sexual abuse is comparatively minor in relation to neglect, which is associated with parental alcohol use.

7. Most often, Indian Child Welfare Act (ICWA) cases involve children outside the territorial jurisdiction of the Navajo Nation. The grounds for ICWA cases involve the same conduct as is addressed in child abuse and neglect and termination of parental rights cases.

8. Probate, quiet title, and validation of marriage actions most often involve disputes over property, usually grazing permits and land leases. How they are handled affects the caseload figures for criminal cases, particularly assaults, and the peacemaker court. Navajos are very adept in selecting the legal tool that is most effective for reinforcing their position in a property dispute.

9. The Navajo Peacemaker Court had one case where a wife resorted to violence to get payments from her husband; she was driven to frustration and assault by her inability to get a court order to require maintenance. A restraining order against her in domestic violence proceedings was resolved in the peacemaker court, which helped the woman negotiate a maintenance agreement from her husband—what she wanted in the first place.

10. See the summary of recommendations of the National Research Council (1993). They include (1) problem-solving initiatives, (2) modifying and expanding violence measurement systems, (3) research projects, and (4) a multicommunity research program. The recommendations require a great deal of planning and coordination of existing programs, initiatives the Navajo Nation should adopt.

11. Leonardo Boff (1982) develops this theory for use in modern times in *St. Francis: A Model for Human Liberation.* He says that an individual can be "poor" in the sense of not being able to participate in public affairs or speak out against felt injustices, and there is hence a general obligation to support poor and oppressed peoples. Boff is a leading proponent of liberation theology and a "preferential option for the poor" as well as Indian issues.

12. A divorce filing fee is waived, but not bankruptcy fees or fees in seeking judicial review of an administrative ruling reducing payments. *Boddie v. Connecticut,* 401 U.S. 371 (1971); *United States v. Kras,* 409 U.S. 434 (1973); and *Ortwein v. Schwab,* 410 U.S. 371 (1973).

13. The leading modern case in point involved a North Dakota statute that required Indian nations to waive sovereign immunity as a condition for bringing a civil suit in that state's courts. *Three Affiliated Tribes of Ft. Berthold Reservation v. Wold Engineering,* 90 L. Ed. 2d 881 (1986).

14. See Commission on Tribal Court Performance Standards (1990), standards 1.1 (open proceedings), 1.2 (adequate facilities), 1.3 (effective participation), 1.4 (courtesy, responsiveness, and respect) and 1.5 (affordability).

15. That struggle continues up to these days, and modern Spanish republics in the Americas still attempt to frame Indian affairs policies. In Mexico, there are armed Indian uprisings as a result of ignoring Indian nation government.

16. See also Parry (1990), MacLachlan (1988), Haring (1975), and Simpson (1982).

17. Chinle, 31 (27 male, 4 female); Crownpoint, 37 (23 male, 14 female); Shiprock, 40 (32 male, 8 female); Tuba City, 34 (26 male, 8 female); and Window Rock, 95 (56 male, 39 female). Source: Department of Corrections, Navajo Nation Division of Public Safety, January 26, 1998.

18. For the purposes of this policy, the term "defendant" includes respondents in delinquency or other individuals who are the subject of court process for their actions.

References

Antieau, Chester James. 1969. *Modern Constitutional Law.* Rochester, N.Y.: Lawyers Co-Operative Publishing Company.

Barsh, Russel Lawrence, and J. Youngblood. 1976. Tribal Courts, the Model Code, and the Police Idea in American Indian Policy. In *American Indians and the Law,* ed. Lawrence Rosen, 25–60. New Brunswick, N.J.: Transaction.

Berman, Harold J. 1983. *Law and Revolution: The Formation of the Western Legal Tradition.* Cambridge, Mass: Harvard University Press.

BIA Says Tribal Self-Determination and Tribal Courts Grants Are "No Longer a High Priority." 1993. *Tribal Court Record* 6 (2): 9.

Boff, Leonardo. 1982. *Saint Francis: A Model for Human Liberation [São Francisco de Assis].* Trans. John W. Diercksmeier. New York: Crossroad.

Borah, Woodrow W. 1983. *Justice by Insurance: the General Indian Court of Colonial Mexico and the Legal Aides of the Half-real.* Berkeley: University of California Press.

Commission on Tribal Court Performance Standards. 1990. *Trial Court Performance Standards with Commentary.* Williamsburg, Va.: National Center for State Courts.

Fahey, John. 1975. Native American Justice: The Courts of the Navajo Nation. *Judicature* 59 (1): 110–17.

Ferguson, Francis N. 1968. Navajo Drinking: Some Tentative Hypotheses. *Human Organization* 27: 159–67.

Gibbs, Nancy, and James Carney. 1993. Laying Down the Law. *Time* 142, no. 8 (August 23): 22–23.

Haring, C. H. 1975. *The Spanish Empire in America.* San Diego: Harvest/HBJ.

Jensen, Gary F., Joseph H. Stauss, and V. H. Harris. 1977. Crime, Delinquency, and the American Indian. *Human Organization* 36 (3): 252–57.

Judicial Branch of the Navajo Nation. n. d. Annual Case Activity Report, April 1, 1992, to March 31, 1993.

Kaplan, Bert, and Dale Johnson. 1964. The Social Meaning of Navaho Psychopathology and Psychotherapy. In *Magic, Faith and Healing: Studies in Primitive Psychiatry Today,* ed. Ari Kiev, 203–29. New York: Free Press of Glencoe.

Levy, Jerrold E., Stephen J. Kunitz, and Michael Everett. 1969. Navajo Criminal Homicide. *Southwestern Journal of Anthropology* 25: 124–52.

Lubben, Ralph A. 1975. Anglo Law and Navajo Behavior. *Kiva* 29 (3): 60–75.

MacAndrew, Craig, and Robert B. Edgerton. 1969. *Drunken Comportment: A Social Explanation.* Chicago: Aldine.

MacLachlan, Colin M. 1988. *Spain's Empire in the New World: The Role of Ideas in Institutional and Social Change.* Berkeley: University of California Press.

May, Philip A. 1982. Contemporary Crime and the American Indian: A Survey and Analysis of the Literature. *The Plains Anthropologist* 27: 225–38.

Nader, Laura. 1980. Old Solutions for Old Problems. In *No Access to Law: Alternative to the American Judicial System,* ed. Laura Nader, 57–110. New York: Academy Press.

National Minority Advisory Council on Criminal Justice. 1982 (January). *The Inequality of Justice: A Report on Crime and the Administration of Justice in the Minority Community.* Washington, D.C.: Government Printing Office.

National Research Council. 1993. *Understanding and Preventing Violence.* Washington: National Academy Press.

Notestein, Wallace. 1962. *The English People on the Eve of Colonization, 1603–1630.* New York: Harper. (Orig. pub. 1954.)

Parry, J. G. 1990. *The Spanish Seaborne Empire: The History of Human Society.* New York: Knopf. (Orig. pub. 1966.)

Sewell, C. Mack., Thomas M. Becker, Charles L. Wiggins, Charles R. Keys, and Jonathan Samet. 1993. Injury Mortality. In *Racial and Ethnic Patterns of Mortality in New Mexico,* ed. Thomas M. Becker et al., 118–31. Albuquerque: University of New Mexico.

Simpson, Lesley Byrd. 1982. *The Encomienda in New Spain: The Beginning of Spanish Mexico.* Berkeley: University of California Press.

Singer, Geraldine. 1993. Memorandum on Senate Committee on Indian Affairs Hearing on P.L. 101-630, the Indian Child Protection and Family Violence Prevention Services Act, and Other Indian Child Abuse Issues, October 28, 1993.

Topper, Martin D. 1980. Drinking as an Expression of Status: Navajo Male Adolescents. In *Drinking Behavior among Southwestern Indians,* ed. Jack O. Waddell and Michael W. Everett, 103–47. Tucson: University of Arizona Press.

United States Commission on Civil Rights. 1991. *Indian Civil Rights Act.* Washington, D.C.: U.S. Commission on Civil Rights.

Waddell, Jack O., and Michael W. Everett, eds. 1980. *Drinking Behavior among Southwestern Indians: An Anthropological Perspective.* Tucson: University of Arizona Press.

12 Epilogue and Dream

A Look Backward and Forward

James W. Zion

"No epilogue, I pray you; for your play needs no excuse. Never excuse; for when the players all are dead, there need none to be blamed."
—Shakespeare, *A Midsummer Night's Dream,* 5.1

This collection of articles on Navajo peacemaking should not require an epilogue because the chapters need no excuse; they speak for themselves. However, examining the broad sweep of the history of American Indians, and particularly looking at failed experiments to "civilize" Indians (such as the General Allotment Act of 1887 and controlled courts of Indian offenses), an epilogue to look at the future, the "dream," of peacemaking is appropriate.

Peacemaking requires a leap of faith for acceptance by those who are used to Western law and adjudication. This book collects over twenty years of observations of Navajo peacemaking. But we must still ask—will peacemaking last into the future, or will it be only a midsummer night's dream?

Reviewing the foundations for a dream of the future is important, because in Navajo linguistics and philosophy, what you dream can become real.

What is this dream?

Chief Justice Yazzie once explained how Navajo healers can look into the future using a multisided crystal. He explained that as you look at each facet of the crystal, as a metaphor for examining problems, you are able to "see" the crystal as a whole—the examination of the elements of a problem carefully combined with stepping back to see it as a whole allows you to look into the future. What facets of peacemaking can we observe today?

Why are some Navajo Nation judges "gatekeepers," and why do some resist peacemaking? We can only speculate. Some Navajos talk about others as being "BIA" thinkers (referring to the regulation of Indian affairs by the Bureau of Indian Affairs), but there are Navajos who are leery of using traditional processes in modern judicial systems out of fear of injuring traditions. There are some, such as Navajo attorney Sarah Foster, who say that they remember peacemaking being done within the family as children, and they would never go to a peacemaker stranger. Some Navajo Nation judges express their feeling that peacemaking should be taken out of the court system and returned to communities. That can be done under the Navajo Nation Local Governance Act of 1998, which provides that one of the powers of the Navajo Nation's chapters is to set up and regulate peacemaking; however, no chapter has exercised that power to date (because of other problems in implementing the act).

When the peacemaking rules were adopted in 1982, they were carefully worded to avoid any attempt to define peacemaking or establish how it would operate. That was partly because of ignorance of what it was, but more important, the rules made a policy choice that an unwritten traditional process should remain unwritten. There is also a growing awareness that since the foundations of peacemaking lie in the Navajo language and base values expressed in Navajo philosophy, it is something more than a *method* of dispute resolution—it is a philosophy of life. A lot of what is being written and said about peacemaking today reinforces that, so part of the dream is reviving the thinking and attitudes of peacemaking in daily Navajo life.

There are two substance and process issues that are in the dreaming stage just now. The first, involving the substance of peacemaking, is an attempt by the judiciary committee of the Navajo Nation Council to get Hózhǫ́ǫ́jí Naat'áanii, the Peacemaker Division, to adopt a "plan of operations" for peacemaking under 2001 legislation that gives a statutory base to the process and the program. Some peacemakers think the move is controversial and may adversely affect their work—some have said that they do not want to give up Zion and McCabe's 1982 *Navajo Peacemaker Court Manual* as the guiding document, although it carefully avoids discussing what the peacemakers are actually doing. Is this affection for the manual because its use has become a "tradition," or is it because the manual avoids telling peacemakers what to do? What makes it more desirable to them? That leads to a subtheme about substance—has peacemaking become overbureaucratized? Aside from those who feel that peacemaking may be damaged if taken out of its original context or that it belongs in families or communities, there are those who express fears that it is being controlled by "Big Navajo" (the slang term for the central government in Window Rock) and that the standards being proposed for adoption by the judiciary committee restrict what peacemakers actually do.

One of the major process issues is the emergence of an identity for peacemakers. That is, as peacemakers do their work, share what they do with others, and talk about who they are and what they do, there is a certain degree of professionalism creeping into peacemaker organization. One of the major policy decisions Chief Justice Yazzie had to make when he was in office was whether to allow or endorse formal peacemaker organizations.

Initially he feared that peacemakers, in formal organizations, would be political and challenge the oversight authority of the judges. Yazzie relented after meetings with peacemakers, and today, they are incorporating by judicial district (with some discussion of a Navajo Nation–wide coalition of local organizations). Thus far the activities of the new corporations have been limited, largely because of the inability to obtain funding for their operations, but there is some potential for their work. For example, in 1998 an organization of peacemakers in the Eastern Agency of the Navajo Nation in New Mexico entered into an agreement with the McKinley County Sheriff's Office to establish a peacemaker's program as part of the county's multi-jurisdictional domestic violence response team so that peacemakers could be used for intervention and counseling in off-reservation domestic violence cases involving Navajos. That shows that peacemaker organizations need not rely upon Navajo Nation funding or bureaucracy to support their work.

The final facet is the problem of the Navajo culture being at a crossroad, the junction where a growing Navajo population that is mobile and passes freely between the rural Navajo Nation and urban centers (as far away as Los Angeles or Chicago) bring more (and sometimes destructive) cultural elements to add to the mix of an integrative Navajo culture that may be changing Navajo society. Navajo society is already experiencing the traumas of language and culture loss. Chief justice Claudeen Bates Arthur took her oath of office in January 2004, and she intentionally focused on the fact that her grandchildren do not speak Navajo, asking for their acceptance. Language and culture loss can be negative, as with its impact on Navajo Nation gangs and crews, many of whose members do not speak Navajo and consider themselves to be only "Indians" (raising fears such as those expressed by Claudeen Bates Arthur as a lawyer of generic "pan-Indianism," with the implication that Navajos will become another American "minority" and fall into the hands of assimiliationists who want to abolish Indian tribes and reservations to promote that process).

The positive side is that Navajo culture has always changed, is ever-changing, and will change in the future. It is a dynamic society that takes the best of what it sees, rejects that which does not work, survives adversity, and adapts to change. We do not "know" how peacemaking worked in prehistoric times, and the conqueror who wrote the history (showing the importance of the Indian "voice" expressed by individuals such as Chief Justice Tom Tso, Chief Justice Robert Yazzie, and Philmer Bluehouse in these pages) did not notice it or record it for the most part. There are only hints of it in the historical literature. Today's version of peacemaking may be a combination of cultural survivals and elements that are inherent in language and traditions. Observers of contemporary young Navajos have reason to be optimistic, because, as Gross noted, many self-identify as "Navajo," and many are proud of their Navajo identity as they accept the modern yet retain a thirst for the traditional.

Navajo peacemaking has entered the mainstream of restorative justice and other humanist initiatives to change the way we look at conflict and dispute and respond to it. Will such movements fade away as fads, or will they become firmly established? There is a growing international ethic that we can construct a better world using consensus, respect, interdependence, and other values that Navajos talk about. Peacemaking should be here to stay.

We who wrote these pages need not excuse what we have done, and we need not give excuses for our play to avoid blame. Surely there have been mistakes along the way—perhaps injuring peacemaking by taking it out of its original context, overbureaucratizing it, or possible dangers of overprofessionalization. Despite any such mistakes, peacemaking is an integral part of Navajo life, and it will continue to be because, as Yazzie said, "life comes from it." The boundaries of peacemaking will be limited by the ability to dream, and dreaming is a Navajo way of bringing reality into existence.

Commentary on the Peacemaking Readings

Marianne O. Nielsen and James W. Zion

In lieu of the impossible task of reprinting in this book every document ever written about peacemaking, we have put together a reading list that contains all book chapters, papers, and scholarly and journalistic articles (as far as we know) about peacemaking. We chose to include a number of readings that provide contextualization for the Navajo Nation courts, Navajo common law, and peacemaking. As we argue in the introduction, it is difficult to understand peacemaking without knowing something about the legal history of the Navajo people, general Native American law, and the history and impact of colonialism. Rather than overwhelm the reader with references, we chose a few that seem most relevant to the chapters. Please note that this list contains the original sources of the reprinted chapters, as do the first notes to those chapters. Some conference papers can be obtained by contacting the editors. If the reader is aware of any additional readings that should be included in this list, please contact us through the University of Arizona Press.

Peacemaking Reading List

Austin, Raymond D. 1992. Incorporating Tribal Customs and Traditions into Tribal Court Decisions. Paper presented at the Federal Bar Association Indian Law Conference, Albuquerque, New Mexico, April 11 (approx.).

———. 1993. Freedom, Responsibility and Duty: ADR and the Navajo Peacemaker Court. *The Judges' Journal* 32 (2): 8–11.

———. n. d. Navajo Common Law Principle and Alternative Dispute Resolution. Unpublished manuscript.

Barker, Michael L. 1989. *Policing in Indian Country.* Guilderland, N.Y.: Harrow and Heston: 119–23.

Barnard, Phyllis E. 1996. Community and Conscience: The Dynamic Challenge of Lawyer's Ethics in Tribal Peacemaking. *University of Toledo Law Review* 27: 821–51.

Barsh, Russel L. 1991. Navajo Tribal Courts, Property and Probate Law, 1940–1972. *Law and Anthropology* 6: 169–95.

Benally, Herbert J. 1987. *Dine' Bo'ohoo'aah Bindii'a*: Navajo Philosophy of Learning. *Dine' Be'iina' Journal* 1 (1): 133–48.

———. 1988. Dine' Philosophy of Learning. *The Journal of Navajo Education* 6 (1): 10–13.

Bielski, Vine. 1995. The Navajo Model. *California Lawyer Magazine,* November, 39.

Bluehouse, Philmer. 1996. The Ceremony of Making Peace: Excerpt from *People of the Seventh Fire,* edited by Dagmar Thorpe. *Native Americas* 13 (3): 54–57.

———. 2003. Is It "Peacemakers Teaching"? or Is It "Teaching Peacemakers"? *Conflict Resolution Quarterly* 20 (4): 495–500.

Bluehouse, Philmer, and James W. Zion. 1993. *Hozhooji Naat'aanii*: The Navajo Justice and Harmony Ceremony. *Mediation Quarterly* 10 (4): 327–37.

Bradford, William C. 2000. Reclaiming Indigenous Legal Autonomy on the Path to Peaceful Coexistence: The Theory, Practice, and Limitations of Tribal Peacemaking in Indian Dispute Resolution. *North Dakota Law Review* 76: 551–604.

———. 2003. "With a Very Great Blame on Our Hearts": Reparations, Reconciliation, and an American Plea for Peace and Justice. *American Indian Law Review* 27: 1.

Brakel, Samuel. 1976. American Indian Tribal Courts: Separate? "Yes," Equal? "Probably Not." *American Bar Association Journal* 62: 1002–6.

Brown, Howard. 2000. The Navajo Nation's Peacemaker Division: An Integrated, Community-Based Dispute Resolution Forum. *American Indian Law Review* 24 (2): 297–308. (Reprinted in 2002, *Dispute Resolution Journal* 57: 42–48, 50.)

Campbell, Murray. 1991. "Taking the Law into Their Own Hands." *The Toronto Globe and Mail,* September 13.

Coker, Donna. 1999. Enhancing Autonomy for Battered Women: Lessons from Navajo Peacemaking. *U.C.L.A. Law Review* 47: 1–111.

Collins, Richard B., Ralph W. Johnson, and Kathy Imig Perkins. 1977. American Indian Courts and Tribal Self-Government. *American Bar Association Journal* 63: 808–15.

Conn, Stephen. 1978. Mid-passage, the Navajo Tribe and Its First Legal Revolution. *American Indian Law Review* 21: 329–70.

Coulter, Robert T. 1978. Indian Conflicts and Nonjudicial Dispute Settlement. *Arbitration Journal* 33: 28–31.

Deloria, Vine, Jr., ed. 1985. *American Indian Policy in the Twentieth Century.* Norman: University of Oklahoma Press.

Deloria, Vine, Jr., and Clifford M. Lytle. 1983. *American Indians, American Justice.* Austin: University of Texas Press.

Driscoll, Lisa. 1993. Tribal Courts—New Mexico's Third Judiciary, Part 3: Navajo Nation. *New Mexico Bar Bulletin* 22 (11): 1, 3–4, 6.

Fahey, Richard P. 1975. Native American Justice: The Courts of the Navajo Nation. *Judicature* 59 (1): 10–17.

Farella, John R. 1984. *The Main Stalk: A Synthesis of Navajo Philosophy.* Tucson: University of Arizona Press.

French, Laurence. 1982. *Indians and Criminal Justice.* Totowa, N.J.: Allenheld Osmun.

Frye, Paul. 1991. Lender Recourse in Indian Country: A Navajo Case Study. *New Mexico Law Review* 21: 275–326.

Goldberg, Carole E. 1997. Overextended Borrowing: Tribal Peacemaking Applied to Non-Indian Disputes. *Washington Law Review* 72: 1003–19.

Gould, Larry A. 1998. Conflicts in Spirituality of the Navajo Police Officer. In *The Refereed Proceeding of the 14th International Congress of the Commission on Folk Law and Legal Pluralism,* edited by Melanie G. Wiber. Conference of the International Union of Anthropological and Ethnological Sciences, Williamsburg, Virginia, July 26–August 1.

———. 1999. The Impact of Working in Two Worlds and Its Effect on Navajo Police Officers. *Journal of Legal Pluralism* 44: 53–71. (This article was also published in *The Refereed Proceeding of the Eleventh International Congress of the Commission on Folk Law and Legal Pluralism,* ed. Keebet von Benda-Beckmann and Harald W. Finkler, 348–57. Ottawa, ON: Department of Indian Affairs).

———. 2002. Indigenous People Policing Indigenous People: The Potential Psychological and Cultural Costs. *The Social Science Journal* 39 (2): 171–88.

Griggs, Thelma Butts. 1995. "The Navajo Peacemaker Court El Jazgado del Obrador de la Paz: Mediacion en la Nacion de los Navajos." In *Mediacion: Una Alternative Extrajoridica,* ed. Colegio Oficial De Psicologos, 69–78. Madrid: Colegio Oficial De Psicologos.

Grohowski, Laura. 1995. Cognitive-Affective Model of Reconciliation: Navajo Family in Peacemaker Ceremony. Master's thesis, Antioch University of Ohio.

Hagan, William T. 1966. *Indian Police and Judges.* New Haven, Conn.: Yale University Press.

Haile, Berard. 1938. Navajo Chantways and Ceremonials. *American Anthropologist* 40 (14): 639–52.

———. 1943 [reprinted 1975]. *Soul Concepts of the Navaho.* St. Michaels, Ariz.: St. Michaels Press.

Innes, Stephanie. 1995. Peace, Not Punishment: Focus of Navajo System. *Arizona Daily Sun,* October 21.

Johnson, William Bluehouse. 1990. Navajo Peacemaker Court: Impact and Efficacy of Traditional Dispute Resolution in the Modern Setting. Doctor of Law Thesis, University of New Mexico School of Law.

Kickingbird, Kirke. 1990. In Our Image . . . After Our Likeness: The Drive for Assimilation. *American Criminal Law Review* 13: 675–700.

Kluckhohn, Clyde. 1968. The Philosophy of the Navajo Indians. In *Readings in Anthropology,* 2nd ed., ed. Morton H. Fried. New York: Crowell. [Orig. pub. 1949. In *Ideo-*

logical Differences and World Order, ed. F. S. C. Northrop, 356–84. New Haven, Conn.: Yale University Press.]

Ladd, John. 1957. *Structure of a Moral Code: A Philosophical Analysis of Ethical Discourse Applied to the Ethics of the Navajo Indians.* Cambridge, Mass.: Harvard University Press.

Lednicer, Oliver. 1959. Peacemaker Court in New York State. *New York University Intramural Law Review* 14: 188–95.

LeResche, Diane. 1993a. Editors' Notes. *Mediation Quarterly* 10: 321–25.

———. 1993b. There Are at Least Four Reasons for Revitalizing Tribal Peacemaking (TPM). *Indian Law Support Center Reporter* 16 (1): 1–6.

Lopez, L. 1984. Taking Care of Their Own: Navajos Dispense Traditional Justice to Retain Harmony. *Arizona Republic,* August 6.

Lowery, Daniel L. 1993. Developing a Tribal Common Law Jurisprudence: The Navajo Experience, 1969–1992. *American Indian Law Review* 18: 379–439.

McCold, Paul. 2000. Overview of Mediation, Conferencing, and Circles. Paper presented to the Tenth United Nations Congress on Crime Prevention and the Treatment of Offenders, Vienna, April 10–17.

Melton, Ada Pecos. 1995. Indigenous Justice Systems and Tribal Society. *Judicature* 79 (3): 126–33.

Meyer, Jon'a. 1998a. History Repeats Itself: Restorative Justice in Native American Communities. *Journal of Contemporary Criminal Justice* 14: 42–57.

———. 1998b. Peacemaking as Restorative Routine. *The Forum* 6 (2): 16–17.

———. 2001. The Hunt for Leges Henrici and Restorative Justice, Navajo Style. *The Forum* 9 (1): 1–5.

———. 2002a. It Is a Gift from the Creator to Keep Us in Harmony: Original (Versus Alternative) Dispute Resolution on the Navajo Nation. *International Journal of Public Administration* 25: 1379–1401.

———. 2002b. Restoration and the Criminal Justice System. In *Controversies in Victimology,* ed. L. J. Moriarty, 81–90. Cincinnati, Ohio: Anderson.

Meyer, Jon'a, and Richard Paul. 1999. Fighting a New Nayee: Domestic Violence on the Navajo Reservation. *The Forum* 7 (2): 4–7.

Meyer, Jon'a, and James W. Zion. 2000. Old Solutions to New Problems: Crime Control in the Navajo Nation. In *Crime and Crime Control,* ed. Gregg Barak, 103–115. Westport, Conn.: Greenwood Press.

Mirsky, Laura. 2004. Restorative Justice Practices of Native American, First Nation and Other Indigenous People of North America: Part One. International Institute for Restorative Practices, http://iirp.org/library/natjust1.html (accessed May 18, 2004).

Morris, Loretta. 2001. Conflict Resolution. Paper presented to the Commission on Navajo Government Development and Training Committee of the Navajo Nation Bar Association.

Navajo Nation, Division of Community Development. 1995. *Navajo Nation Profile* (Spring): 1–6.

Navajo Nation, Judicial Branch. n. d. Judicial Branch of the Navajo Nation [brochure]. Window Rock, Ariz.: Judicial Branch.

Nielsen, Marianne O. 1996a. A Comparison of Developmental Ideologies: Navajo Peacemaker and Canadian Native Justice Committees. In *Restorative Justice: International Perspectives,* ed. Burt Galaway and Joe Hudson, 207–23. Monsey, N.Y.: Criminal Justice Press.

———. 1996b. Indigenization versus Self-Determination: The Role of Traditionally Based Native Criminal Justice Services in the Development of Native Self-Government in Canada and the United States. Paper presented at the Western Social Sciences Association Annual Meeting, Reno, Nevada, April 17–20.

————. 1997. The Re-emergence of Indigenous Social Control Mechanisms: Traditional Contextualization for Two Justice Programs. Paper presented at the Western Society of Criminology Annual Meeting. Honolulu, Hawaii, February 27–March 2.

————. 1998. A Comparison of Canadian Native Youth Justice Committees and Navajo Peacemakers: A Summary of Results. *Journal of Contemporary Criminal Justice* 14 (1): 6–25.

————. 1999. Navajo Nation Courts, Peacemaking, and Restorative Justice Issues. *Journal of Legal Pluralism* 44: 105–26.

————. 2000a. The Impact of Colonialism on Leadership in Indigenous-Operated Criminal Justice Organizations: Some Preliminary Thoughts. CINSA Conference Proceedings. School of Native Studies, University of Alberta, Canada [CD-ROM].

————. 2000b. Stolen Land, Stolen Lives: Native Americans and the Criminal Justice System. In *Investigating Difference: Human and Cultural Relations in Criminal Justice,* ed. the CJ Collective, 47–58. Needham Heights: Allyn and Bacon.

————. 2001a. A Comparison of the Community Roles of Indigenous Operated Criminal Justice Organizations in Canada, the USA and Australia. Paper presented at the Modern Native America Conference, Flagstaff, Arizona, August 15–17. Published 2004: *American Indian Culture and Resource Journal* 28:3: 57–75.

————. 2001b. Organizational Strategies for Overcoming the Impact of Racism on Indigenous Justice Organizations. Indigenous Peoples and Racism: Conference of Indigenous Peoples of Australia, New Zealand, Canada, Hawaii and the United States (Regional Meeting for the United Nations World Conference Against Racism, Racial Discrimination, Xenophobia and Related Intolerance), Sydney, Australia, February 20–22. Published 2003: *International Journal of Comparative Criminology* 3(2): 191–221.

————. 2003. The Role of Indigenous-Operated Criminal Justice Organizations in Political Activism in Australia, Canada, New Zealand and the USA. Paper presented at the American Society of Criminology Conference, Denver, Colorado, November 19–22.

Nielsen, Marianne O., and Larry A. Gould. 2003. Developing the Interface between the Navajo Nation Police and Navajo Nation Peacemaking. *Police Practice and Research* 4 (4): 429–43.

Nielsen, Marianne O., and Lindsay Redpath. 2000. Working in Two Worlds: The Interface Between Indigenization and Homogeneity in Indigenous Criminal Justice Service Organizations. Paper presented at the Modern Native America Conference, Flagstaff, Arizona, August 16–18.

Norrell, Brenda. 1996. Federal Court System Alien to American Indians. *Indian Country Today,* February 12–19.

O'Connor, Sandra Day, 1996. Lessons from the Third Sovereign: Indian Tribal Courts. *Tribal Court Reporter* 9 (1): 12–14.

Peacemaker Court. *Independent* [Gallup, New Mexico], July 27, 1991.

Peacemaker Initiative Works with Troubled Youth. 1996. *Indian Country Today,* August 26–September 2.

The People's Law Conference, Canada. 1983. *The People's Law: What Canadians Want from the Law.* Ottawa, ON: The People's Law Conference.

Pinto, Jeanmarie. 1998. Original Dispute Resolution: An Analysis of the Peacemaker System of the Navajo Nation. Master's thesis, Nova Southeastern University, Ft. Lauderdale, Florida.

Pommersheim, Frank. 1995. *Braid of Feathers: American Indian Life and Contemporary Tribal Life*. Berkeley: University of California Press.

Porter, R. B. 1997. Strengthening Tribal Sovereignty through Peacemaking: How the Anglo-American Legal Tradition Destroys Indigenous Societies. *Columbia Human Rights Law Review* 28: 235–305.

Price, Richard T., and Cynthia Dunnigan. 1995. *Toward an Understanding of Aboriginal Peacemaking*. Victoria, B.C.: UVic Institute for Dispute Resolution.

Ramo, Roberta C. 1995. Lawyers as Peacemakers: Our Navajo Peers Could Teach Us a Thing or Two about Conflict Resolution. *American Bar Association Journal* 81: 6.

Reichard, Gladys A. 1977. *Navajo Religion: A Study of Symbolism*. Princeton, N.J.: Princeton University Press. [Revised edition 1983, Tucson: University of Arizona Press.]

Reno, Janet. 1999. Remarks of Honorable Janet Reno, Attorney General, to the Department of the Navy, Office of General Counsel Conference, Arlington, Virginia, May 6.

Roche, Declan. 2003a. *Accountability in Restorative Justice*. Oxford: Oxford University Press.

Roche, Declan, ed. 2003b. *Restorative Justice*. Burlington, Vt.: Ashgate.

Royal Commission on Aboriginal People. 1996. The United States Tribal Court Experience, Past and Present. In *Bridging the Cultural Divide: Report on Aboriginal People and Criminal Justice in Canada*, 180–91. Ottawa, ON: Royal Commission on Aboriginal People.

Roybal, G. E. 1998. Mediation, Street Courts Making Headway. *Arizona Daily Sun*, October 12.

Rubin, H. Ted. 1990. Tribal Courts and State Courts: Disputed Civil Jurisdiction Concerns and Steps Toward Resolution. *State Court Journal* (Spring): 9–15.

Scala, L. S., 1998. Yazzie Proposes Justice Reform Plan. *Navajo-Hopi Observer*, May 13.

Scow, Alfred J. N. d. A Brief Visit to the Navajo Justice System. Unpublished paper.

Sedillo Lopez, Antoinette. 2000. Evolving Indigenous Law: Navajo Marriage, Cultural Traditions and Modern Challenges. *Arizona Journal of International and Comparative Law* 17 (2): 283–307.

Seidschlaw, Kurt D. 1997. Peacemaking and Mediation. Paper presented at the Western Social Sciences Association Annual Meeting, Albuquerque, New Mexico, April 23–26.

Shepardson, Mary. 1962. Value Theory in the Prediction of Political Behavior: The Navajo Case. *American Anthropologist* 64: 742–49.

———. 1963. *Navajo Ways in Government: A Study in Political Process*. Vol. 65 (3), Part 2. Washington, D.C.: American Anthropological Association

———. 1965. Problems of the Navajo Tribal Courts in Transition. *Human Organization* 24 (3): 250–53.

Sitts, Richard. 1991. Navajo Peacemaking Makes a Comeback. *Independent* [Gallup, New Mexico], July 27.

Sullivan, Dennis. 2002. Navajo Peacemaking History, Development and Possibilities for Adjudication-Based Systems of Justice: An Interview with James Zion. *Contemporary Justice Review* 5 (2): 167–88.

Sullivan, Dennis, and Larry Tifft. 1997. Criminology as Peacemaking: A Peace-Oriented Perspective on Crime, Punishment and Justice That Takes into Account the Needs of All. *The Justice Professional* 11: 5–34.

———. 2001. Navajo Peacemaking. In *Restorative Justice: Healing the Foundations of Our Everyday Lives,* ed. Dennis Sullivan and Larry Tifft, 52–59. Monsey, N.Y.: Willow Tree Press.

Taraschi, Shruti Gola. 1998. Peacemaking Criminology and Aboriginal Justice Initiatives as a Revitalization of Justice. *Contemporary Justice Review* 1 (1): 103–21.

Toledo, Irene. 2000. Tribal Justice: The Practice and Development of American Indian Courts. Paper presented to Shaking the Foundations 2000 Conference, Stanford University School of Law, November 8–10.

———. 2001. Peacemaking: Applications in Family Court. Paper presented to the Lodestar Symposium 2001, Phoenix College, Phoenix, Arizona, March 23–24.

Tso, Tom. 1986. The Tribal Court Survives in America. *Judges' Journal* 25: 22–25, 52–56.

———. 1989a. The Navajo Concept of Justice. Paper presented at the American Association of Law Schools Conference, New Orleans, Louisiana, August 4 (approx.).

———. 1989b. The Process of Decision Making in Navajo Tribal Courts. *Arizona Law Review* 31 (2): 225–35.

———. 1992a. Looking to the Future: An Interview with the Retiring Chief Justice of the Navajo Nation. *Arizona Attorney* (May): 9–10.

———. 1992b. Moral Principles, Traditions and Fairness in the *Navajo Nation Code of Judicial Conduct. Judicature* 76 (1): 15–21.

U.S. Department of Justice, Bureau of Justice Statistics. 1999. *American Indians and Crime.* Washington, DC: U.S. Department of Justice (NCJ 173386).

Van Valkenburgh, Richard. 1936. Navajo Common Law I: Notes on Political Organizations, Property and Inheritance. *Museum Notes* [Museum of Northern Arizona] 9 (4): 17–22.

———. 1937. Navajo Common Law II: Navajo Law and Justice. *Museum Notes* [Museum of Northern Arizona] 9 (10): 51–54.

———. 1938. Navajo Common Law III: Etiquette-Hospitality-Justice. *Museum Notes* [Museum of Northern Arizona] 10 (12): 37–45.

———. 1945. The Government of the Navajos. *Arizona Quarterly* 1: 63–73.

Vicenti, Dan, Leonard B. Jimson, Stephen Conn, and M. J. L. Kellogg. 1972. *The Law of the People—Dine' Bibee Haz'a'anii: A Bicultural Approach to Legal Education for Navajo Students.* Vol. 2. Ramah, N.Mex.: Ramah Navajo High School Press.

White, Richard. 1983. *The Roots of Dependency: Subsistence, Environment, and Social Change among the Choctaws, Pawnees, and Navajos.* Lincoln: University of Nebraska Press.

Wilkins, David E. 1987. *Dine'Bebeehaz'aahii: A Handbook of Navajo Government.* Tsaile, Ariz.: Navajo Community College Press.

———. 1999. *The Navajo Political Experience.* Tsaile, Ariz.: Dine' College Press.

Witherspoon, Gary. 1975. *Navajo Kinship and Marriage.* Chicago: University of Chicago Press.

Witmer, Sharon. 1996. Making Peace, the Navajo. *Tribal College Journal* (Summer): 24–26.

Yazzie, Robert. 1992. The Navajo Peacemaker Court: Contrasts of Justice. Unpublished manuscript.

———. 1993a. Law School as a Journey. *Arkansas Law Review* 41 (1): 271–74.

———. 1993b. Navajo Justice Experience—Yesterday and Today. In *Aboriginal Peoples and the Justice System: National Roundtable on Aboriginal Justice Issues,* ed. Royal Commission on Aboriginal Peoples, 407–14. Ottawa, ON: Canada Communications Group.

————. 1994. Life Comes from It: Navajo Justice Concepts. *New Mexico Law Review* 24 (2): 175–90.

————. 1996. *Hozho Nahasdlii*—We Are Now in Good Relations: Navajo Restorative Justice. *St. Thomas Law Review* 9: 117–24.

————. 1997. Navajo Peacekeeping: Technology and Traditional Indian Law. *St. Thomas Law Review* 10: 95–101.

————. 1998a. The Healing and Community Justice Policy of the Judicial Branch of the Navajo Nation. Talk given at public forum, Northern Arizona University, Flagstaff, Arizona, May 1.

————. 1998b. Navajo Peacemaking: Implications for Adjudication-Based Systems of Justice. *Contemporary Justice Review* 1 (1): 123–31.

————. 2000a. Approaches to Aboriginal Offenders. Paper presented to the Association of Paroling Authorities International, Ottawa, Ontario, November 4 (approx.).

————. 2000b. Indigenous Peoples and Post-Colonial Colonialism. In *Reclaiming Indigenous Voice and Vision,* ed. Marie Battiste, chapter 2. Vancouver: University of British Columbia Press.

————. 2000c. Navajo Indian Mediation Issues. Paper presented to Mediation and Minority Cultures, Islamic Legal Studies Program, Harvard Law School, July 15 (approx.).

————. 2000d. Navajo Justice: Navajo Nation Peacemakers are Taking the Place of Judges, Prosecutors, and Prisons. *Yes! A Journal of Positive Futures* 15: 36–38.

————. 2000e. Navajo Nation Dispute Settlement Methods. Paper presented to the United States–Mexico Law Institute, International Law Section, American Bar Association, Santa Fe, New Mexico, September 19 (approx.).

————. 2000f. Navajo Perspectives of Alternative Dispute Resolution. Paper presented to the Alternative Dispute and Natural Resources: Building Consensus and Resolving Conflicts in the Twenty-First Century Conference, Tucson, Arizona, November 11.

————. 2000g. Sovereign Knowledge: On What Do We Base Legal Knowledge if God and Reason Are Dead as Universal Epistemologies—A Navajo Response. Paper presented to the American Association of Law Professors, San Francisco, California, August 20 (approx.).

————. 2000h. Tribal Justice: The Practice and Development of American Indian Courts. Paper presented to Shaking the Foundations 2000 Conference, Stanford Law School, November 8–10.

————. 2001a. Healing Circles, Peacemaking, and Original Dispute Resolution. Paper presented at National Law Day, California Western School of Law, San Diego, California, May 1.

————. 2001b. A New Look at Navajo Peacemaking. Paper presented to the Lodestar Symposium 2001, Phoenix College, Phoenix, Arizona, March 23–24.

————. 2001c. The Promise of Restorative Justice. Paper presented to the National Criminal Justice Association Conference, ". . . And Justice for All"—Achieving Racial and Ethnic Justice, Sedona, Arizona, May 3 (approx.).

————. 2001d. Rethinking Indian Courts. Paper presented at the University of Denver School of Law, September 29 (approx.).

————. N. d. Reviving Traditional Indian Law. Unpublished manuscript.

Yazzie, Robert, and James W. Zion. 1995. "Slay the Monsters": Peacemaker Court and Violence Control Plans for the Navajo Nation. In *Popular Justice and Community Regeneration,* ed. Kayleen M. Hazlehurst, 67–87. Westport, Conn.: Praeger.

————. 1996. Navajo Restorative Justice: The Law of Equality and Justice. In *Restorative Justice: International Perspectives,* ed. Burt Galaway and Joe Hudson, 157–73. Monsey, N.Y.: Criminal Justice Press.

Young, Robert W. 1978. *A Political History of the Navajo Tribe.* Tsaile, Ariz.: Navajo Community College Press.

Zion, James W. 1983. The Navajo Peacemaker Court: Deference to the Old and Accommodation to the New. *American Indian Law Review* 11: 89–109.

————. 1984. Harmony Among the People: Torts and Indian Courts. *Montana Law Review* 45: 265–79.

————. 1988. Searching for Indian Common Law. In *Indigenous Law and the State,* ed. Bradford W. Morse and Gordon R. Woodman, 121–48. Dordrecht, Netherlands: Foris.

————. 1991. The Use of Navajo Custom in Dealing with Rape. *Law and Anthropology* 6: 131–67.

————. 1992a. The Navajo Peacemaker Court. *Perception* 15 (4)–16 (1): 48–51.

————. 1992b. North American Indian Perspectives on Human Rights. In *Human Rights in Cross Cultural Perspectives: A Question for Consensus,* ed. Abdullah Ahmd An-Na'im, 191–220. Philadelphia: University of Pennsylvania Press.

————. 1993. Taking Justice Back: American Indian Perspectives. In *Aboriginal Peoples and the Justice System: National Roundtable on Aboriginal Justice Issues,* ed. Royal Commission on Aboriginal Peoples, 309–23. Ottawa, ON: Canada Communications Group.

————. 1994. Stories from the Peacemaker Court. *In Context* 38: 31.

————. 1995a. Law as Revolution in the Court of the Navajo Nation. Paper presented at the Federal Bar Association Indian Law Conference, Albuquerque, New Mexico, April 8 (approx.).

————. 1995b. Living Indian Justice: Navajo Peacemaking Today. Paper presented at the Alternative Dispute Resolution Conference, Vancouver, British Columbia, October 15 (approx.).

————. 1997a. Indian Tradition and Custom in Adjudication Under Rules of Evidence. Paper presented at the National Tribal Judicial Conference, Green Bay, Wisconsin, April 30 (approx.).

————. 1997b. The Oral Will. Navajo Common Law Research Paper. Unpublished manuscript.

————. 1997c. Traditional Indian Solutions for Victims of Crime. *Australian Journal of Law and Society* 13: 167–80.

————. 1998. The Dynamics of Navajo Peacemaking. *Journal of Contemporary Criminal Justice* 14 (1): 58–74.

Zion, James W. 1998. The Use of Custom and Tradition in the Modern Justice Setting. *Contemporary Justice Review* 1 (1): 133–48.

————. 1999. Monster Slayer and Born for Water: The Intersection of Restorative and Indigenous Justice. *Contemporary Justice Review* 2 (4): 359–82.

————. 2000. Peacemaking: A Family Affair. *Yes! A Journal of Positive Futures* 15: 38.

————. 2001a. Applications of Navajo Peacemaking Across Disciplines. Paper presented to the Lodestar Symposium 2001, Phoenix College, Phoenix, Arizona, March 23–24.

————. 2001b. Court Lawyering in the Navajo Nation. Class materials, Navajo Supreme Court Clinical Program, Harvard Law School, January 8–9.

————. 2002a. Civil Rights in Navajo Common Law. *University of Kansas Law Review* 50 (3): 523–44.

————. 2002b. How the Infidels Can Save Civilization: Traditional Irish and American Indian Law. Paper presented to the Brehon Law Project Symposium, Dublin, Ireland, January 12.

————. 2002c. Indian Restorative Healing. Paper presented at the Third International Conference on Conferencing, Circles, and Other Restorative Practices, Minneapolis, Minnesota, August 8.

————. 2002d. "Making it Plain and Clear": Navajo Peacemaking Stories. Paper presented at the 44th Annual Western Social Science Association Annual Meeting, Albuquerque, New Mexico, April 10–13.

————. 2002e. Navajo Therapeutic Jurisprudence. *Touro Law Review* 18 (3): 563–640.

Zion, James W., and Philmer Bluehouse. 1993. *Hozhooji Naat'aanii*: The Navajo Justice and Harmony Ceremony. *Mediation Quarterly* 10 (4): 327–37.

Zion, James W., and Nelson J. McCabe. 1982. *Navajo Peacemaker Court Manual*. Window Rock, Ariz.: Navajo Nation.

Zion, James W., and Robert Yazzie. 1996. Completing the Circle: An International Perspective of Aboriginal Justice. Paper presented at the Contemporary Aboriginal Justice Models Conference, Kahnawake, Quebec.

————. 1997. Indigenous Law in North America in the Wake of Conquest. *Boston College International and Comparative Law Review* 20 (1): 55–84.

Zion, James W., and Elsie B. Zion, 1993. Hozho' Sokee'—Stay Together Nicely: Domestic Violence under Navajo Common Law. *Arizona State Law Journal* 25 (2): 407–26.

ABOUT THE CONTRIBUTORS

Philmer Bluehouse is the former director of the Navajo Nation Peacemaker Division. He is a member of the Red House Clan and was born to the To Walk Around You Clan. Bluehouse is also a veteran of seventeen years of law enforcement. He is currently the director of the Bluehouse Peacemaking Institute.

Eric Ken Gross is a Ph.D. candidate at Temple University. His research on Navajo Peacemaking is part of his dissertation. He is currently in the process of creating a peacemaking program with the City of Philadelphia.

Jon'a Meyer is an associate professor of criminal justice in the Department of Sociology at Rutgers University, Camden. An alumnus of the University of California–Irvine's social ecology program, she has published on many aspects of criminal justice, including Native American legal systems, restorative justice, sentencing, criminal courts, decision making in the criminal justice system, child victims, prison industry and reform, and community-oriented policing. She is the author of *Doing Justice in the People's Court, Inaccuracies in Children's Testimony,* and *The Courts in Our Criminal Justice System.*

Marianne O. Nielsen is an associate professor in the Department of Criminal Justice at Northern Arizona University. She received her Ph.D. from the University of Alberta, Canada. She is the editor with Robert A. Silverman of two books on the involvement of indigenous peoples in the criminal justice systems of Canada and the United States, and the author of numerous book chapters and articles on the same topic.

Sandra Day O'Connor was until 2005 a justice of the Supreme Court of the United States. She was formerly a judge in Arizona.

Tom Tso is a former chief justice of the Supreme Court of the Navajo Nation.

Robert Yazzie is a former chief justice of the Navajo Nation. He is a graduate of Oberlin College (B.A., 1973) and the University of New Mexico School of Law (J.D., 1982).

James W. Zion is a graduate of the University of Saint Thomas (B.A., 1966) and the Columbus School of Law, Catholic University of America (J.D., 1969). He is a private jurisconsult who lives in Albuquerque, New Mexico, researching and writing on Indian court matters, traditional Indian law, and Indian country justice initiatives; and he is an adjunct professor at the Department of Criminal Justice at Northern Arizona University. He was solicitor to the courts of the Navajo Nation from 1981 through 1983 and 1991 through 2001. He was a professional in residence with the United States State Department in 1995 for discussions of the role of traditional law and government in relation to the adoption of the Constitution of South Africa. He has written extensively on traditional Indian law and the human rights of indigenous peoples.

INDEX

Editors' note: Because of the growing use of Dine' legal and scholarly concepts in scholarly writing, they are used as the key terms in this index. As an example, if readers wish to learn about the roles of peacemakers, they will be referred to "Naa'táanii, role of" in the index. The only exception is "peacemaking", because of the complexity of its Dine' usage.